I0813027

IMAGES of America

AROUND HOULTON

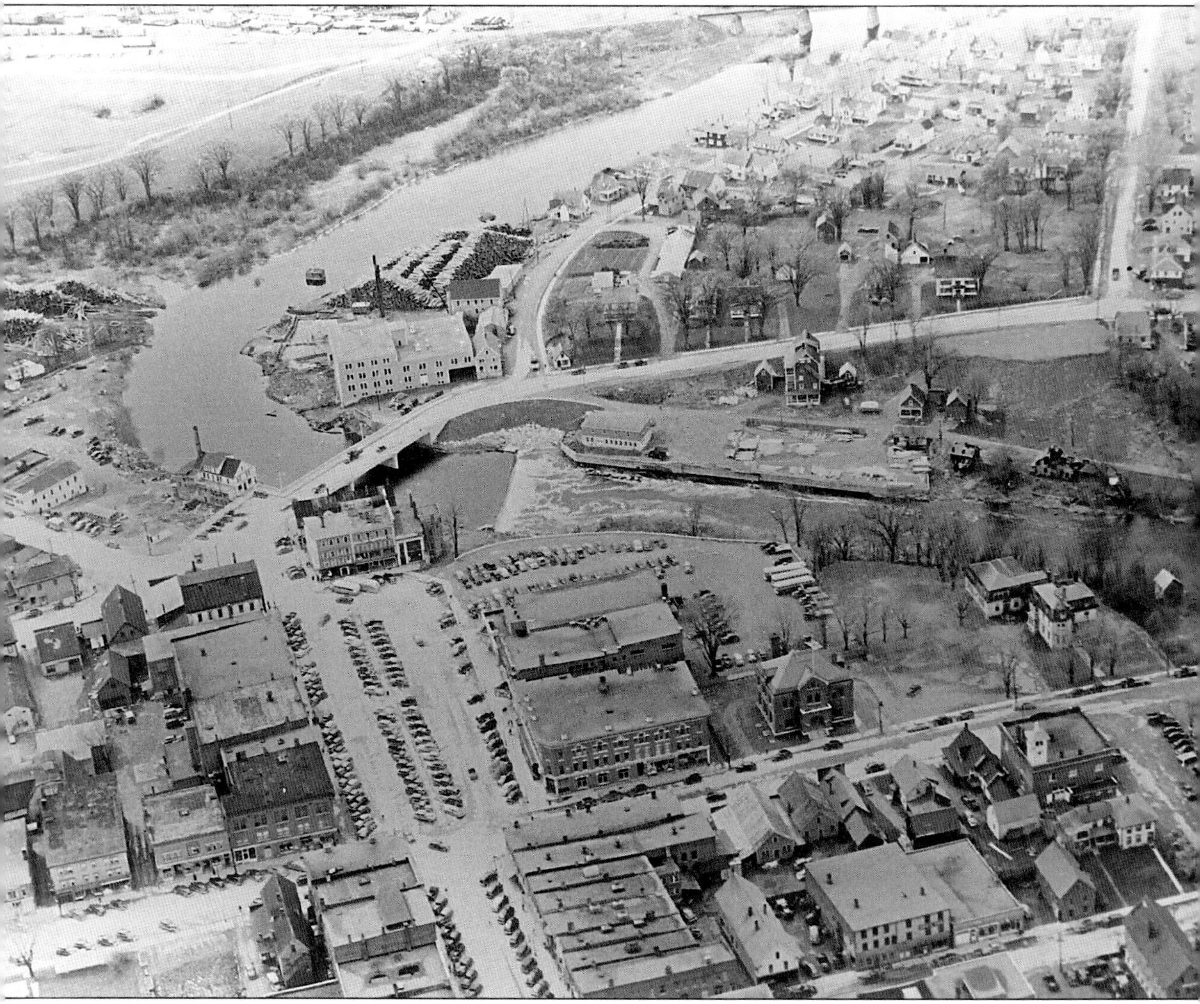

An air view of Houlton in the 1950s.

On the cover: Please see page 57.

IMAGES
of America

AROUND HOULTON

Frank H. Sleeper

ARCADIA
PUBLISHING

ISBN 978-0-7385-4924-8

Published by Arcadia Publishing
Charleston, South Carolina

Printed in the United States of America

Library of Congress Catalog Card Number: 2006930978

For all general information contact Arcadia Publishing at:
Telephone 843-853-2070
Fax 843-853-0044
E-mail sales@arcadiapublishing.com
For customer service and orders:
Toll-Free 1-888-313-2665

Visit us on the Internet at www.arcadiapublishing.com

Contents

Introduction 7

1. Houlton Is Not Isolated 9
2. Houlton Is Business 31
3. Houlton Is Potatoes 57
4. Houlton Is Fun and Recreation 63
5. Houlton Is the Town and Surroundings 89
6. Houlton Is Doers and Shakers 109

Acknowledgements 128

Introduction

The shiretown of Aroostook County is tucked next to the Canadian border at the northeast terminus of this country's vast interstate road network. Pass along that interstate from Old Town up and you see primarily trees with a few lakes, a river here and there and towns invisible off to one side or the other. Houlton seems as isolated as Aroostook when you travel I-95.

But Houlton is not. There were cross border relationships from the first settlers' arrival in 1807. During the War of 1812, while much of the District of Maine was attacked by the British, particularly along the coast, a truce existed between Houlton and Woodstock, New Brunswick. The northeast boundary dispute about thirty years later almost brought war—but the cross border friendships and relationships kept it the "Bloodless Aroostook War." Negotiation and diplomacy set the final border—not war. The Maliseet Indians helped the early settlers of Houlton; they wandered back and forth, then as now, without recognizing any boundary. Folk from New Brunswick moved to Houlton. Some Houltonites moved to Woodstock and points east. As time went on, Houlton was closer to Woodstock in a foreign country than it was to its Aroostook rival, the city of Presque Isle, 30 miles north. The railroad came to Houlton from New Brunswick more than twenty years before it came from Bangor, Houlton experienced economic boom only after the Bangor and Aroostook Railroad opened the town more directly to the American market.

My grandmother, Cora Putnam, had a hand in this cross border relationship, helping establish Eastern Star chapters in New Brunswick as well as in other Aroostook communities. It just could be that the Houlton-Woodstock axis is the strongest example of good relations on the longest undefended border in the world—and was so long before formal trade agreements were worked out. It was and is a relationship most notable for its quietness and lack of publicity.

If you consider Houlton as your home town even though you only spent the first twenty summers of your life there as I did, you are likely to find one of its greatest qualities its open-mindedness. Some of its settlers, by way of Salem and New Salem, Massachusetts (the latter in the western part of that state) were descended from some who took part in the Salem witchcraft trials. Perhaps it was partially in reaction to those trials that such open-mindedness exists in the town. As far as I can determine, only the Maliseets, over the years, were not rewarded as they should have been for their early aid to the Houlton settlers.

With this cross border movement and relationships and this open-mindedness, Houlton maintains a strong feeling of patriotism; of community; of stability. Ingredients contributing to this are education, churches and religion, civic and fraternal organizations and the spirit of voluntarism which was fostered right from the start by the harsh conditions of survival. These factors of stability could almost make up another book on Houlton in the Old Photographs series as this volume can make no claim to cover life in this Maine community completely.

Most communities, especially in rural areas, have their own cultures. Houlton is no exception. As well as the aspects of that culture already mentioned, the town is a market center, a communications center, an educational center for a series of communities surrounding it—Hodgdon, Linneus, New Limerick, Ludlow, Monticello, Littleton, Hammond Plantation, Amity, perhaps even Smyrna, Oakfield, Island Falls, Sherman, Bridgewater and, sometimes, Woodstock. It is also the county seat of Aroostook County, a county larger than the states of Rhode Island and Connecticut. Although Caribou and Presque Isle keep trying to cut into Houlton's shiretown role, the town has managed to hold on to many of the functions of county government. County government has never been as powerful in Maine as in the South, for example, but it has its place. This has appeared especially true in the judicial arena in Houlton, which has had more than its share of eminent jurists, and has also affected politics over the years at the state level. Those politics were almost exclusively Republican up until the Democratic comeback in Maine from 1954 onwards.

My mother and father grew up in Houlton. My ancestors, on my mother's side, were among the founders of this town. I owe Houlton much—and I hope this book will help repay some of this debt. I especially hope this will bring a greater appreciation of their community to the young people who live in Houlton.

There is something to this community nestled next to the Canadian border up in northern Maine. You may not appreciate it now. But if you ever leave Houlton and you return up I-95 just for a visit perhaps, you'll feel a tingle as you cross the line into Aroostook County, a tingle that will increase as you get closer to this small town. And now, to some matters in Houlton not covered in this introduction.

One

Houlton Is Not Isolated

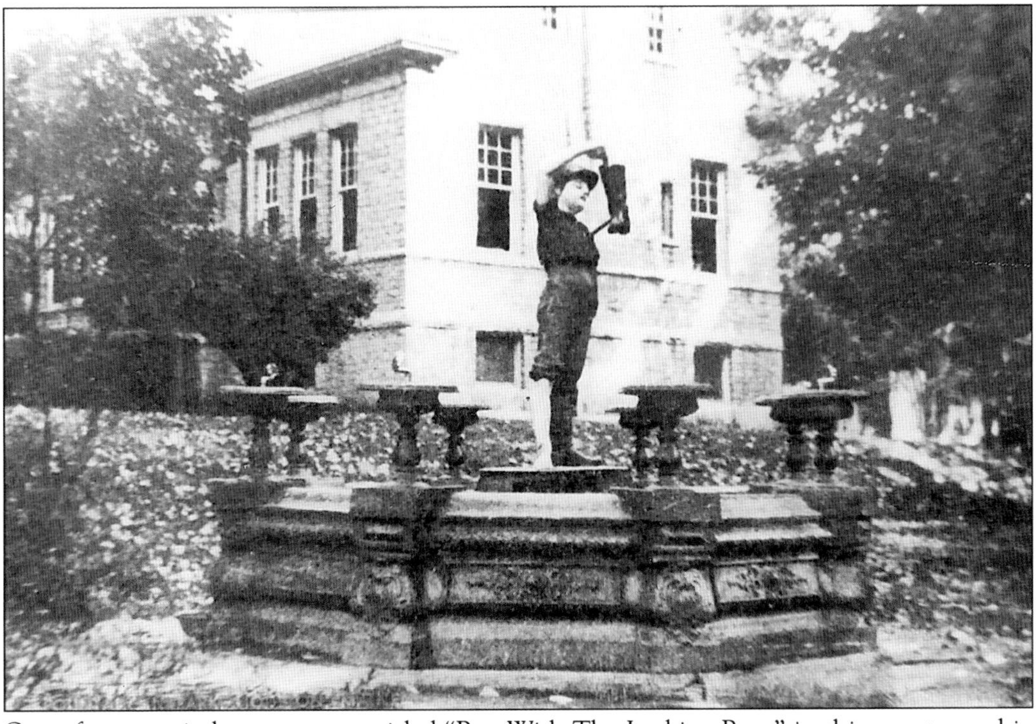

One of twenty-six known statues titled "Boy With The Leaking Boot" in this country and in Sweden, England, Canada and Venezuela, this statue in Houlton was purchased with funds donated by Mrs. Clara P. Frisbie in 1916. It is the only such statue providing water for both man and beast. This sculpture of worldwide cultural importance had to be moved from the location above because of vandalism.

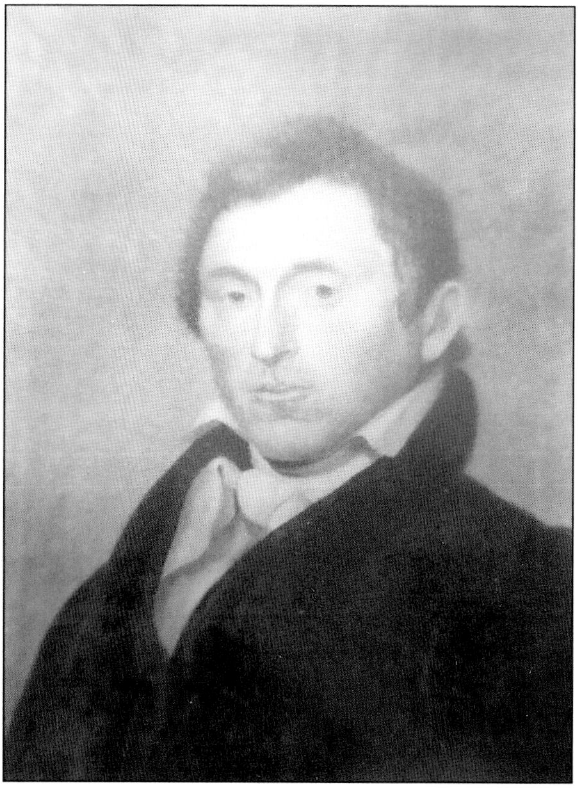

In the "Bloodless Aroostook War," Col. Joshua Carpenter led a group of militia, the Pioneers, to Presque Isle. He reported that he expected no harm unless he crossed the border. There was none. Cross border relationships and friendships won in the end.

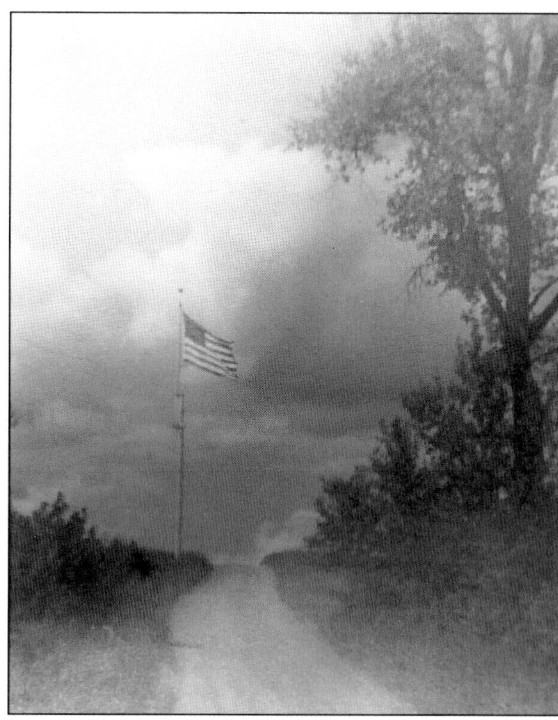

The flag flies above the partial reproduction of the Hancock Barracks in Houlton. Here federal troops were stationed for some years both before and after the "Bloodless Aroostook War." During the period of greatest tensions, those troops' commanders counseled patience and calm. They did much to prevent actual bloodshed.

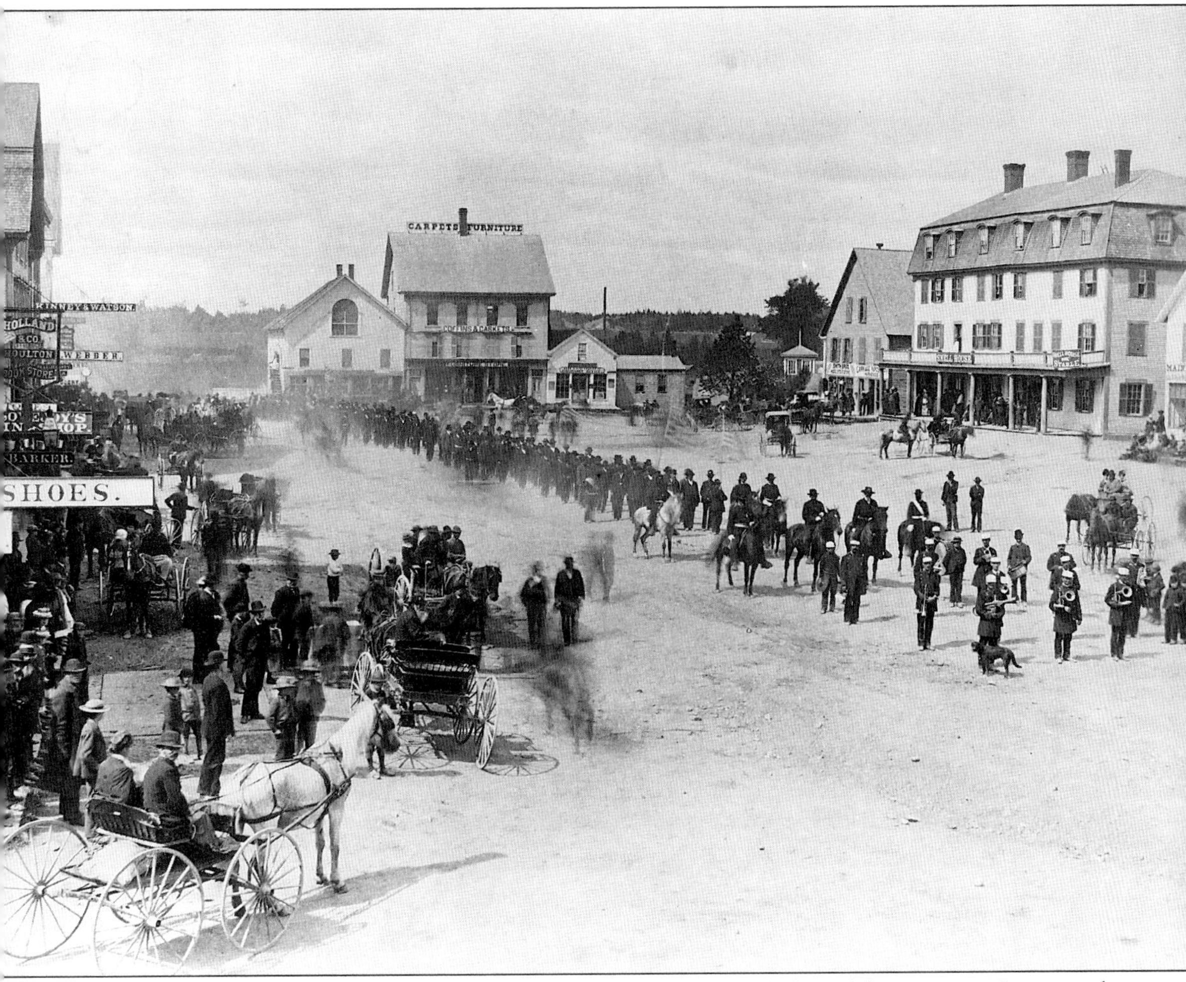

The Civil War brought to many Houlton men a broader knowledge of their nation. It certainly increased patriotism as well as lessening the feeling of isolation from the rest of the country. There were few from Houlton who bought their way out of serving in the war between the States. This photograph shows a parade in Market Square in 1865. This war and, even more so, the First and Second World Wars, brought wider horizons to the Houlton men and women who took part.

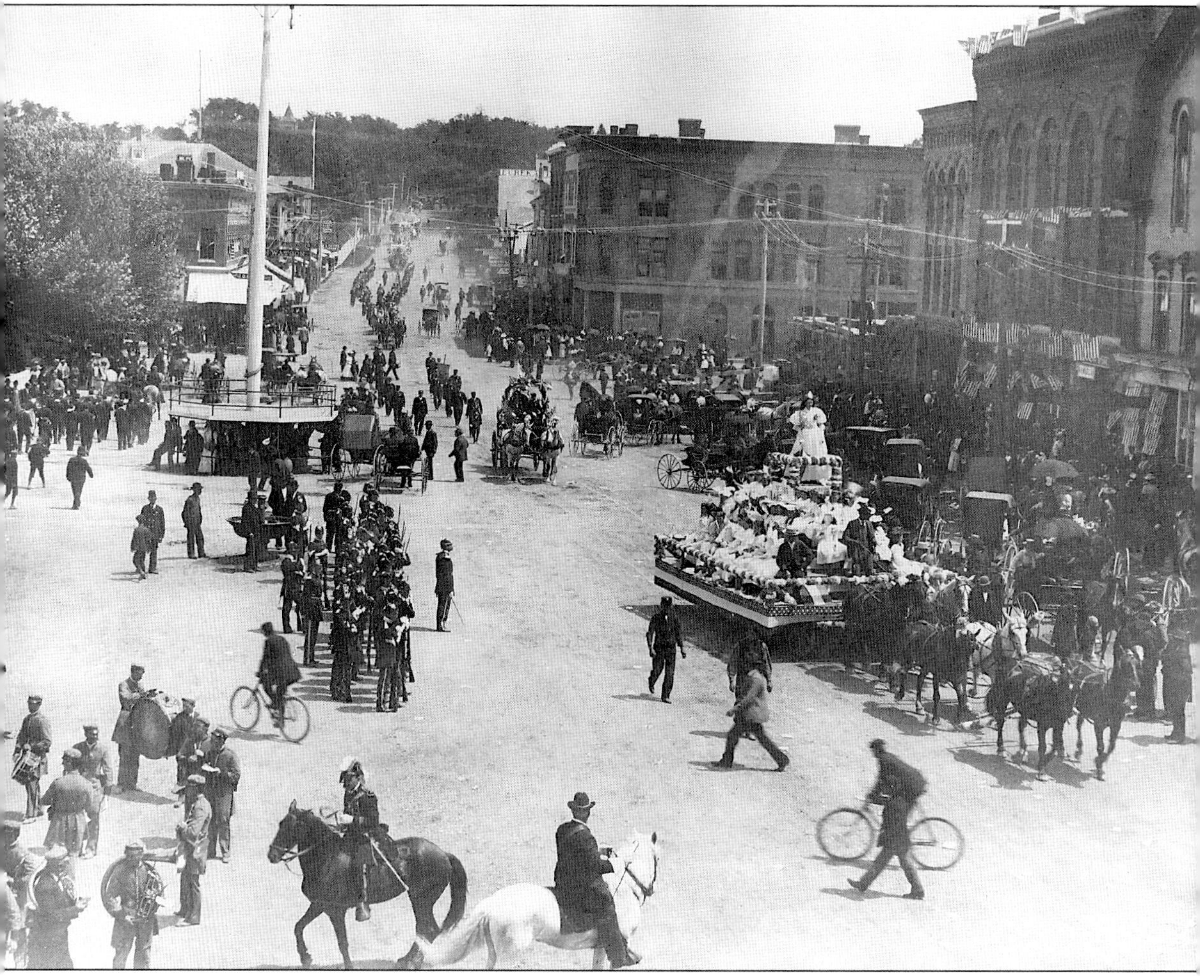

Black Hawk Putnam, foreground, on his white horse, supervises an 1895 parade in Market Square. In 1861, Putnam recruited Company E of the 1st Maine Cavalry in Houlton. He led his company, as a captain, in a famous charge in 1862 at Middleton, Virginia. In that charge, the company lost forty-two men and had sixty-six horses killed. Putnam was wounded. He escaped into the mountains with a few others and wandered for nine days without food before getting away.

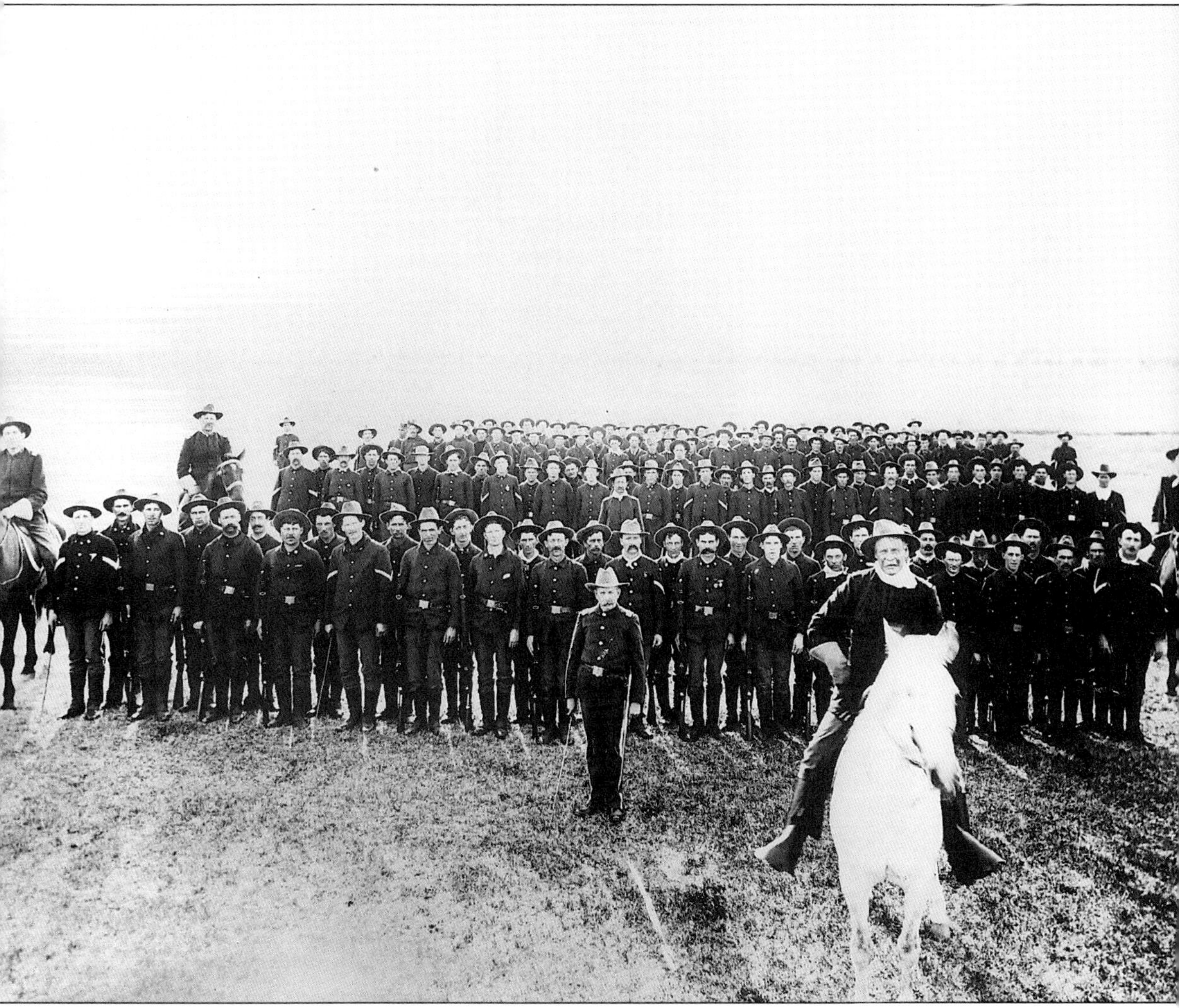

Black Hawk Putnam rides at the head of his troop. Putnam was an enthusiastic Grand Army of the Republic man, according to my grandmother's book *The Story of Houlton*. He was colonel of the Northern Maine Regiment of the GAR for two years. Black Hawk Putnam could put on a good military show, a show which helped the town tucked against the Canadian border keep in mind that it was not cut off from the rest of the United States.

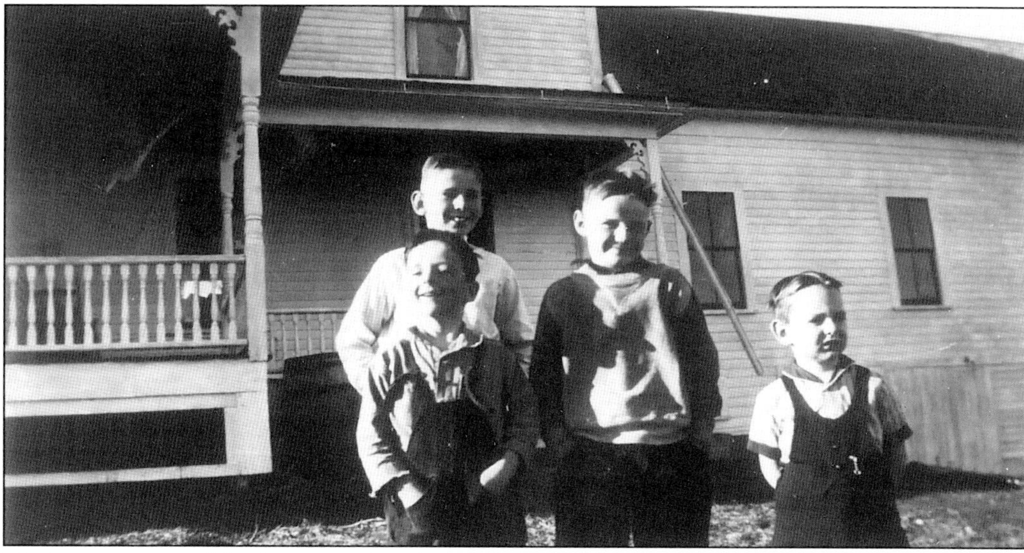

Houlton was not like Boston. The Irish blended in well when they came to Aroostook's shiretown, often becoming farmers but also operating many businesses. The Fitzpatricks, who are probably the largest family of Irish descent in Houlton today, came first to Houlton in 1898 from New Brunswick. Four Fitzpatrick brothers are pictured here in front of the Fitzpatrick farm house on the B Road in Houlton about 1946. Left to right, front: Harold, six, and Francis, four; rear: Robert, ten, and Donald, eight.

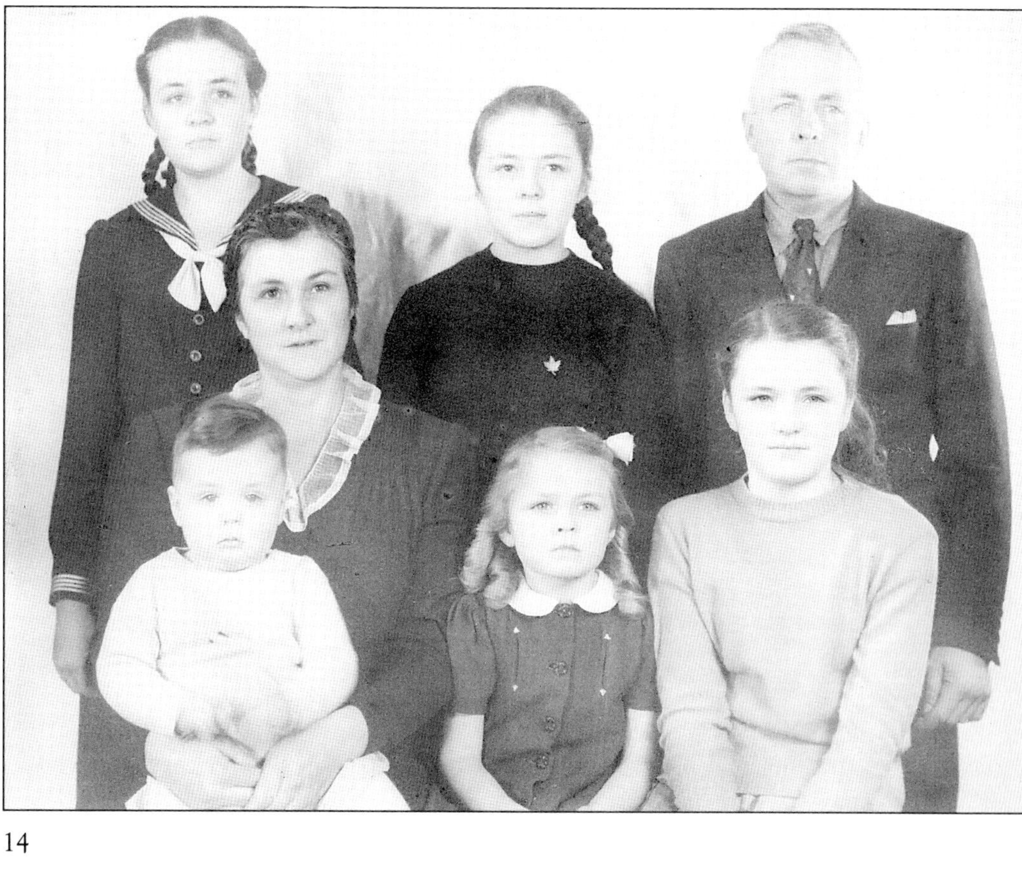

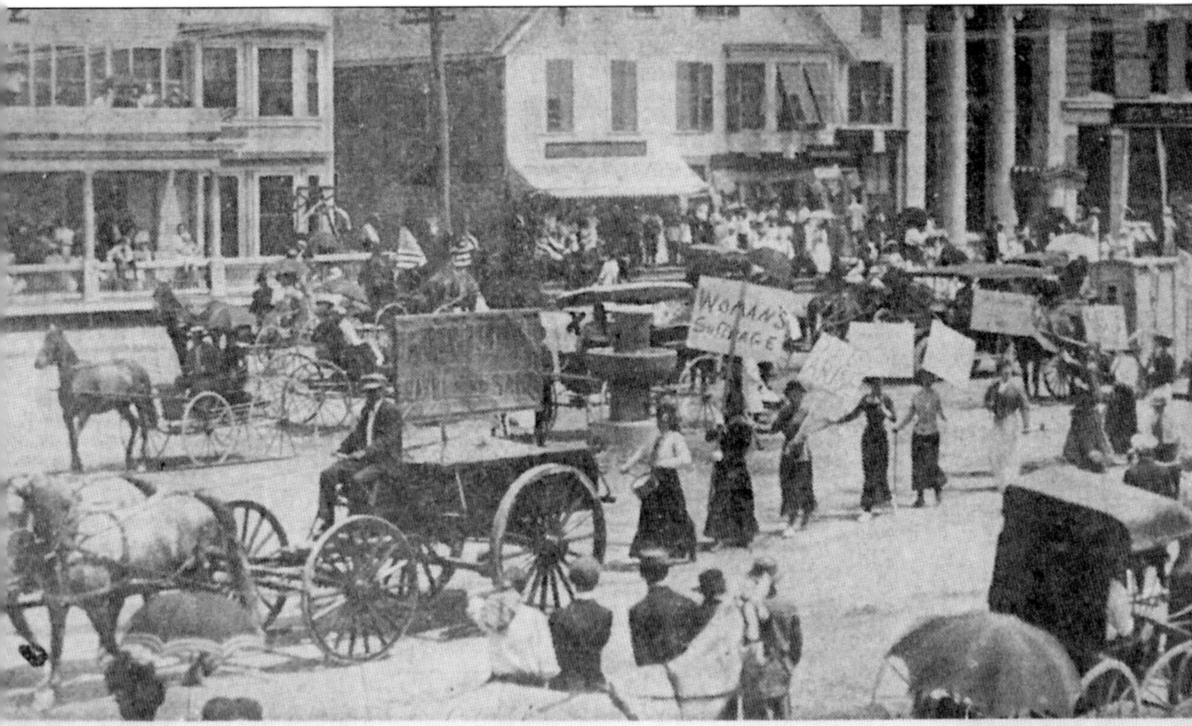

Those Were The Days . . .

Horizons were broadened in Houlton as women sought the vote. These women were marching sometime just before the First World War. Houlton women, like many in Maine, have been leaders in general ever since 1807. The pioneer women could bend with adversity and not break. They were tough, versatile people and many of their descendents have retained those characteristics.

Opposite: The James R. Haley (O'Haley) family in 1945 with, left to right, front: James E. Haley, Dorothy Haley and Ruth Haley; rear: Eleanor Haley, Mary (White) Haley, Gladys Haley and James R. Haley.

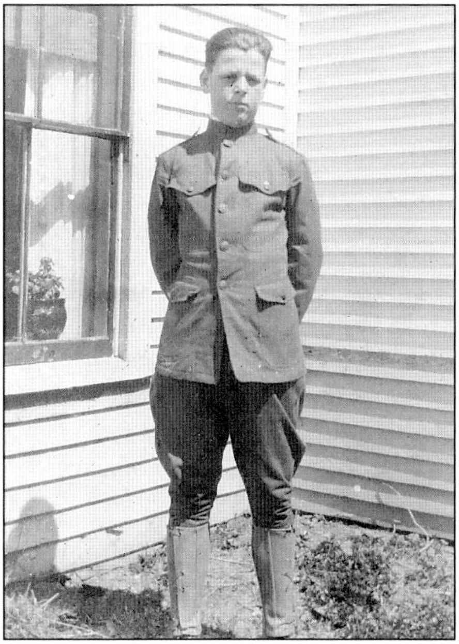

And then came the First World War. This is doughboy Frank Clark of Houlton in 1917. Houlton boys certainly got around in Europe.

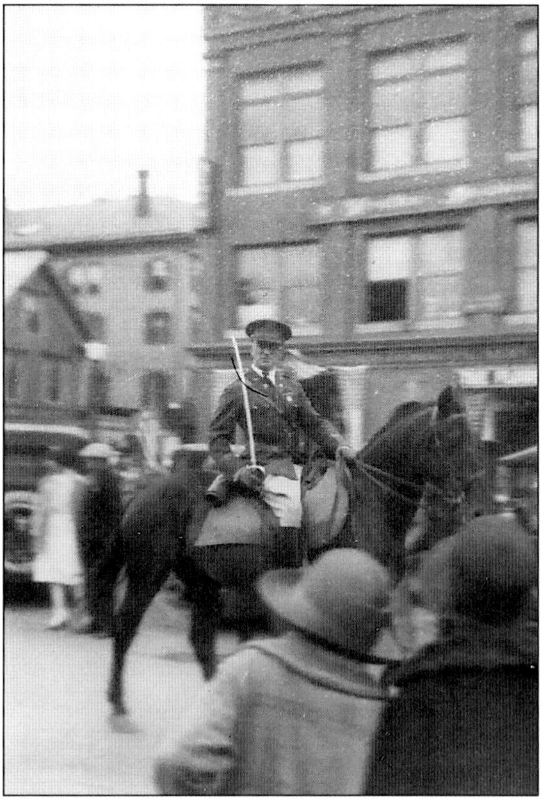

Clement Carroll, Company L, 103rd Infantry, won the Croix de Guerre from France. Winning that medal as a private, Carroll was later to become an officer in the Maine State Guard.

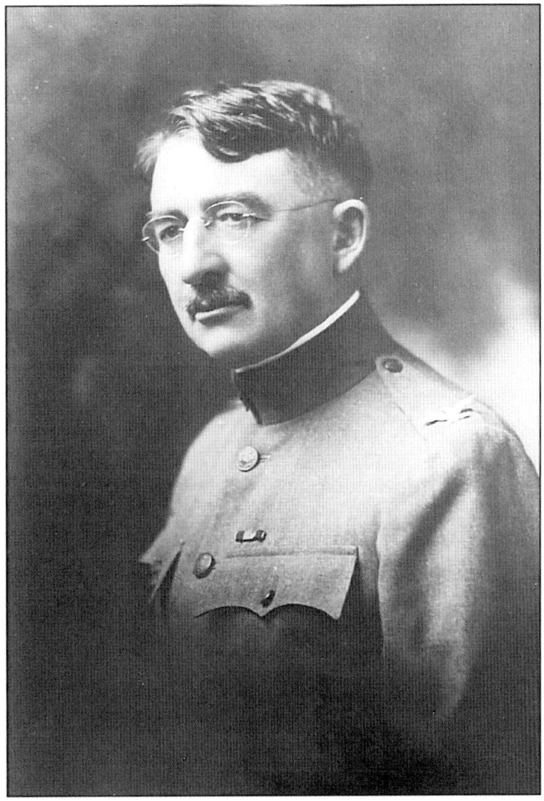

Col. Frank M. Hume was the highest ranking officer from Maine in the First World War. As commander of the 103rd Infantry, he won the Croix de Guerre and Distinguished Service Medal. Hume had also been a Houlton postmaster.

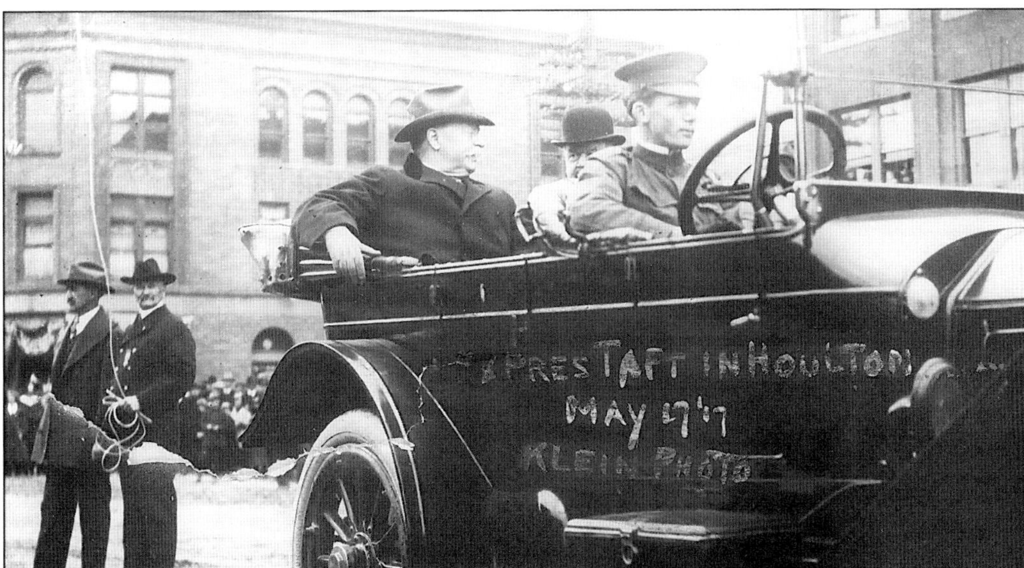

The First World War brought former President William Howard Taft to Houlton in May, 1917. Taft, among other things, visited Ricker Classical Institute. The event is believed to be the only visit to Houlton by a former president.

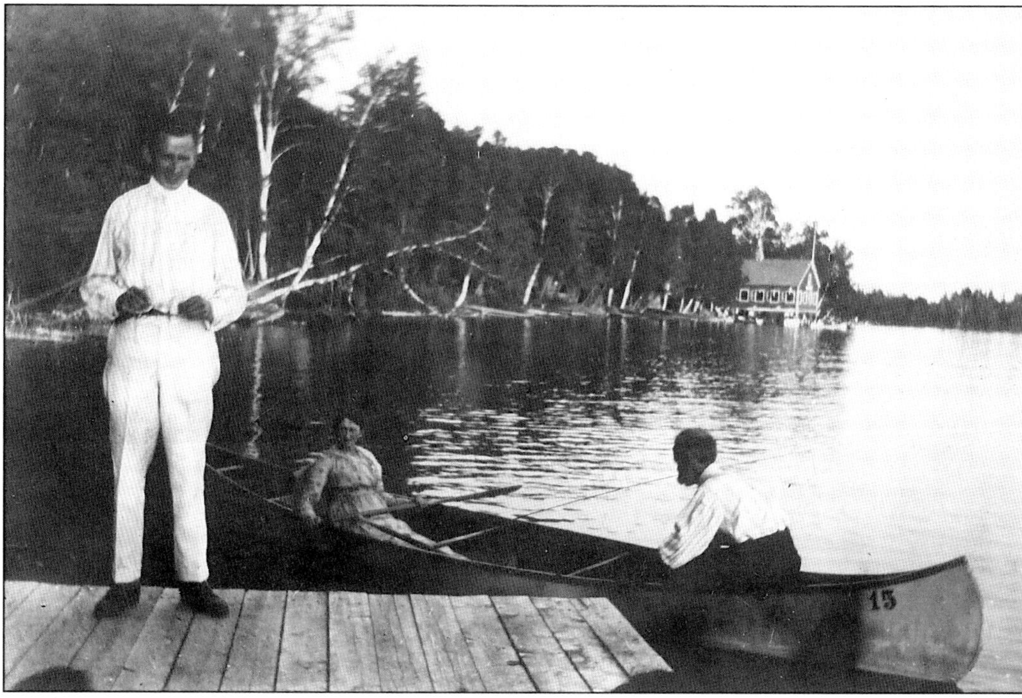

Frank Putnam joined the Canadian Army before the United States entered the First World War and was gassed at Vimy Ridge. Here he is standing while his mother and father, Cora and Amos Putnam, sit in a canoe at Nickerson Lake.

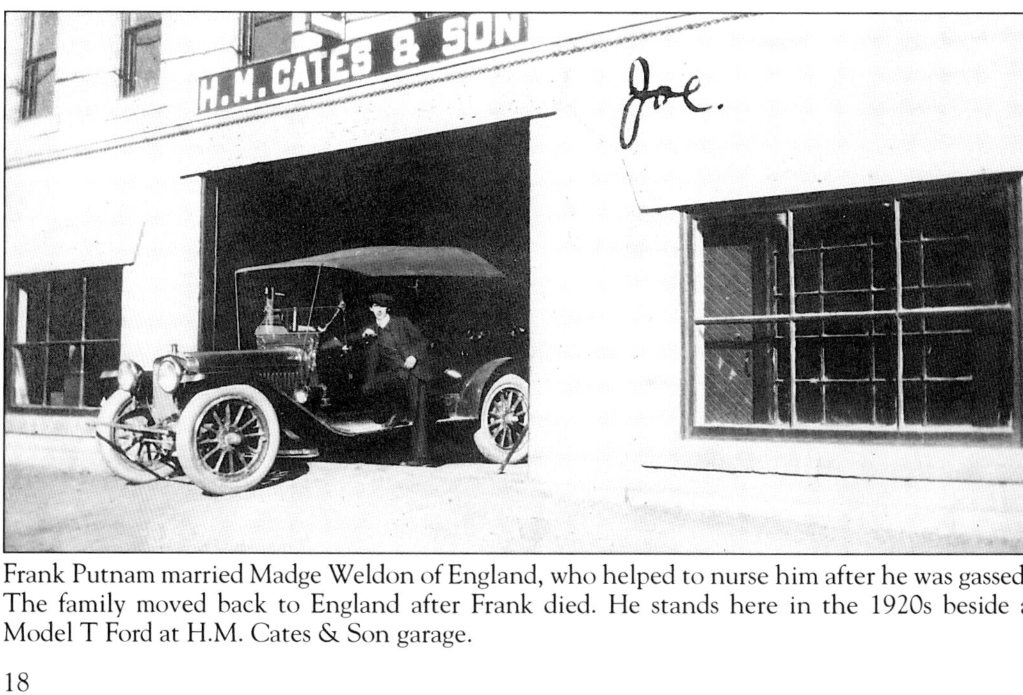

Frank Putnam married Madge Weldon of England, who helped to nurse him after he was gassed. The family moved back to England after Frank died. He stands here in the 1920s beside a Model T Ford at H.M. Cates & Son garage.

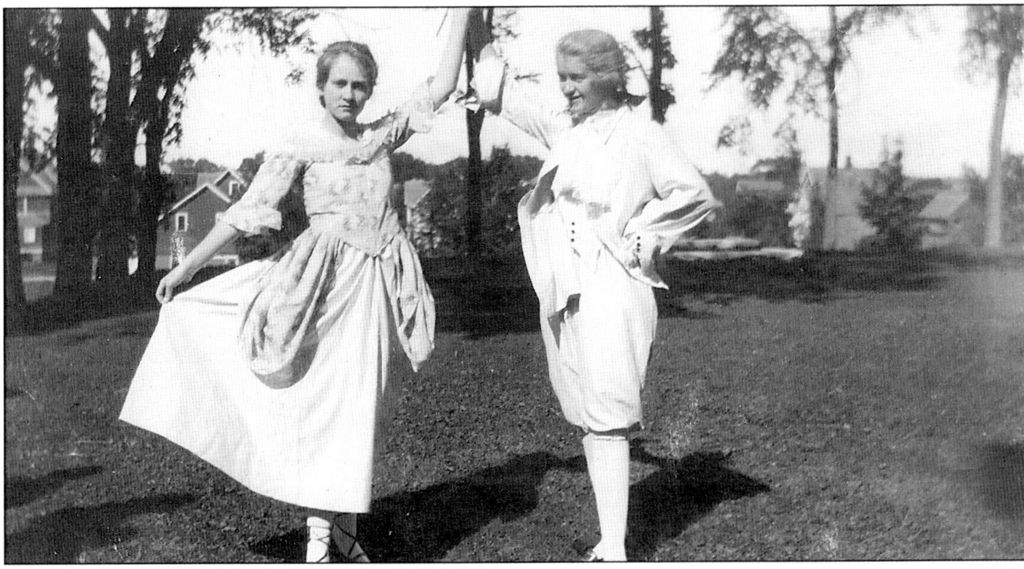

Houlton's horizons expand as Marion Williams and Avery Munroe represent France in a 1918 Red Cross Pageant.

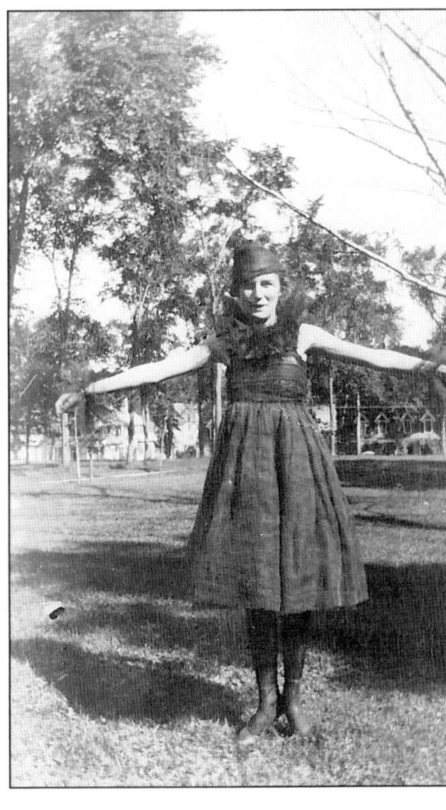

Betty Hume represented coal in that same pageant.

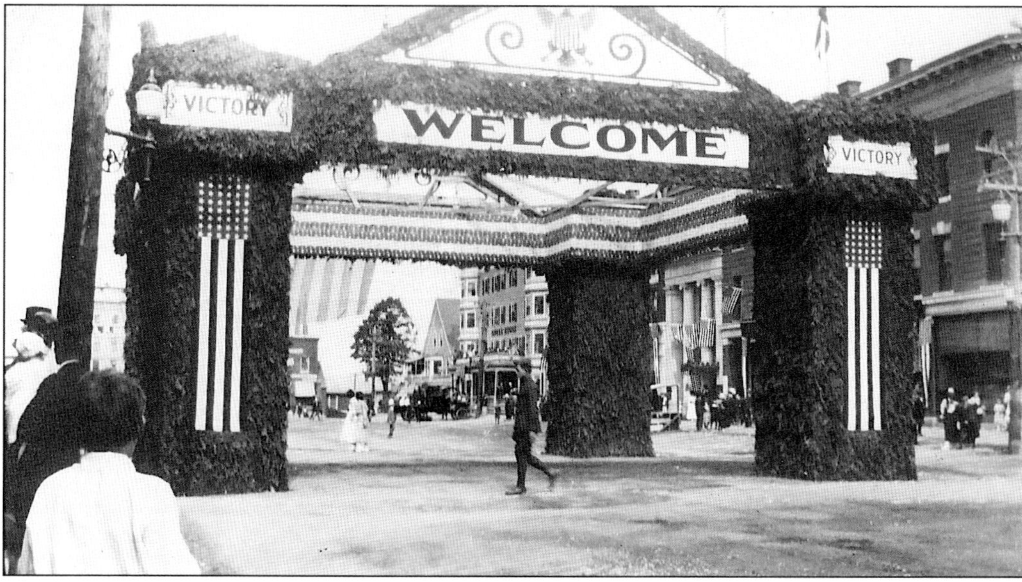

The boys were back from the First World War. A welcome arch for returned soldiers highlighted the 3 July, 1919 parade.

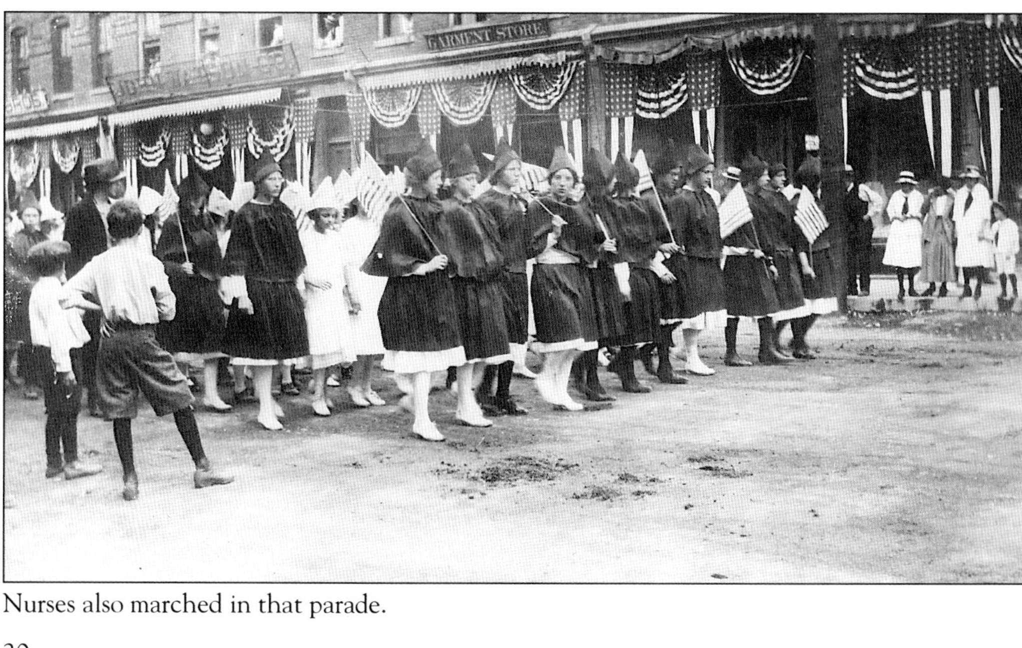

Nurses also marched in that parade.

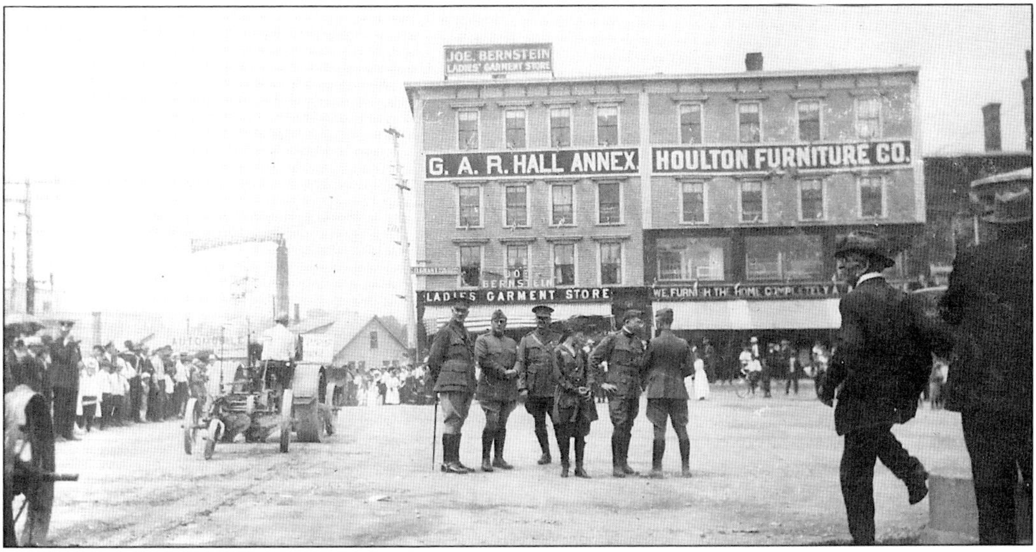

Top officers from Houlton stand together in Market Square on 4 July, 1919.

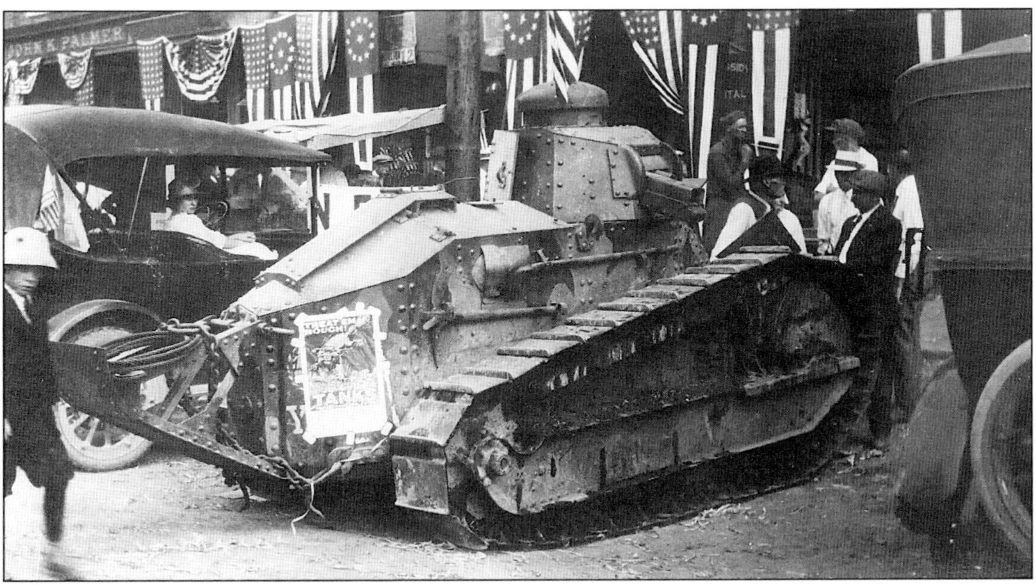

One of the first tanks was a feature of the 4 July, 1919 parade.

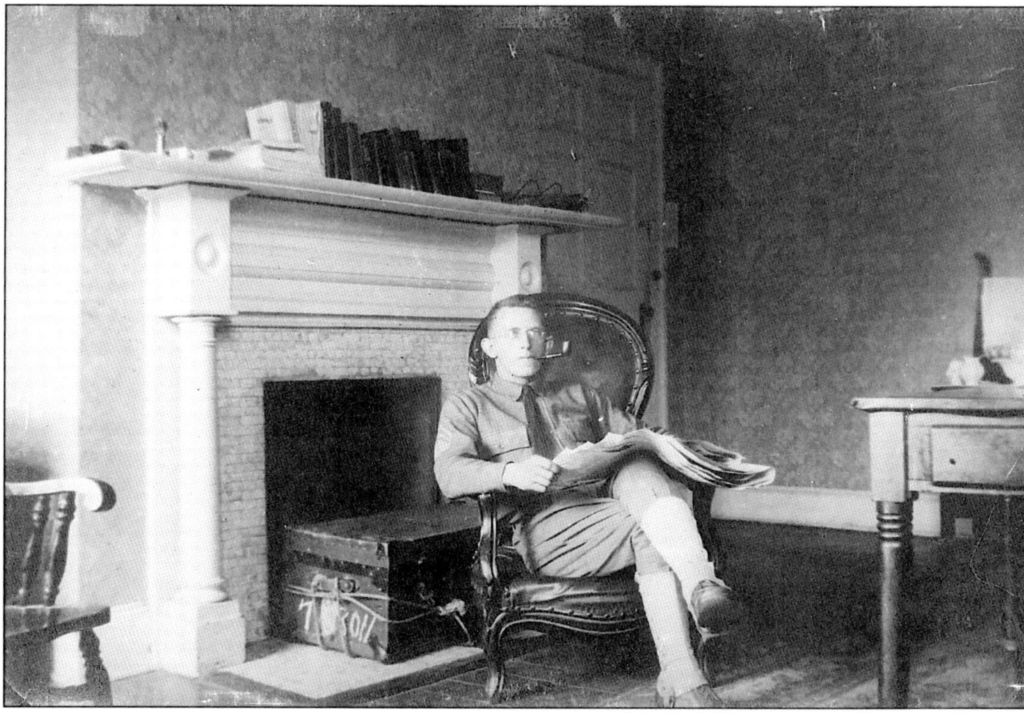

Ervin E. (Mike) Putnam served through the First World War and after, much of the time overseas. Putnam left Houlton to serve as an X-ray technician at the Veterans Administration Hospital in Northampton, Massachusetts. He returned to his native area every summer and guided doctors from the hospital on fishing trips in Maine.

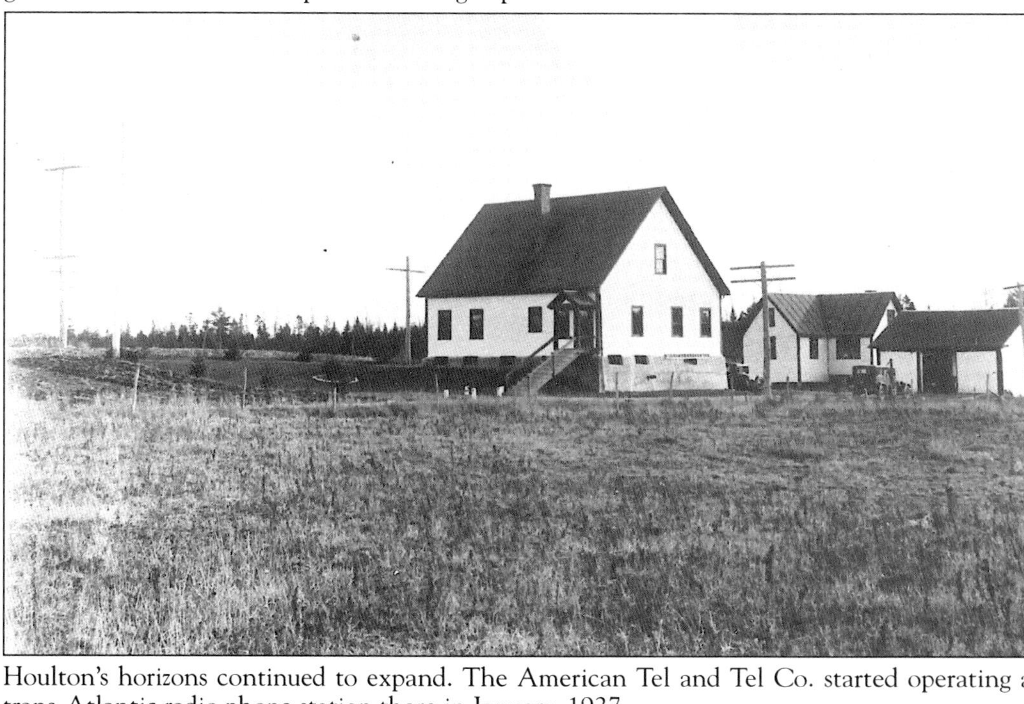

Houlton's horizons continued to expand. The American Tel and Tel Co. started operating a trans-Atlantic radio phone station there in January, 1927.

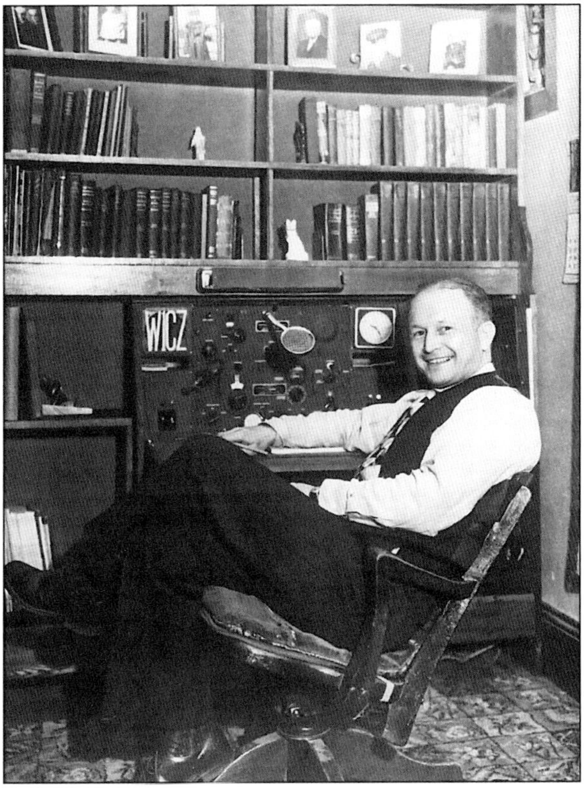

Peter Dombek, one of the AT&T station's employees, sits before his ham radio set. Dombek operated such a set from the early 1920s to 1988.

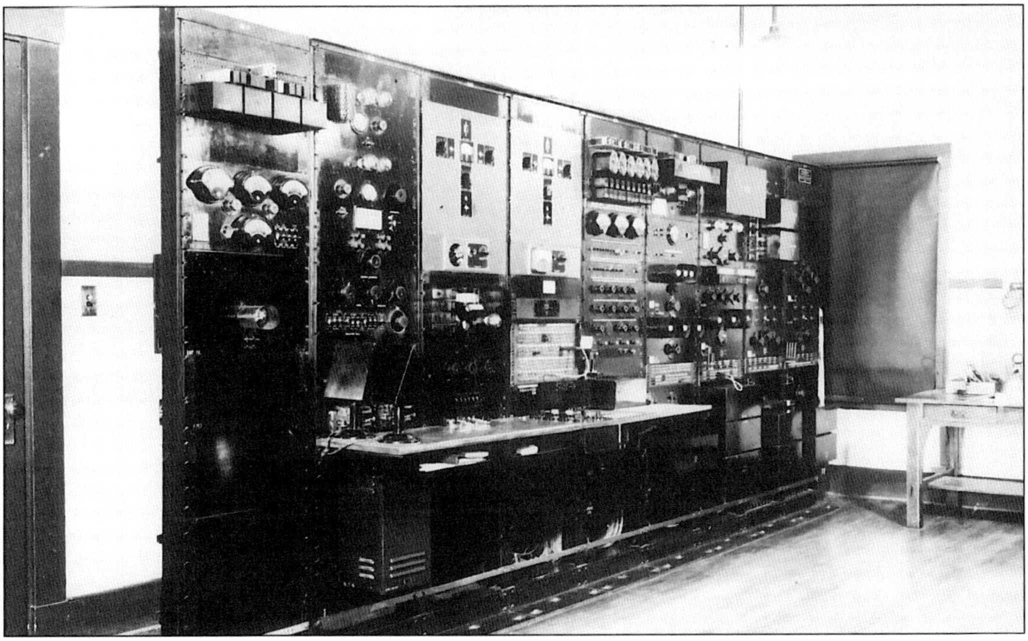

This is the long-wave receiver at the trans-Atlantic radio phone station. It was beamed primarily to England. The installation was placed in Houlton because interference there was found to be the least of all the locations considered. Operated for years, the station building has now been converted into a residence.

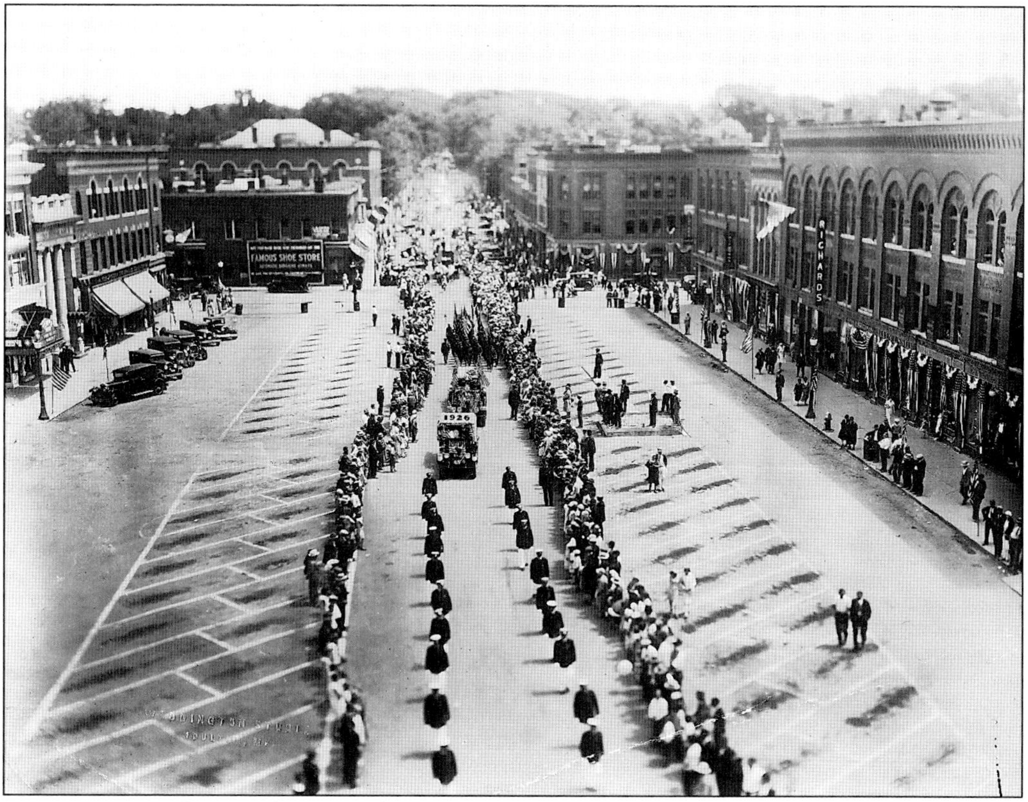

Patriotism stayed strong between the two World Wars. The 4 July, 1926 parade, for example, had strong military units in it.

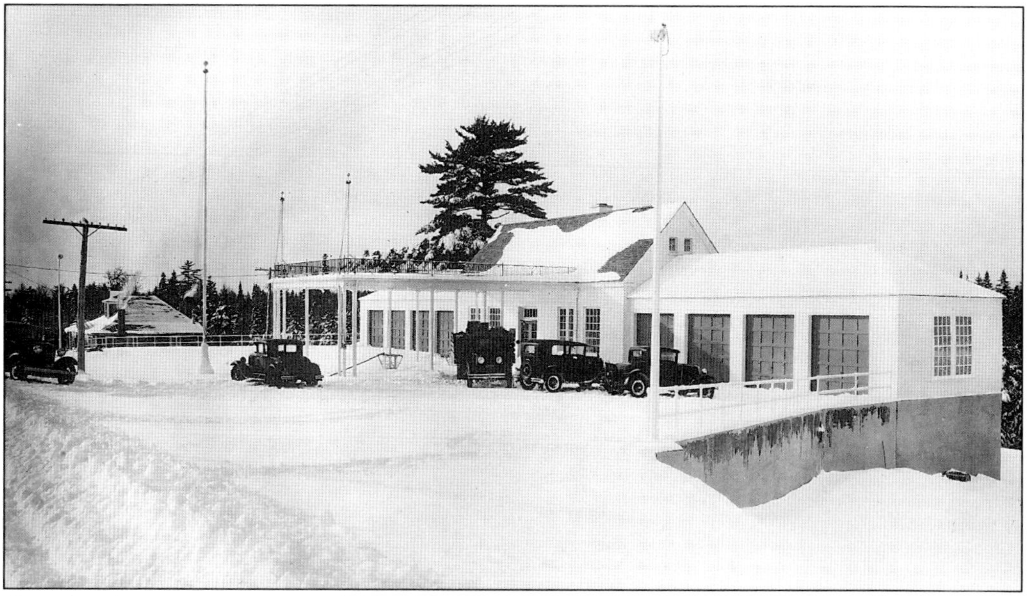

Cross border activity continued. The US Customs Station at the New Brunswick border was in its first day of operation in December, 1933. It replaced another building and has since been replaced by a larger structure.

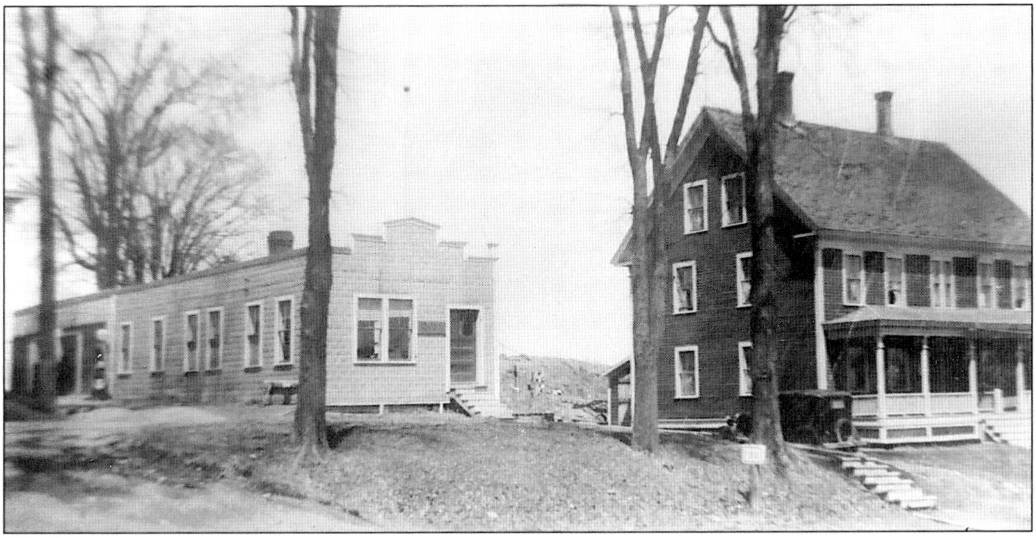

The Border Patrol and Immigration Service headquarters was on Bangor Street about 1937. That headquarters has since been moved.

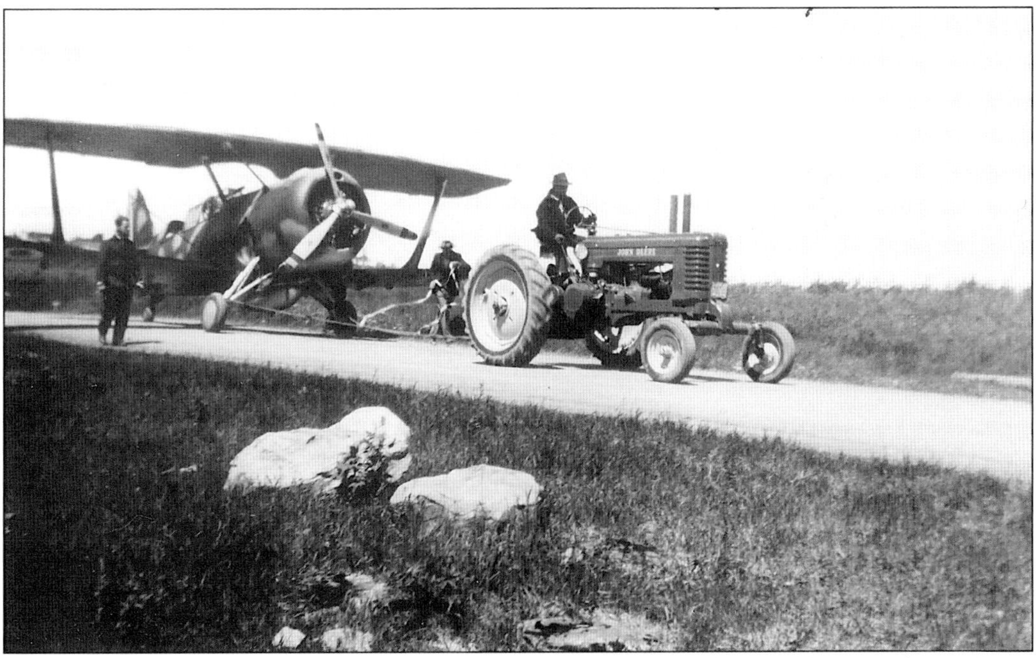

The Second World War came to Houlton before this country had officially entered it. In June, 1940, Arnold Peabody, a great Houlton High and Colby College athlete and later a Houlton town councilor, was one of those on tractors as Stinson 105 planes (thirty-three in just one day) were dragged across the Canadian border from the Houlton Airport.

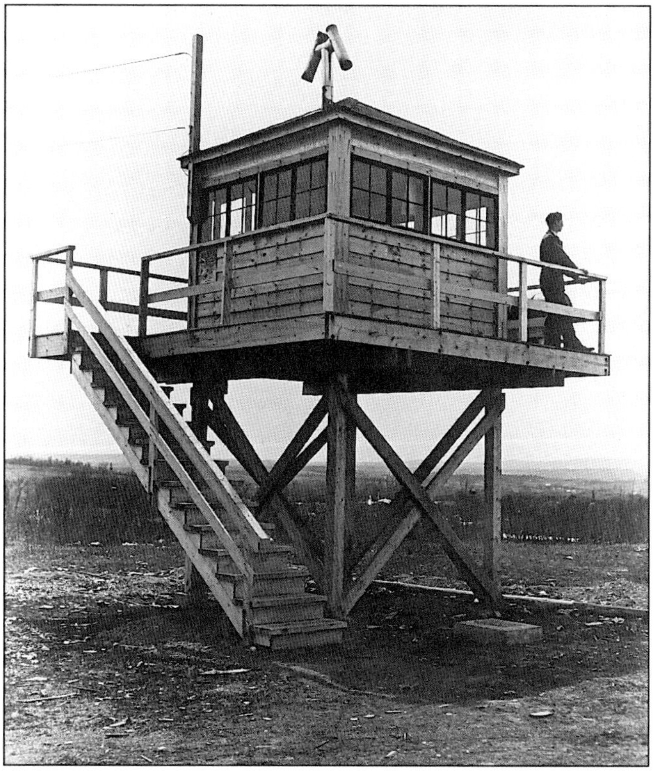

The cross border plane dragging was part of the Neutrality Act of 1939. That act forbade US pilots to fly planes sold to foreign countries directly to those countries. With the support of President Roosevelt, Secretary of State Cordell Hull ruled that the planes could be dragged across the border and then US pilots could fly them again. James M. Pierce had much to do with the Houlton Airport getting such work. Appropriately enough, Garrison Hill was site of a Civil Defense Observation Post, shown here in 1944.

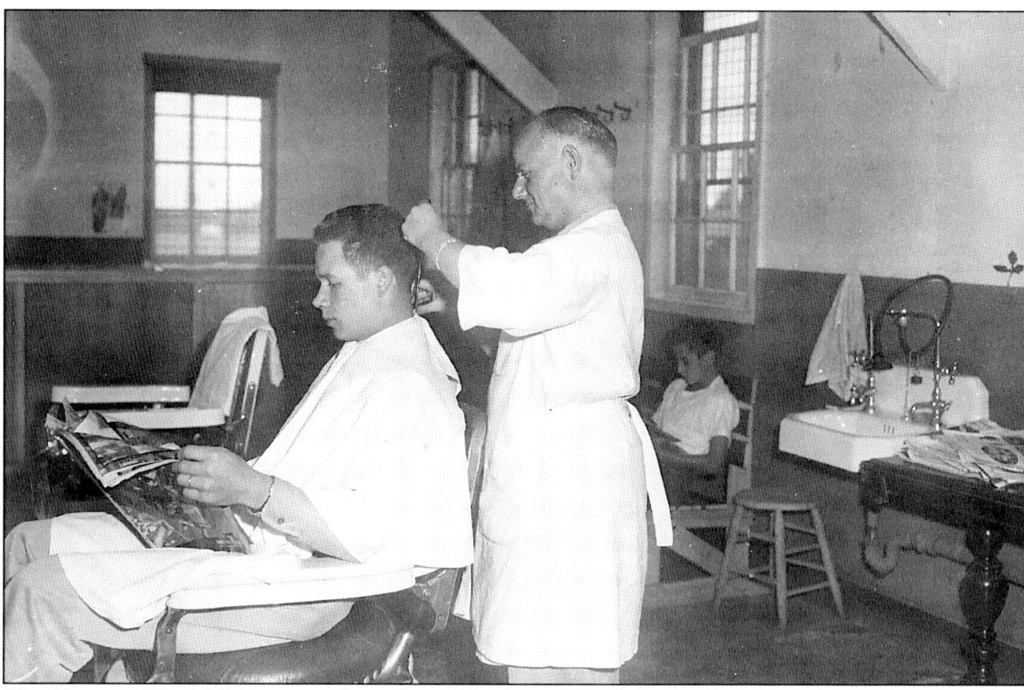

The Second World War came directly to Houlton on 1 July, 1944, when about three hundred German prisoners of war arrived at buildings at the airport. Here a POW cuts the hair of an American GI at the airport.

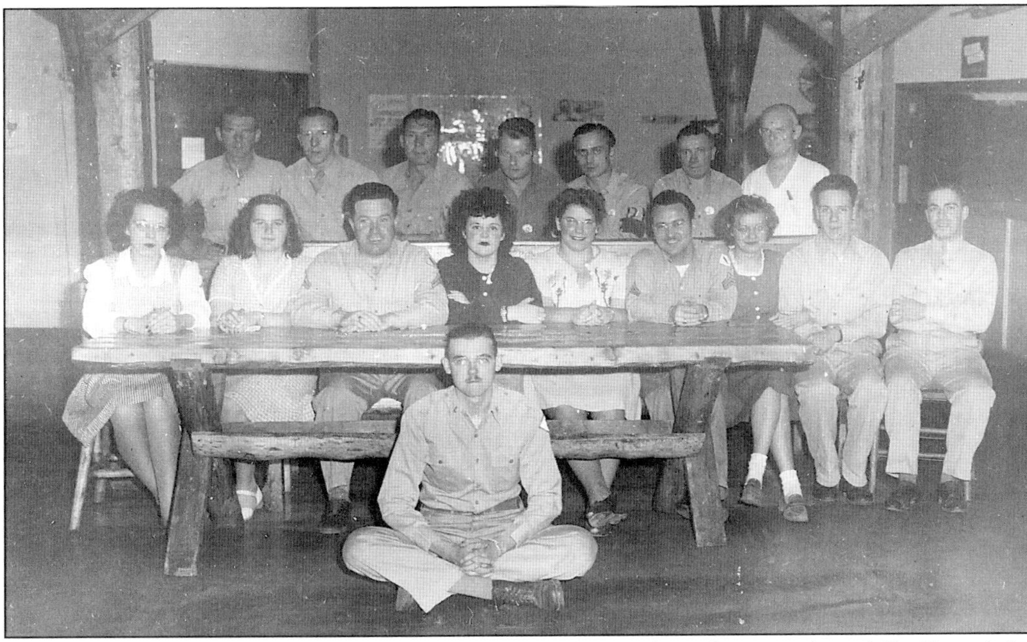

The POWs peaked at about three thousand in Houlton. Then their numbers fell off until the last one left the town early in the spring of 1946. Doris Brown McPherson and Ruth Palmer at the Post Exchange sit with military personnel and POWs in the back row.

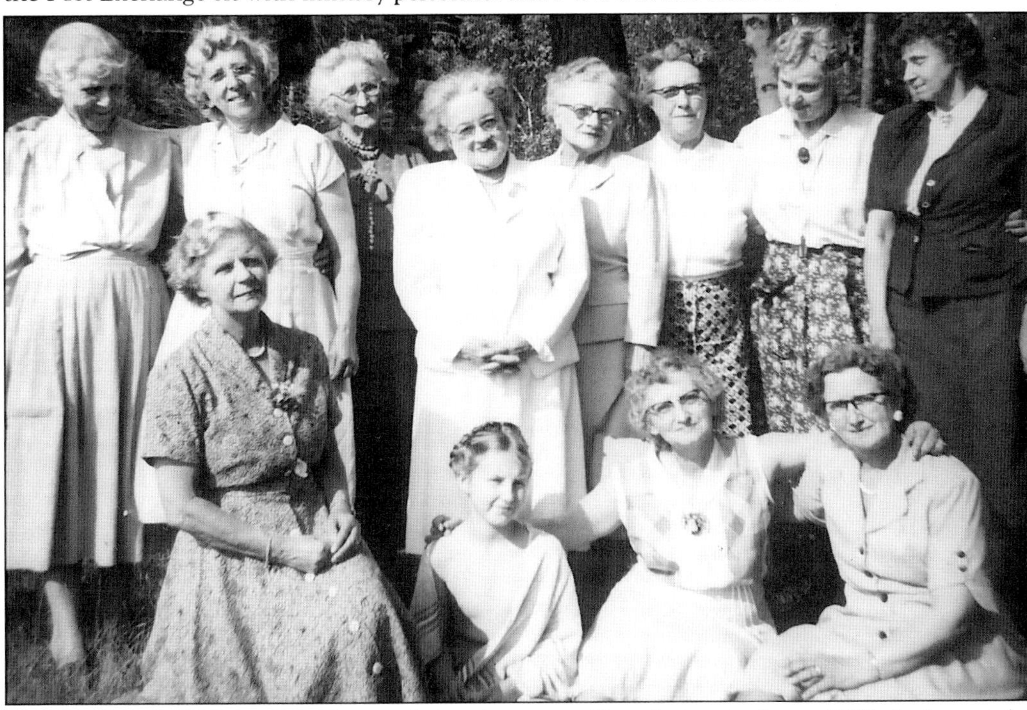

Lydia Putnam Chapter, Daughters of the American Revolution in June, 1953. Left to right, rear: unknown, Elvira Johnson, Cora Putnam, Matilda Lowery, Kathryn Young, Cora Crawford, Isabelle Hess Miller and Frances Richards; front: Madge Putnam, Mardi Abbitt, Margaret Greaves and Harriette Cates.

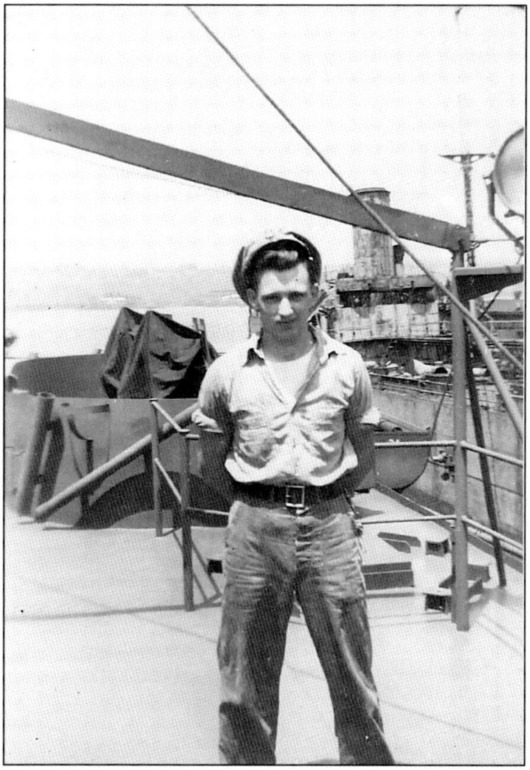

The Second World War ended. Houlton young men and women had their horizons broadened by it. But, with the Cold War and the Korean War, Houlton youth continued to serve. Stanley P. Greaves, a future executive vice-president of the Maine Potato Council, was a seaman on a barracks ship in New York Harbor about 1947.

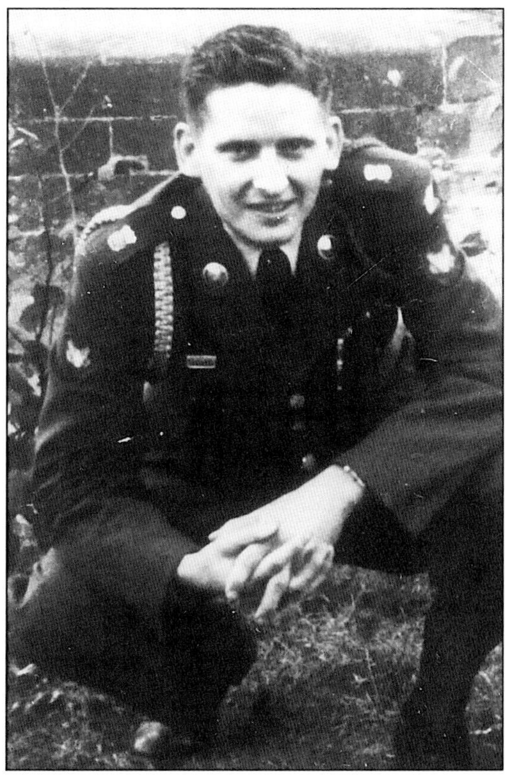

His brother, Joseph F. Greaves, now a teacher and paralegal in El Salvador, was stationed in Germany about 1950.

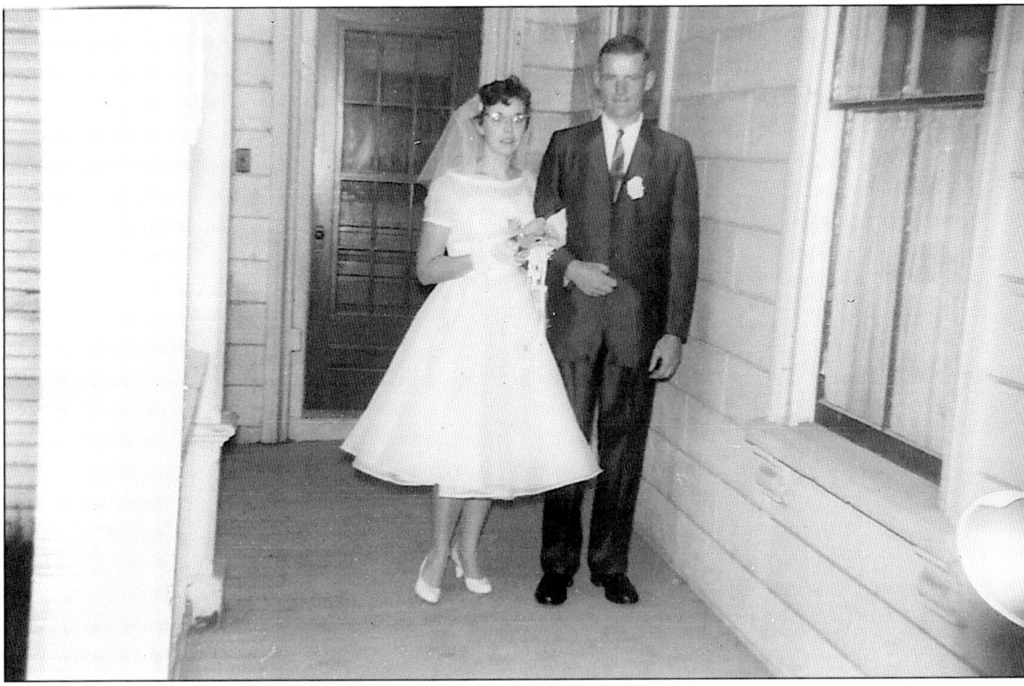

Again illustrating just how well the people of Irish descent have joined in the Houlton community, Donald and Dorothy Fitzpatrick stand on the porch of St. Mary's Convent in Houlton on 15 July, 1958, their wedding day.

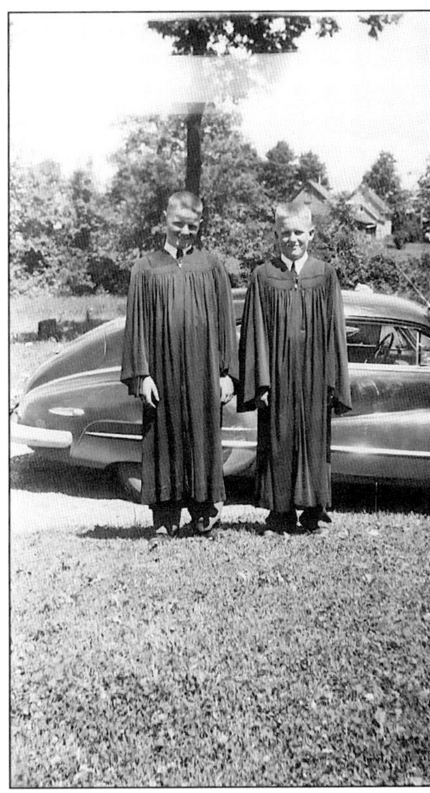

Donald Fitzpatrick, left, and Tommy Watson stand for photographs after their confirmation in 1950.

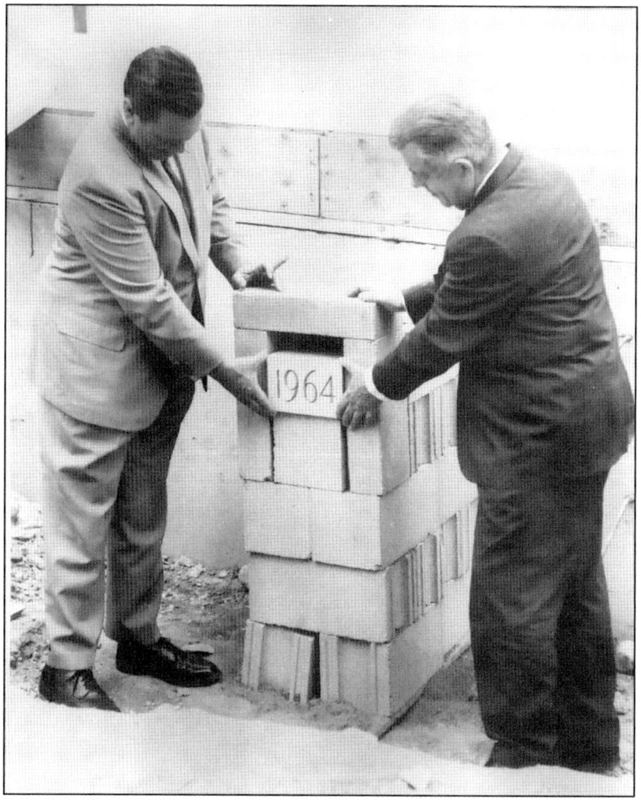

Ricker College, closed in 1978, also broadened Houlton's horizons. Dr. C. Worth Howard, president of Ricker College from 1957 to 1970, was a Middle East expert who came to Houlton from Cairo, Egypt. Howard established a Muslim Studies program, headed by Abdulmunim Shakir, a Saudi Arabian. Here Howard presides at a 1963 cornerstone ceremony with A.R. Tandy, president, Southern Mill and Manufacturing Co.

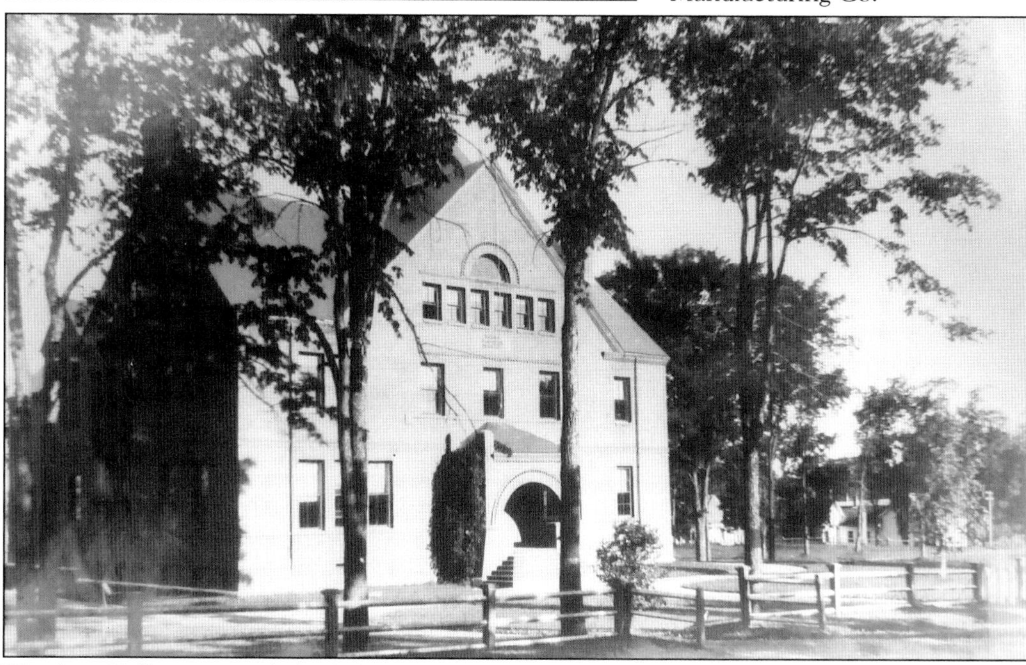

Wording Hall was a symbol of what Ricker College stood for. It eventually almost specialized in recruiting foreign students to come to its campus in Houlton, thus further widening the horizons of the community.

Two

Houlton Is Business

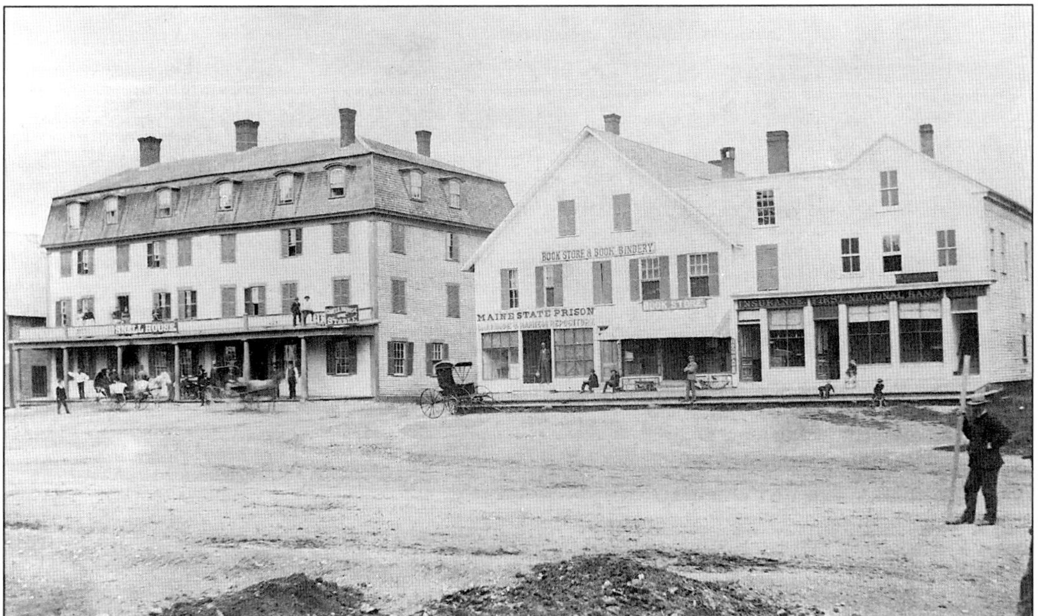

The Snell House, Houlton's leading hotel for years (it was torn down and its land made into a parking lot for the Temple Theater) stands next to the Maine State Prison Book Bindery in this 1884 photograph.

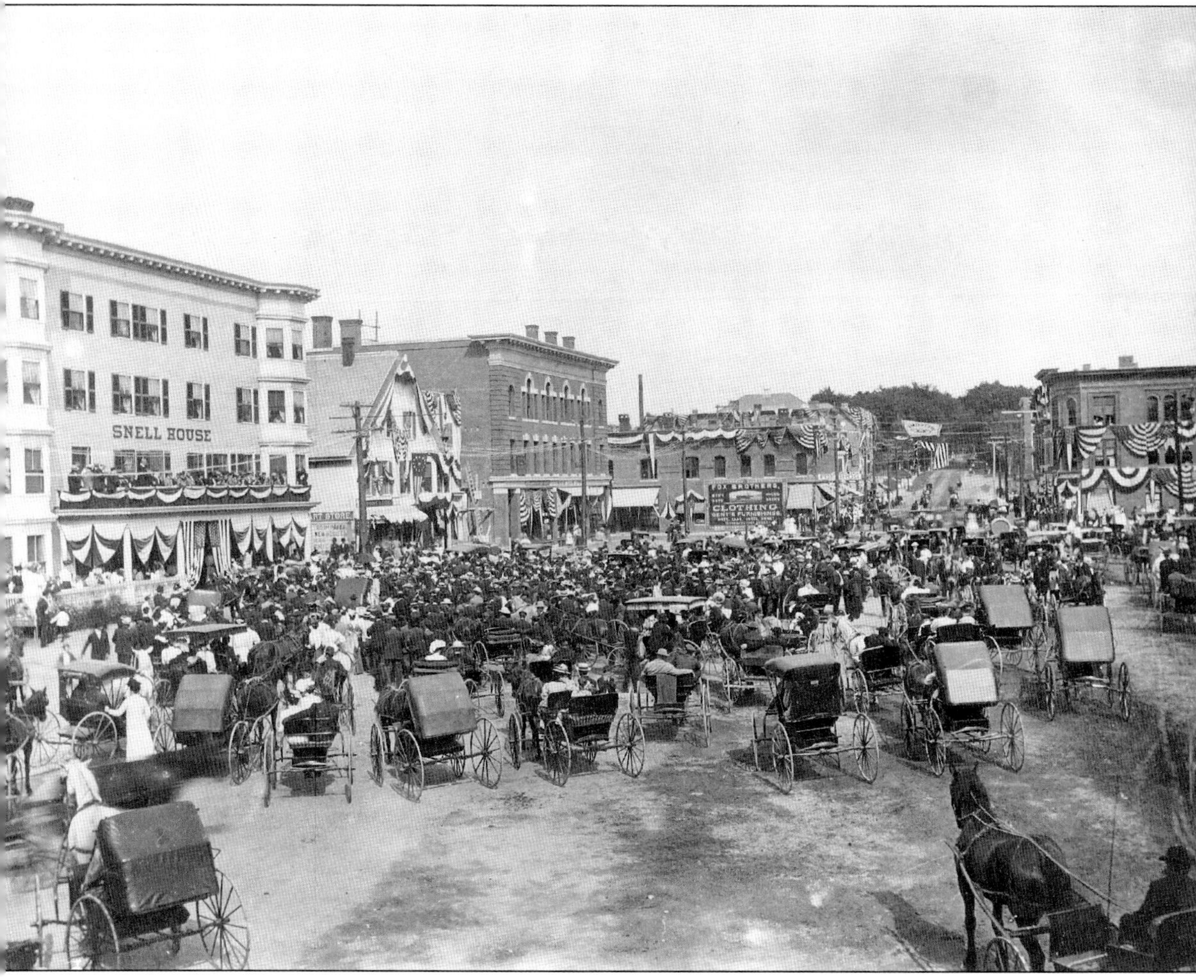

The center of business in Houlton during the period covered here was Market Square. On a Saturday night, the square would be packed with wagons, carriages and buggies as the farmers poured in from the nearby communities to do their shopping for the next week. It was (and is) a wide square like you find in many Aroostook towns. You might swear you were in a Texas town except there were no rolling balls of tumbleweed blowing along! Here's a Market Square scene about 1895, probably on a Saturday.

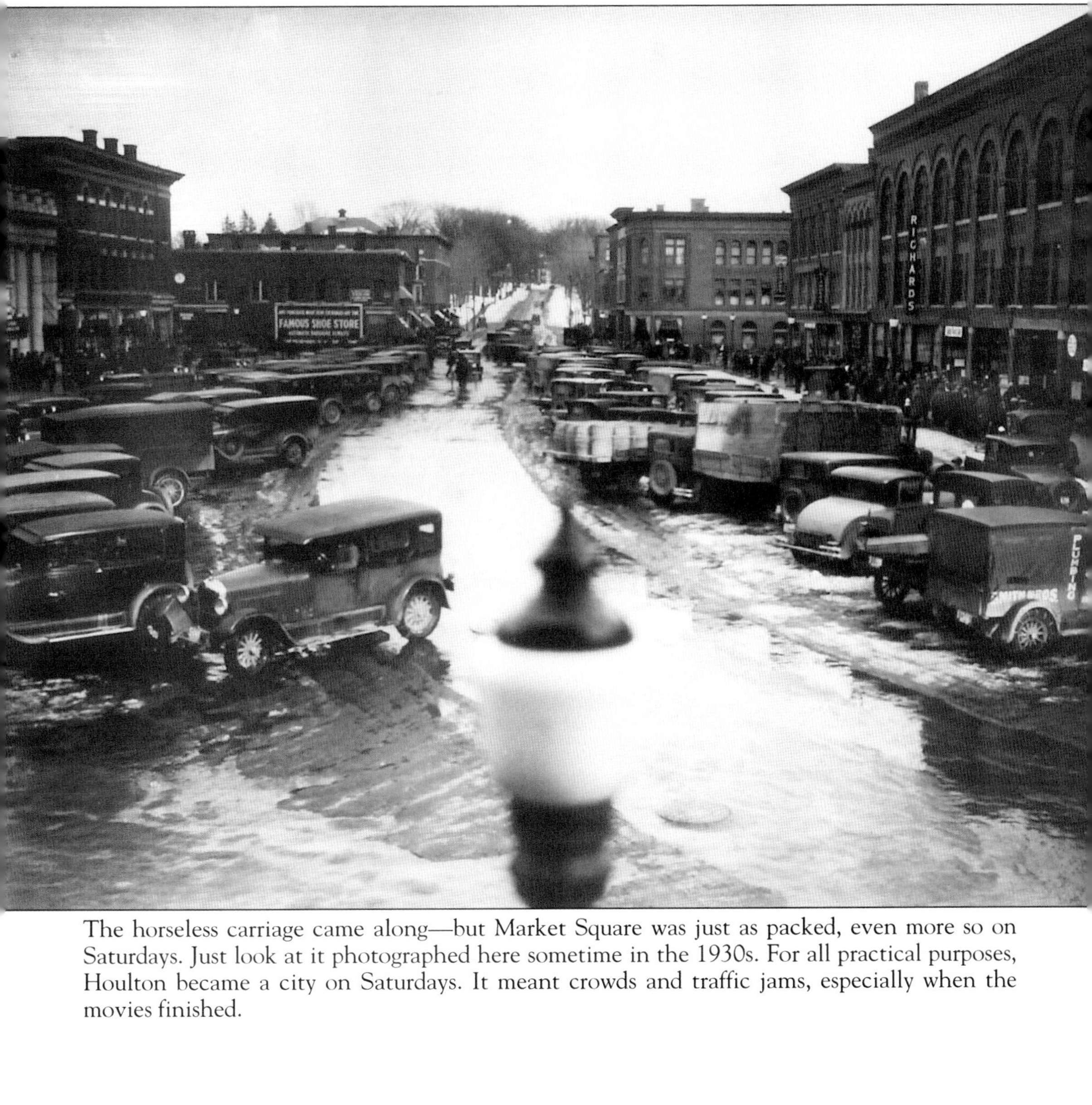

The horseless carriage came along—but Market Square was just as packed, even more so on Saturdays. Just look at it photographed here sometime in the 1930s. For all practical purposes, Houlton became a city on Saturdays. It meant crowds and traffic jams, especially when the movies finished.

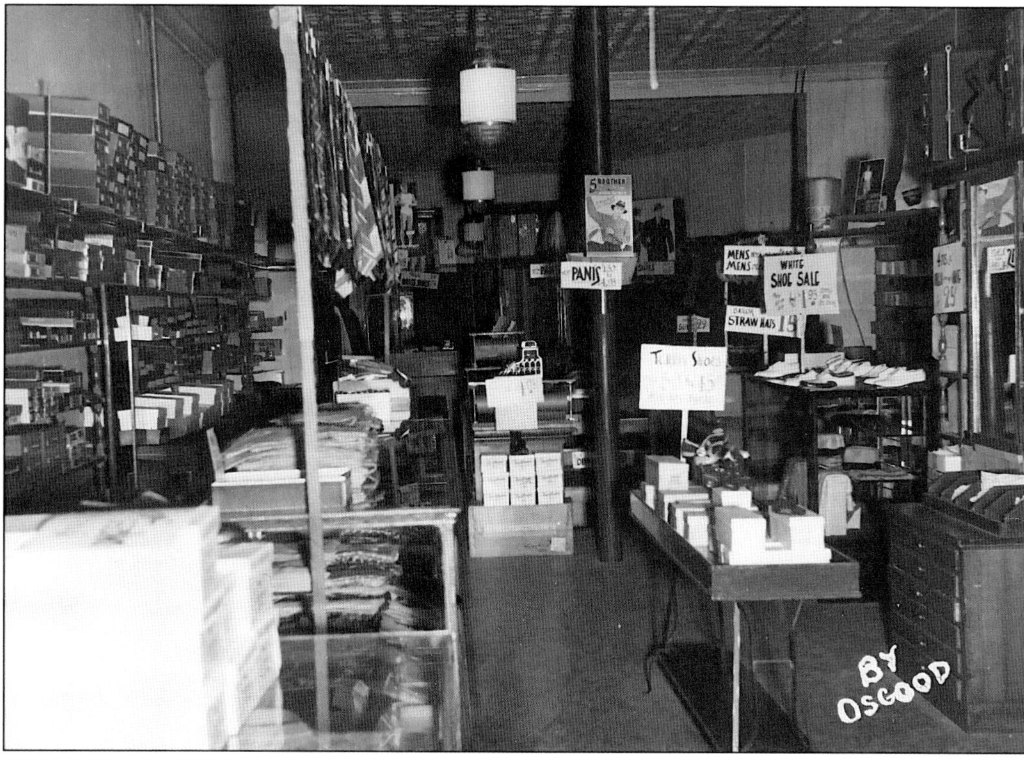

The date is uncertain for this Houlton clothing and shoe store basement photograph. But it was years ago! Note that pants cost $1.50 to $4.95 and straw hats were 15 cents apiece.

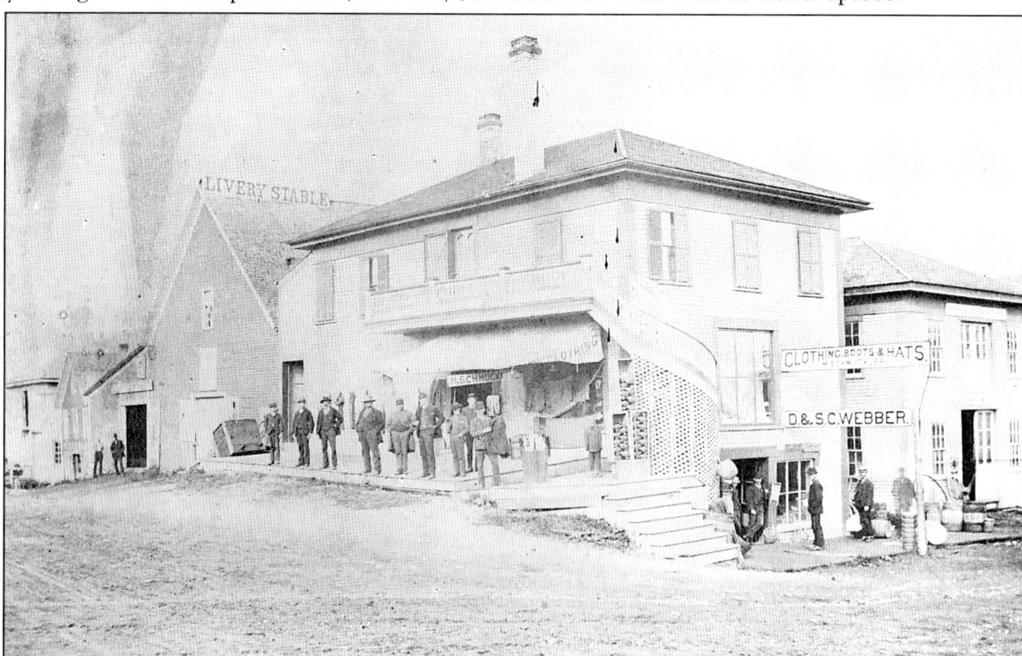

There used to be hotels in Houlton, but they are now all gone and replaced by their motel cousins. This is the Union Square Hotel in the 1850s.

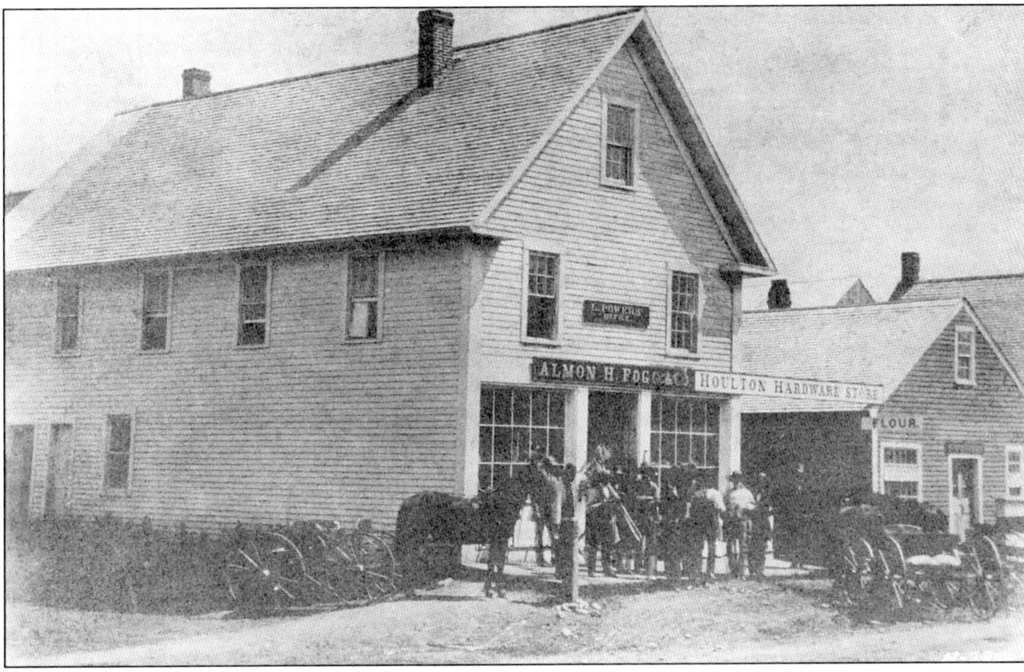

Almon H. Fogg Co., hardware firm, is still going strong. It has largely been controlled by the Pierce family. Its first store was established in 1859.

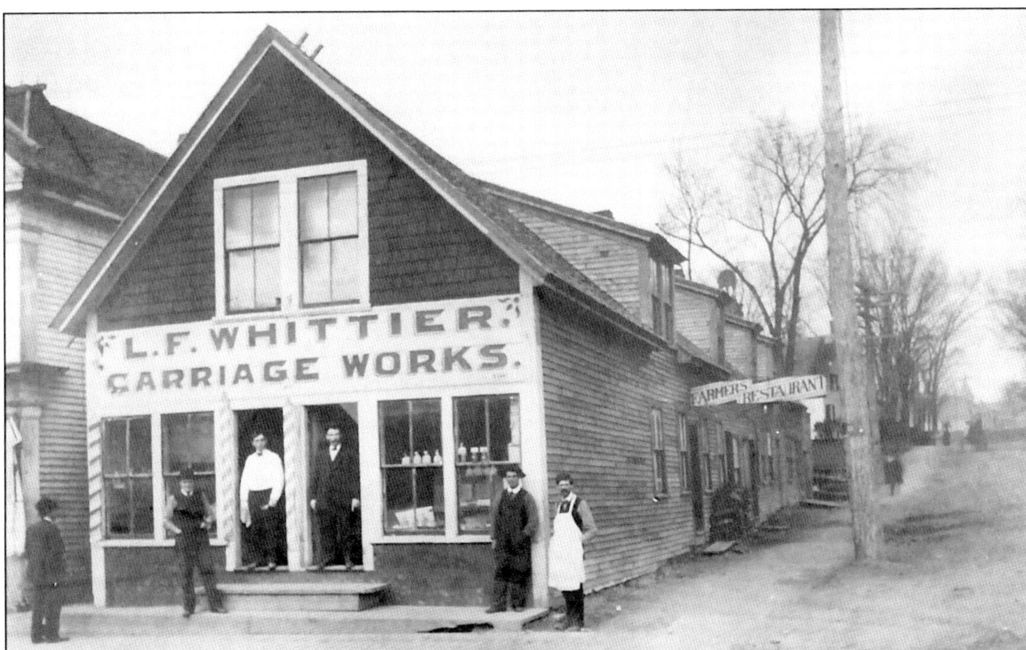

Time and technology pass some businesses by. So it was with L.F. Whittier Carriage Works. Leslie Whittier is second from left and Arthur Kitchen third from left in this 1890s photograph.

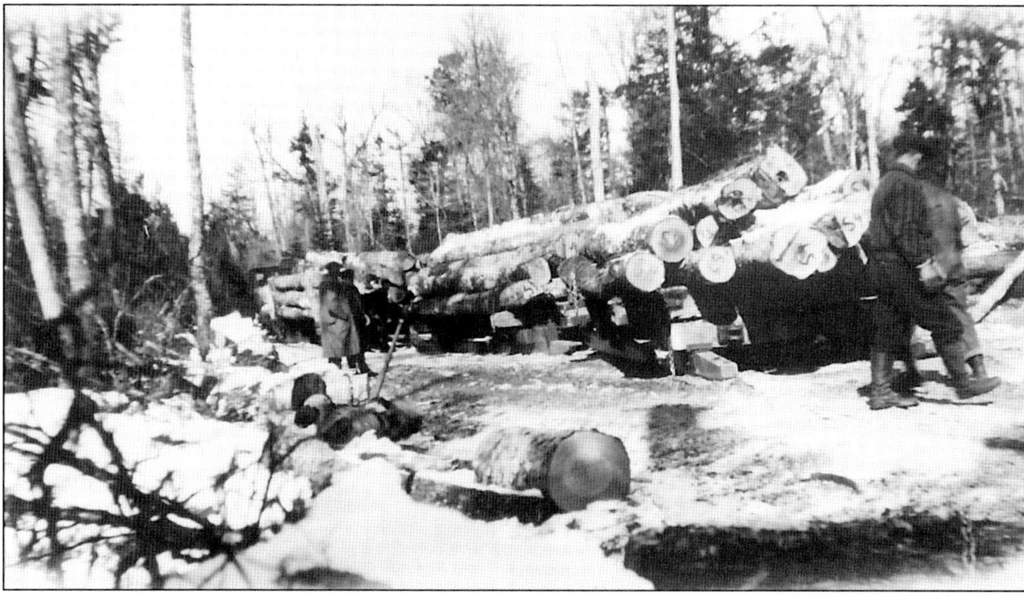
Before there were potatoes en masse in Houlton, there was logging. It still goes on in the area. Here we see possibly Clarence Bither on a skidder.

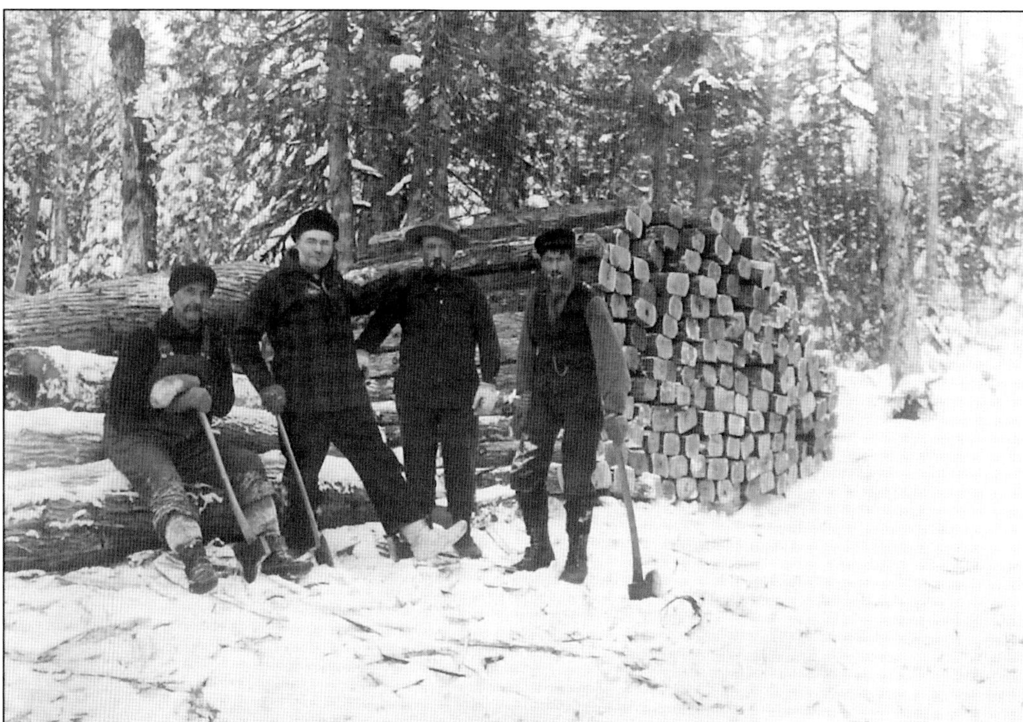
Another Houlton area logging operation, probably in the 1890s. Leslie Whittier may be one of those on the scene.

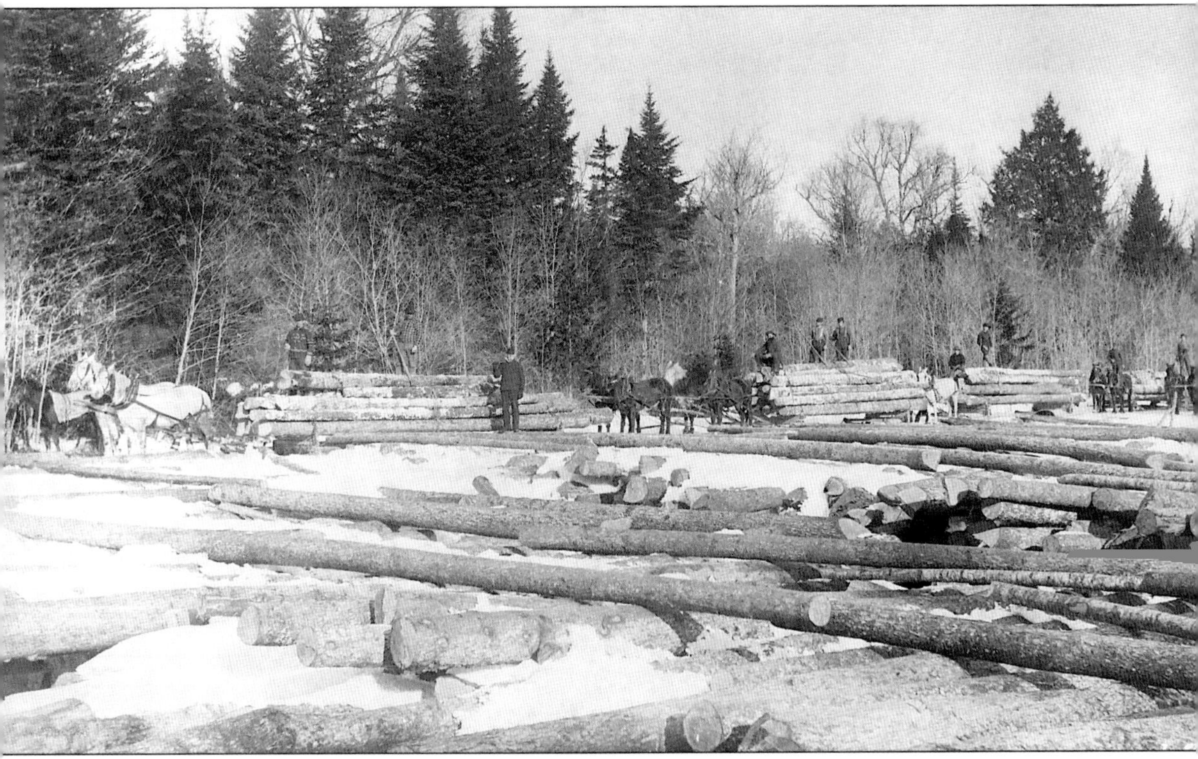

We can pin this good-looking logging operation down. It was conducted by Emerson Brothers in 1891. Maynard Russell of Linneus is driving the first team. Potatoes didn't really get big in Houlton and the County until the Bangor and Aroostook Railroad reached Houlton in December, 1893, but woods work still went on. Now it is done for the Louisiana Pacific plant in New Limerick.

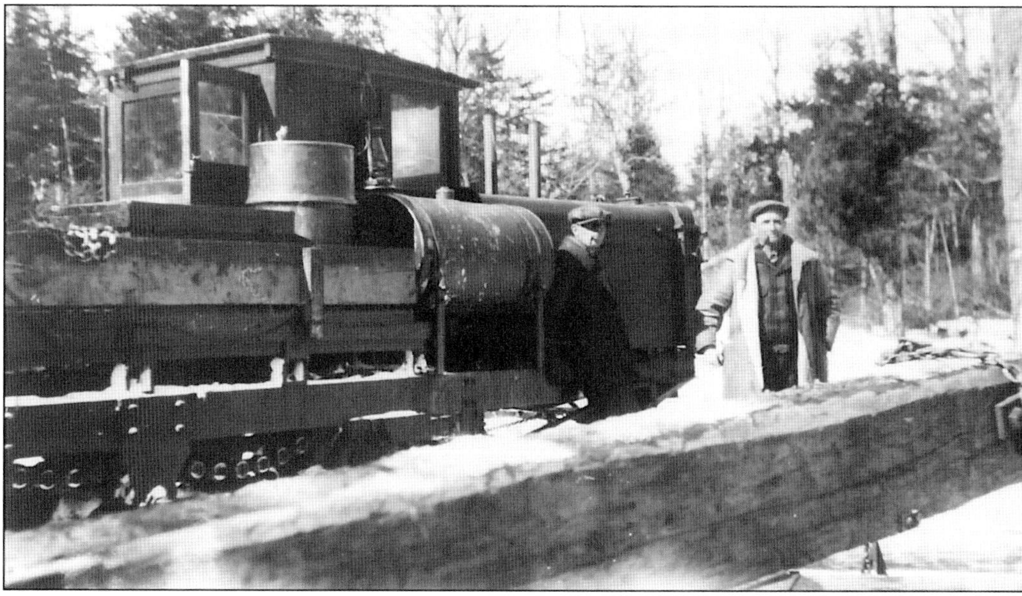

Clarence Bither is on the right in Linneus, probably in the 1890s. That's a regular woods hauler.

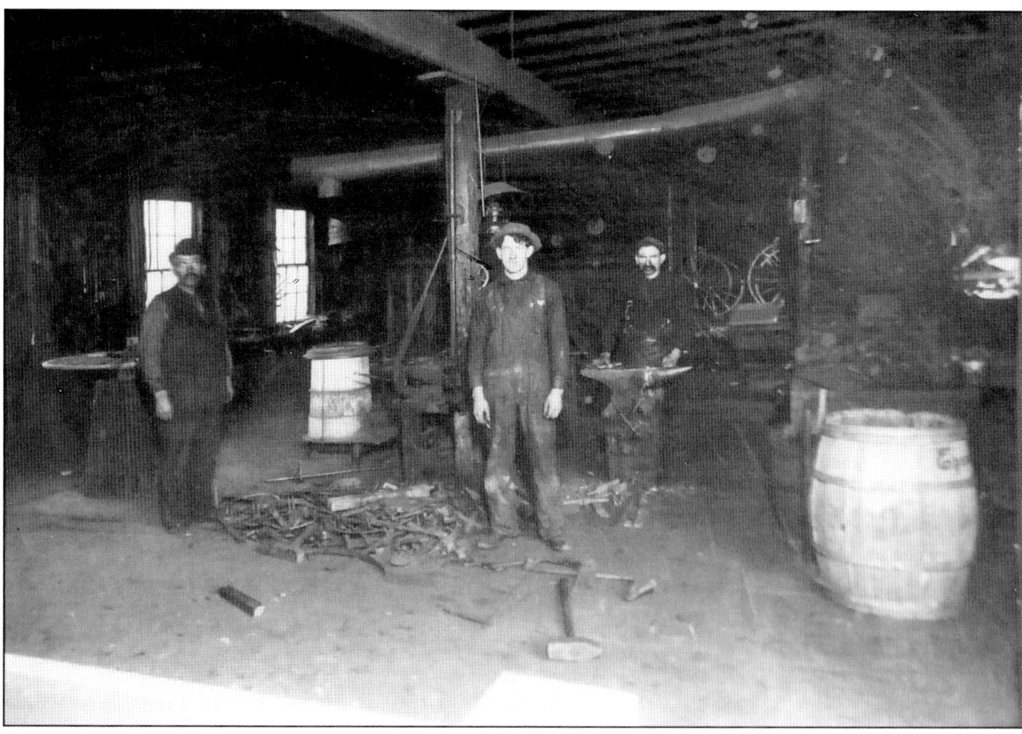

Anson Taber operated a blacksmith shop in Houlton. Silas Taber and Frank McNally can be seen here with Robert Derrah at the anvil.

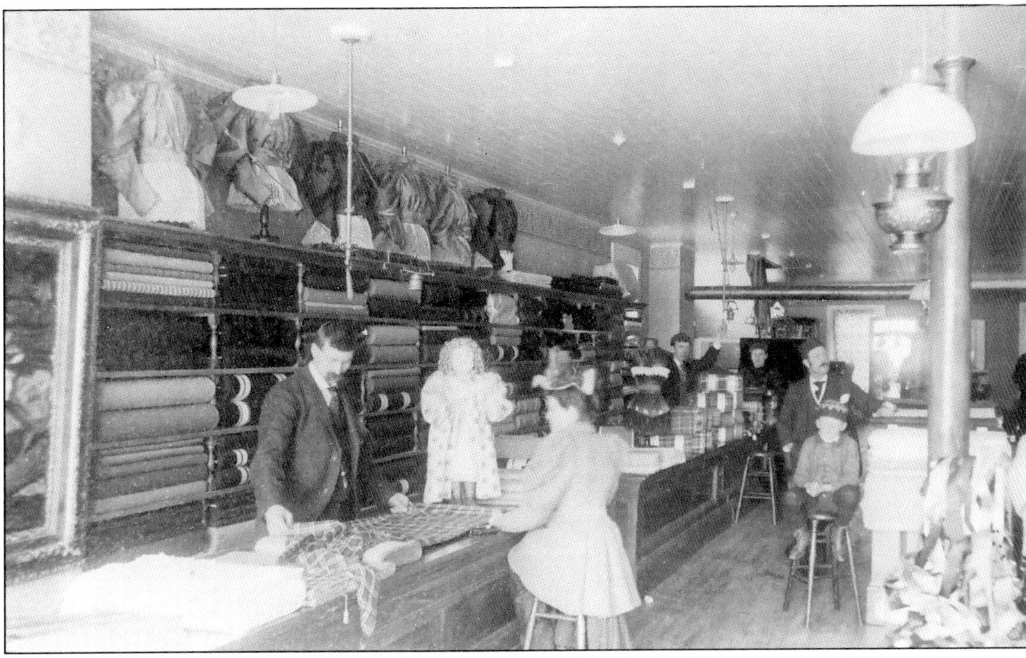

George W. Richards became a merchant prince in Houlton. This was one of his early stores. Here we see Richards with Hobson W. Richards (the small boy), Frank Rogers of Massachusetts behind the counter and Walter Small in the rear behind the counter. Emma Wright is in the rear and there's a partial view of Minnie Yerxa, sitting at the counter on the right.

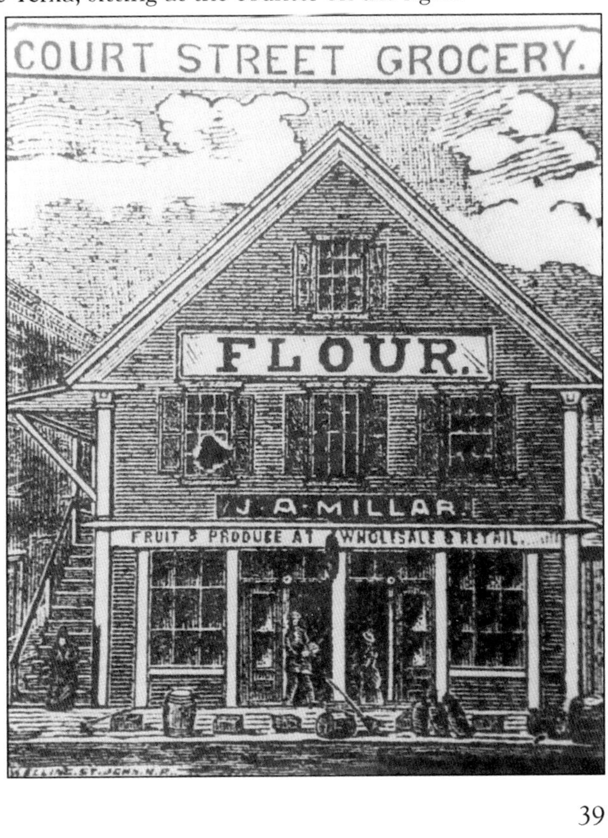

This is a woodcut of the John Millar store about 1870. The store operated for years.

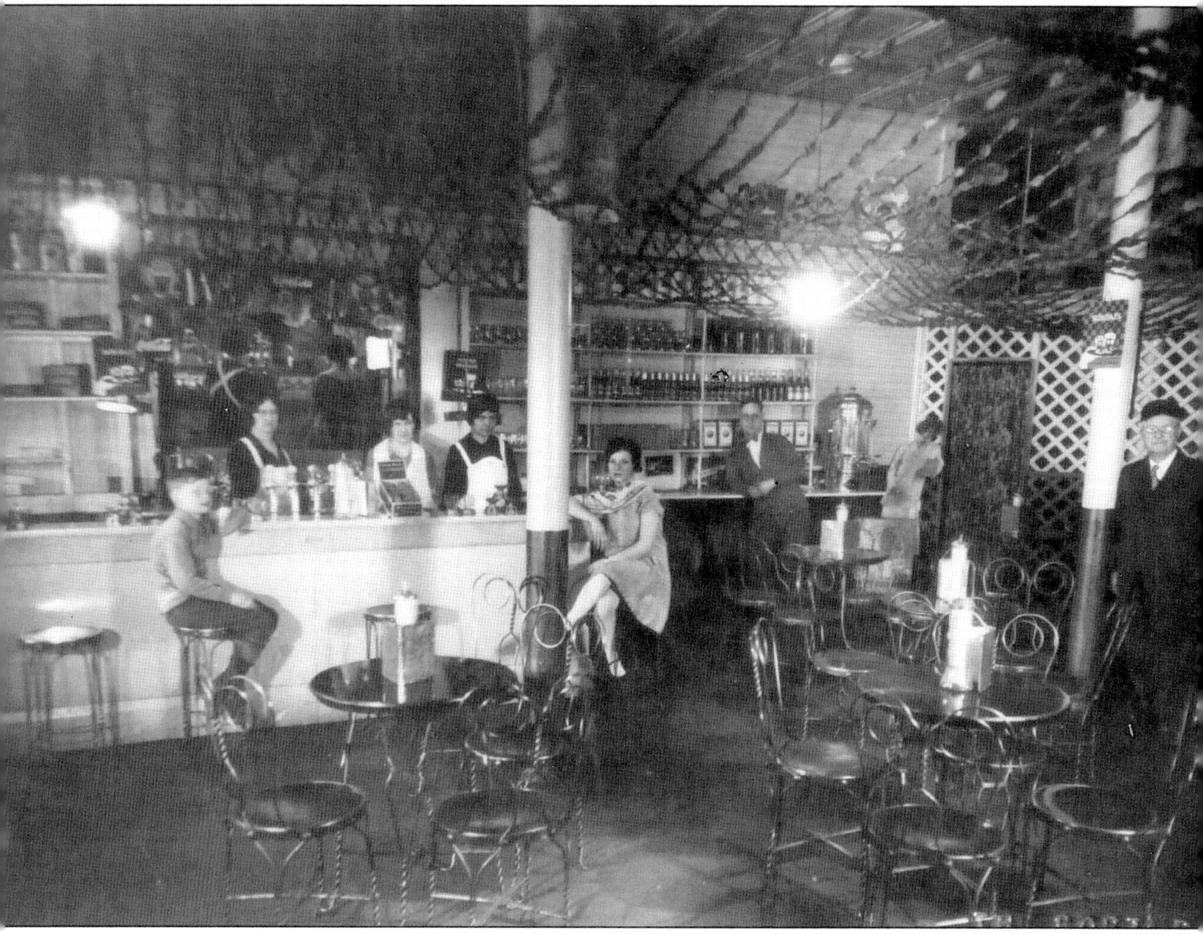

Still going strong in 1930, the Millar store is photographed here crowded with relatives. Young John Millar is on the left with his sister, Leeta Millar (Posey) next to him and their father, Albert G. Millar next. At the right is John A. Millar, then eighty years old.

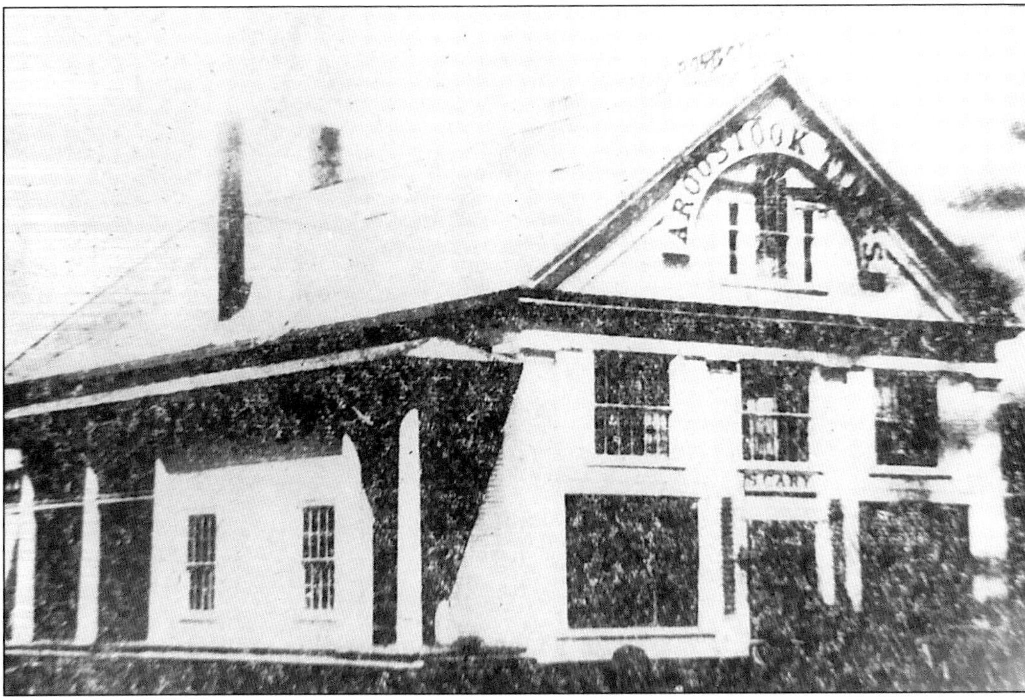

The *Aroostook Times* was published in this building. Newspapers in Houlton have usually had excellent records.

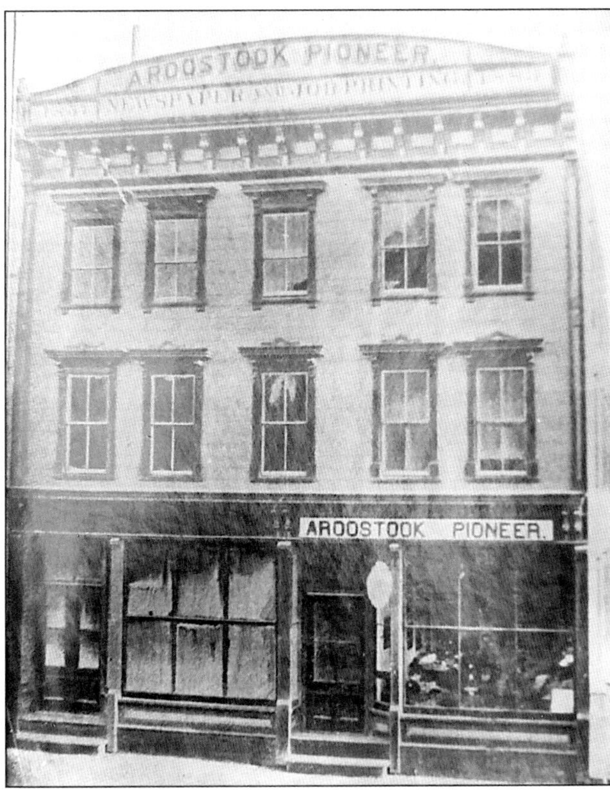

And here the *Aroostook Pioneer* was published.

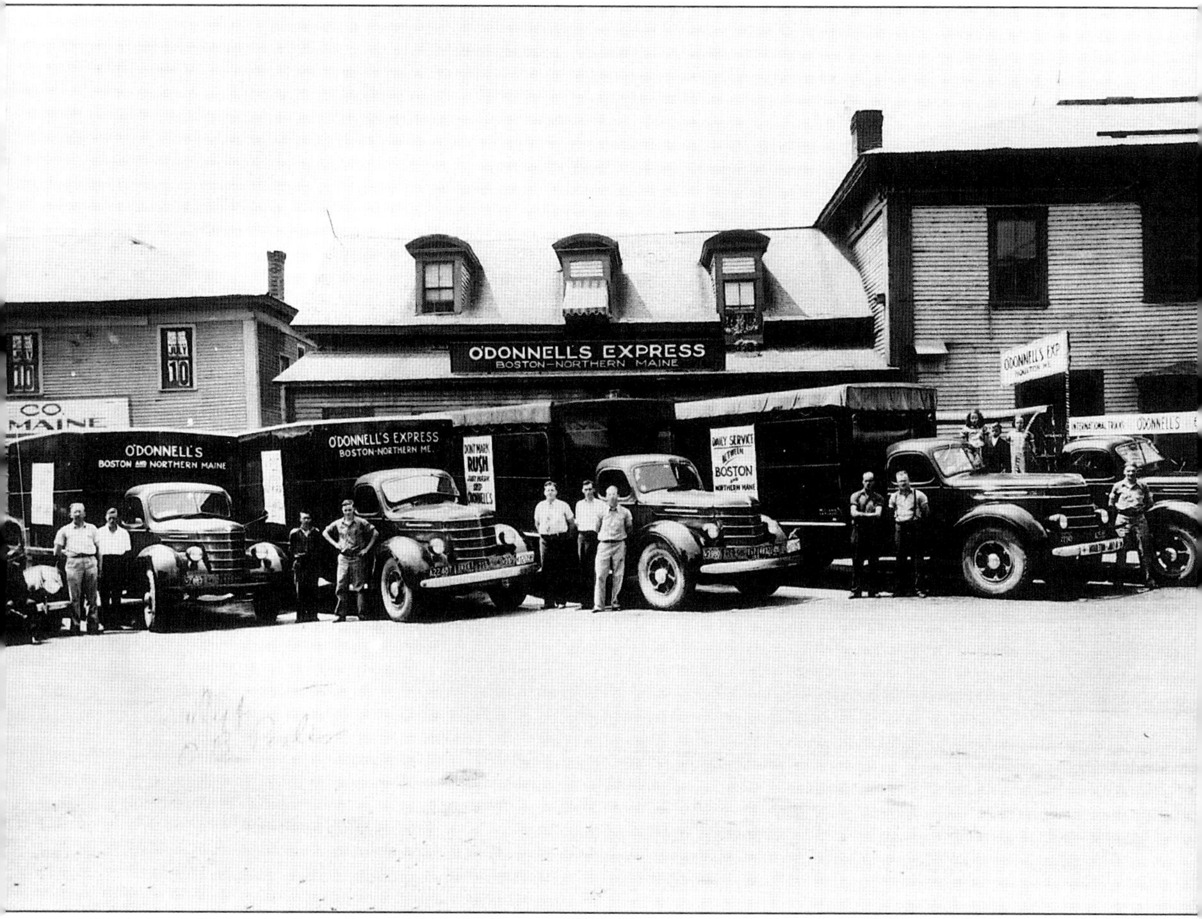

And then there was transportation. O'Donnell's Express operated out of Houlton. Here, before the 4 July, 1939 parade are, left to right: George O'Donnell, Wilfred Hannon, Bernard Swimm, Lee London, Chris O'Donnell, Perley Alexander, Elwood Porter, Lewis London and Sparkie Cummings. The children are: Dorothy O'Donnell Hay, Joseph O'Donnell, Elaine O'Donnell and Barbara O'Donnell.

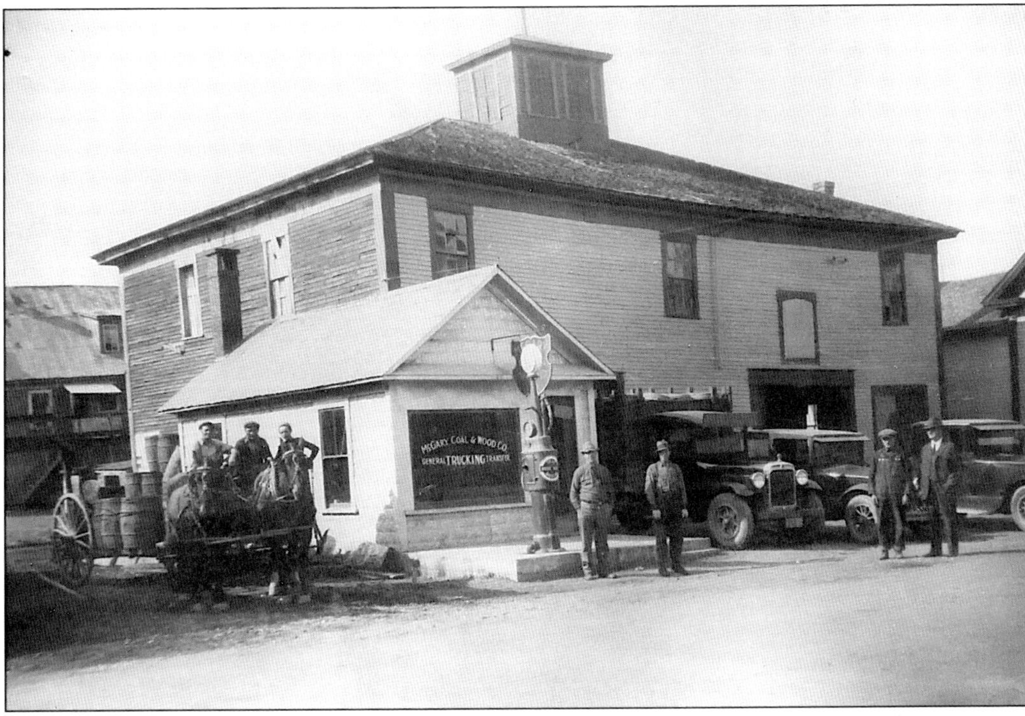

McGary's was another Houlton-based trucking firm. This photograph dates from the 1930s.

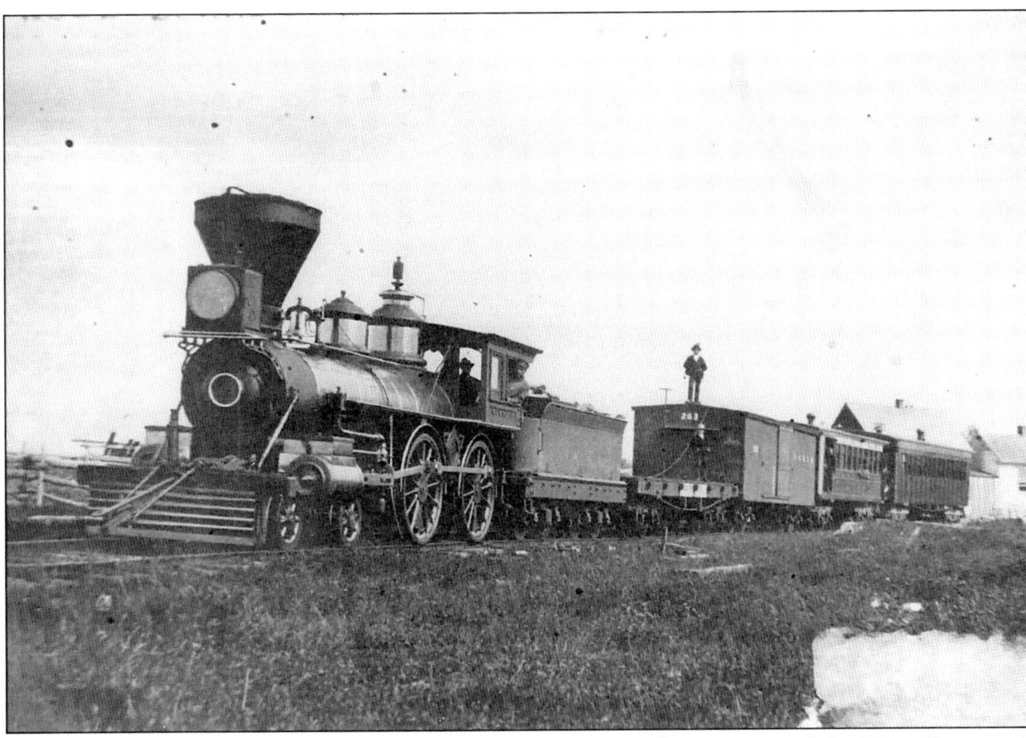

But the railroad came first. This is a wood-burning steam locomotive of the New Brunswick Railway at Houlton some time between 1870 and 1890.

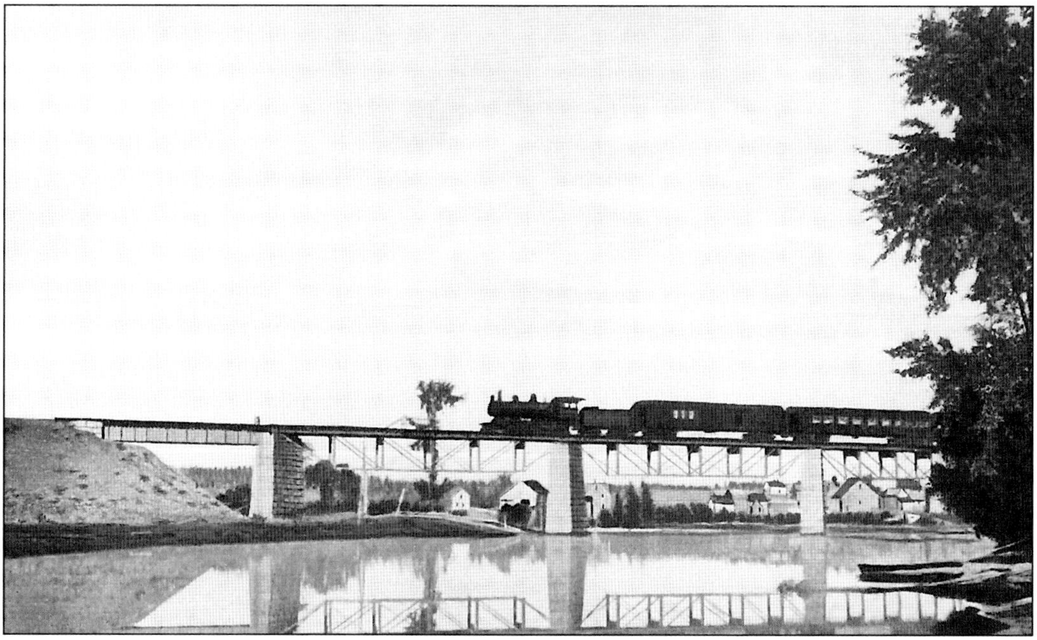

A Bangor and Aroostook Railroad train chugs over the railroad bridge at Houlton.

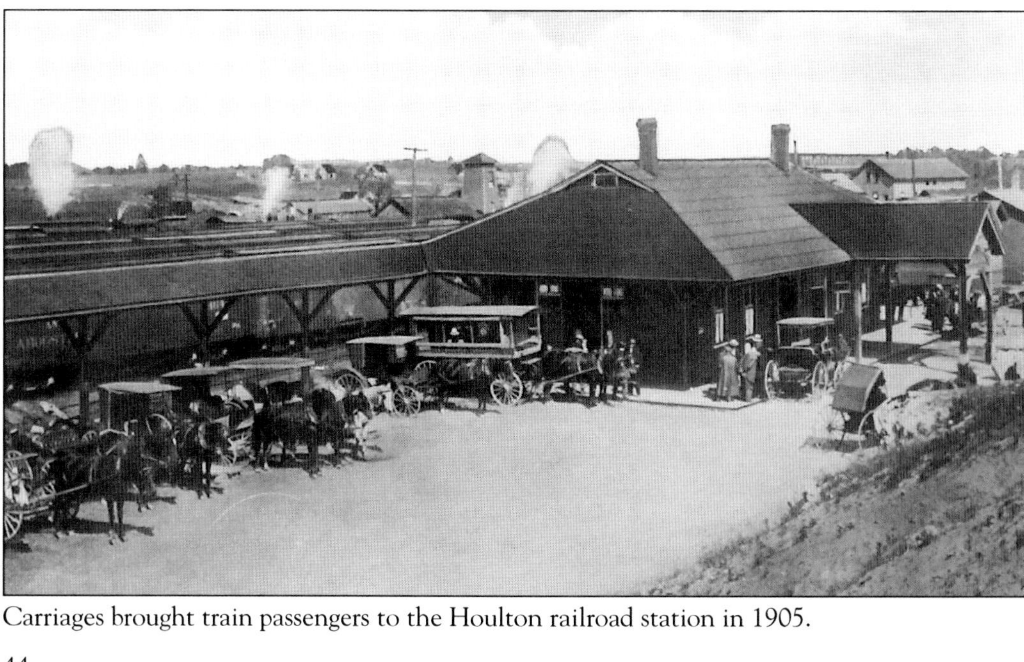

Carriages brought train passengers to the Houlton railroad station in 1905.

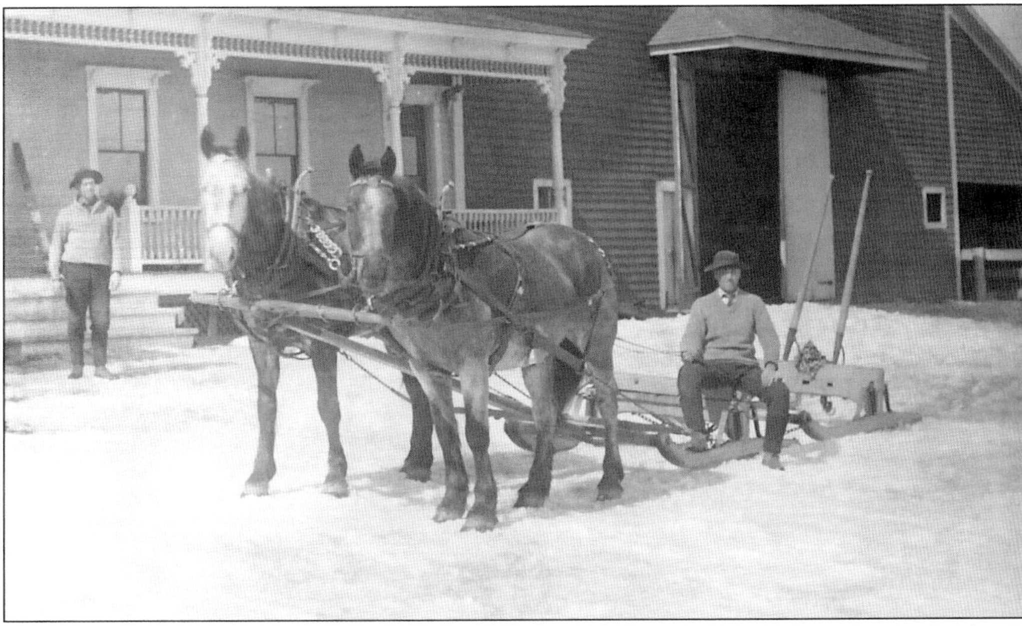

Back on the farms, horses were still being used to take people through and over the heavy snowfalls of Houlton and vicinity.

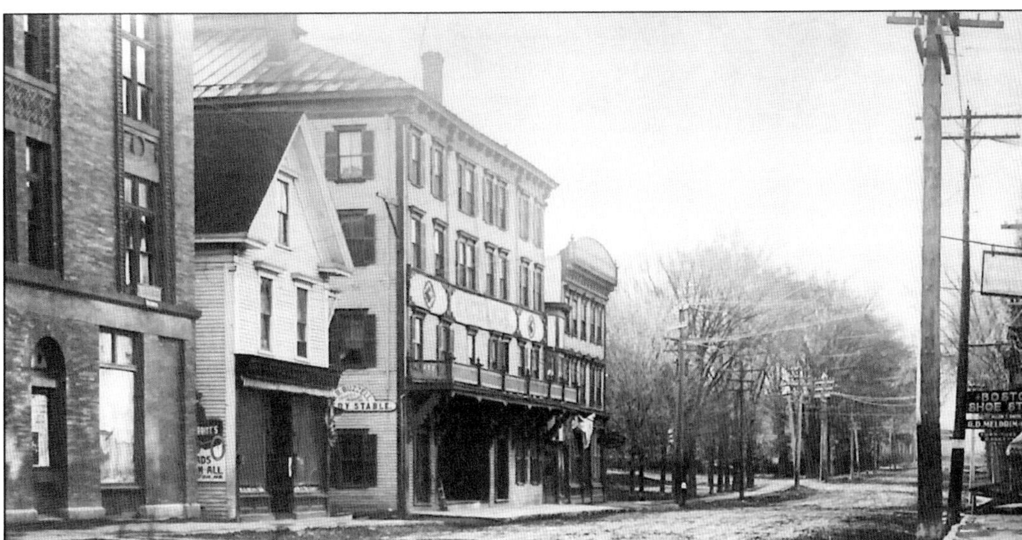

The warmth of hotels was good during the winters and they were often cool in the summers. This was the Hotel Exchange, built in 1880 and burnt to the ground on 3 May, 1942. It was at the corner of Court and Main Streets.

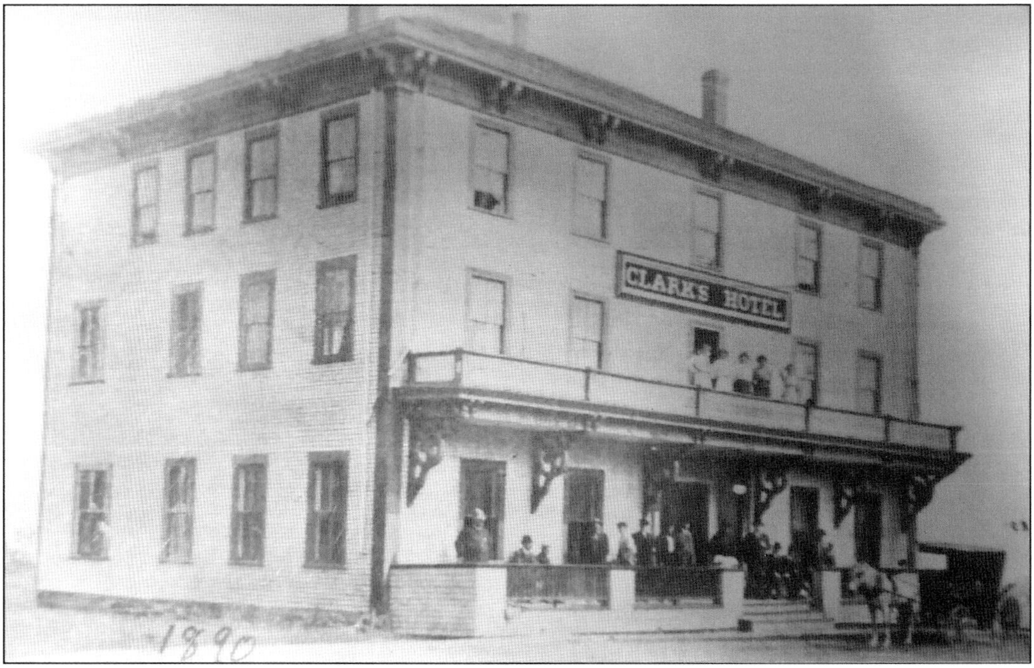

Clark's Hotel was flourishing in 1890.

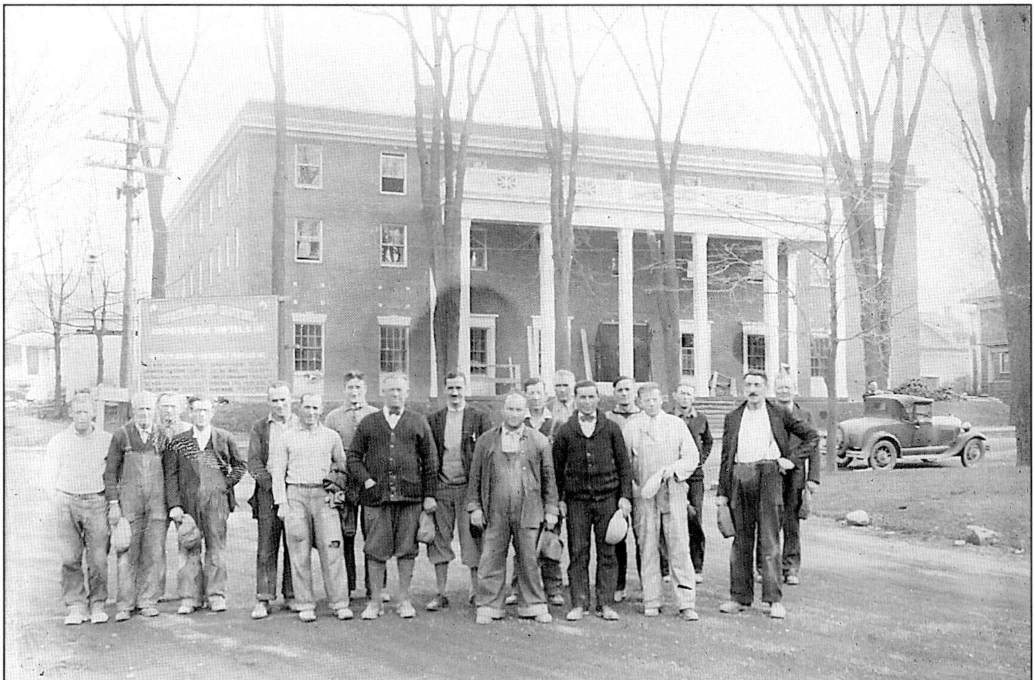

Finally came the Northland Hotel. Here it is pictured in the fall of 1930, shortly before it opened in December of that year. In front of it are some of the owners and some of the construction crew. It has not been a hotel for some years.

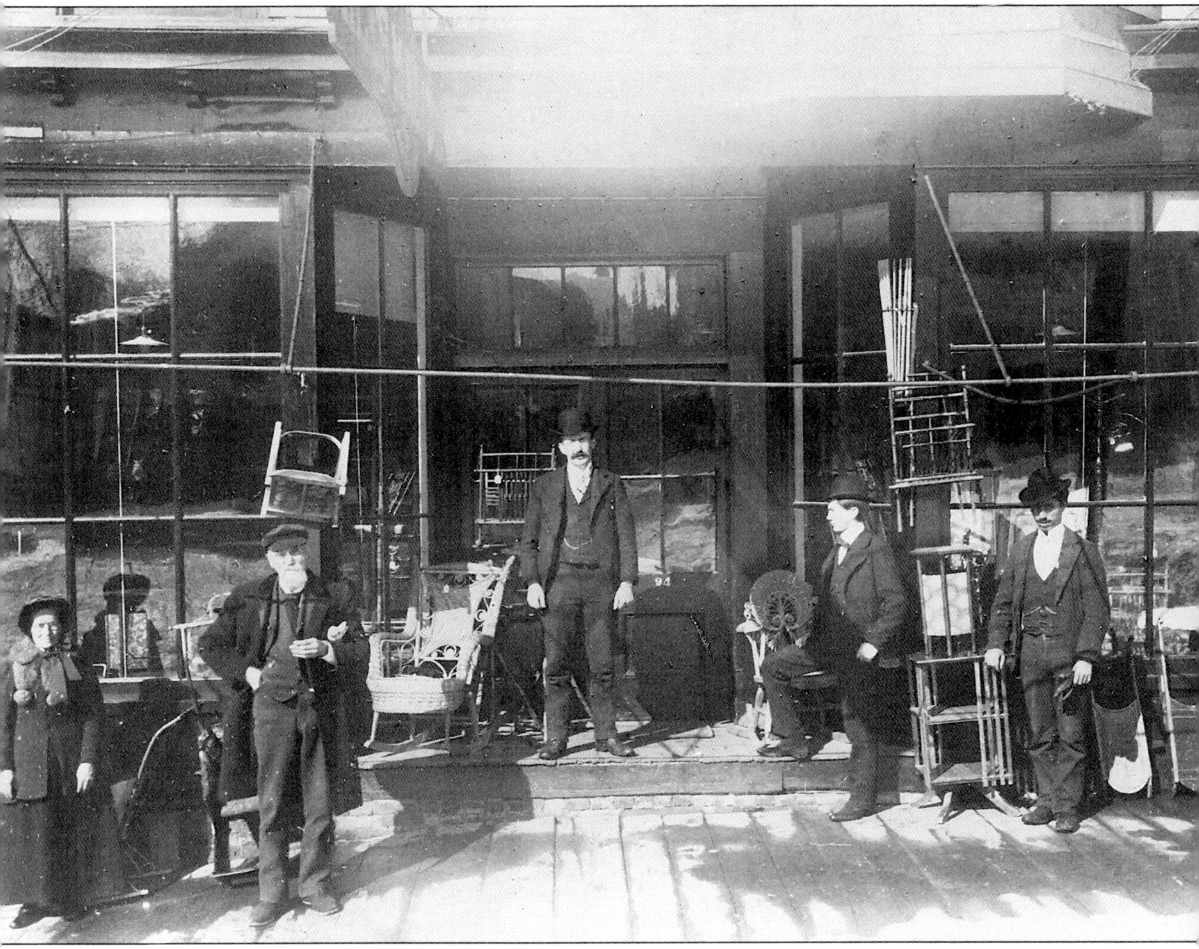

The John M. Rice Furniture Store was the first in Houlton. The man on the far right is Harry F. Mansfield. On the left are John and Eleanor (Stone) Gray, parents of one of Houlton's oldest citizens, Sadie G. Smith, who lived from 1867 to 1972. The furniture industry blended in nicely with wood products. However, for years Houlton people had either made their own furniture or purchased it elsewhere.

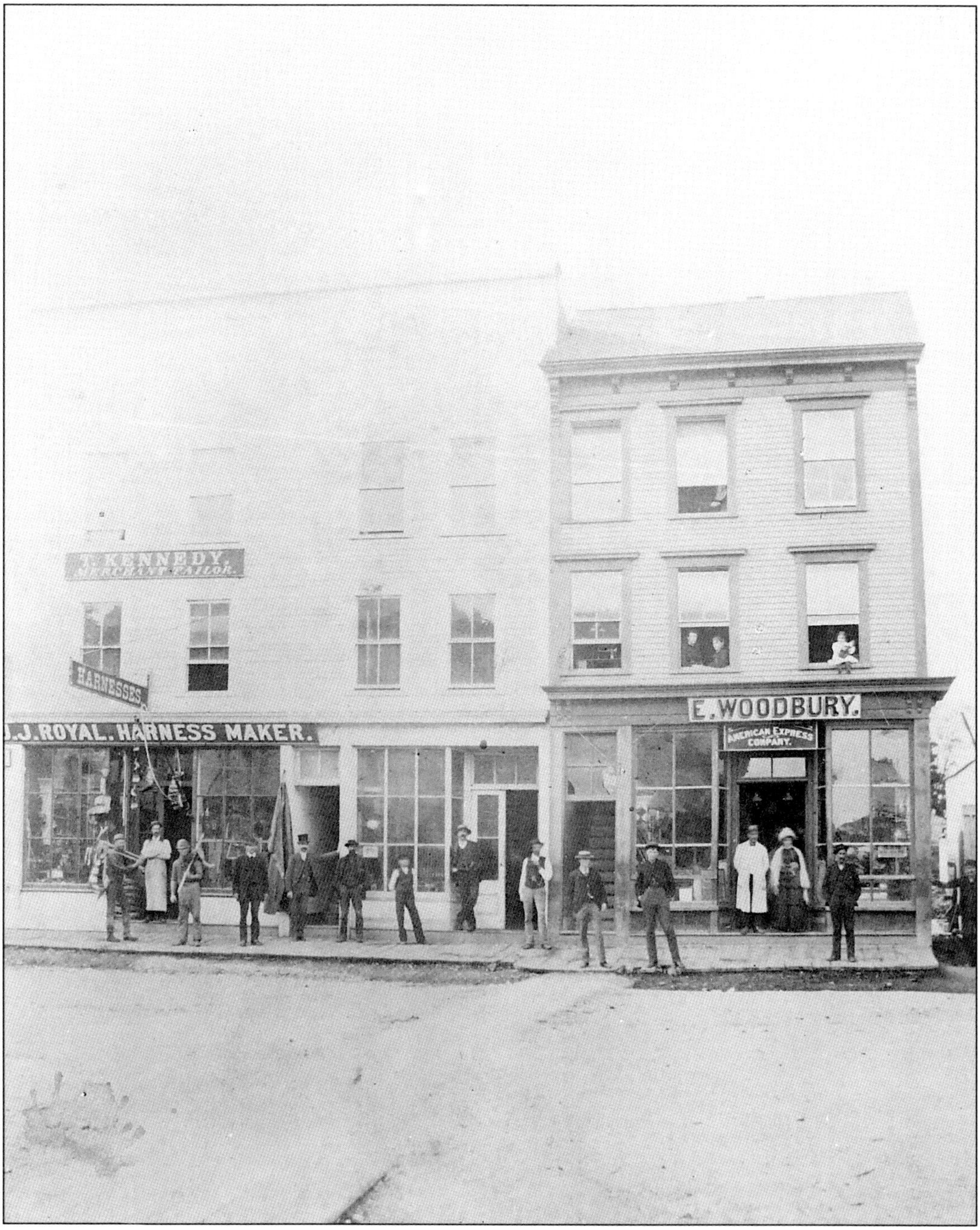

Houlton's first American Express Company outlet and the J.J. Royal harness making firm stand in the 1850s at the site of what was to be the Dunn Block. One thing about downtown Houlton around Market Square—its businesses did change, especially when one looks at them over a long period of time.

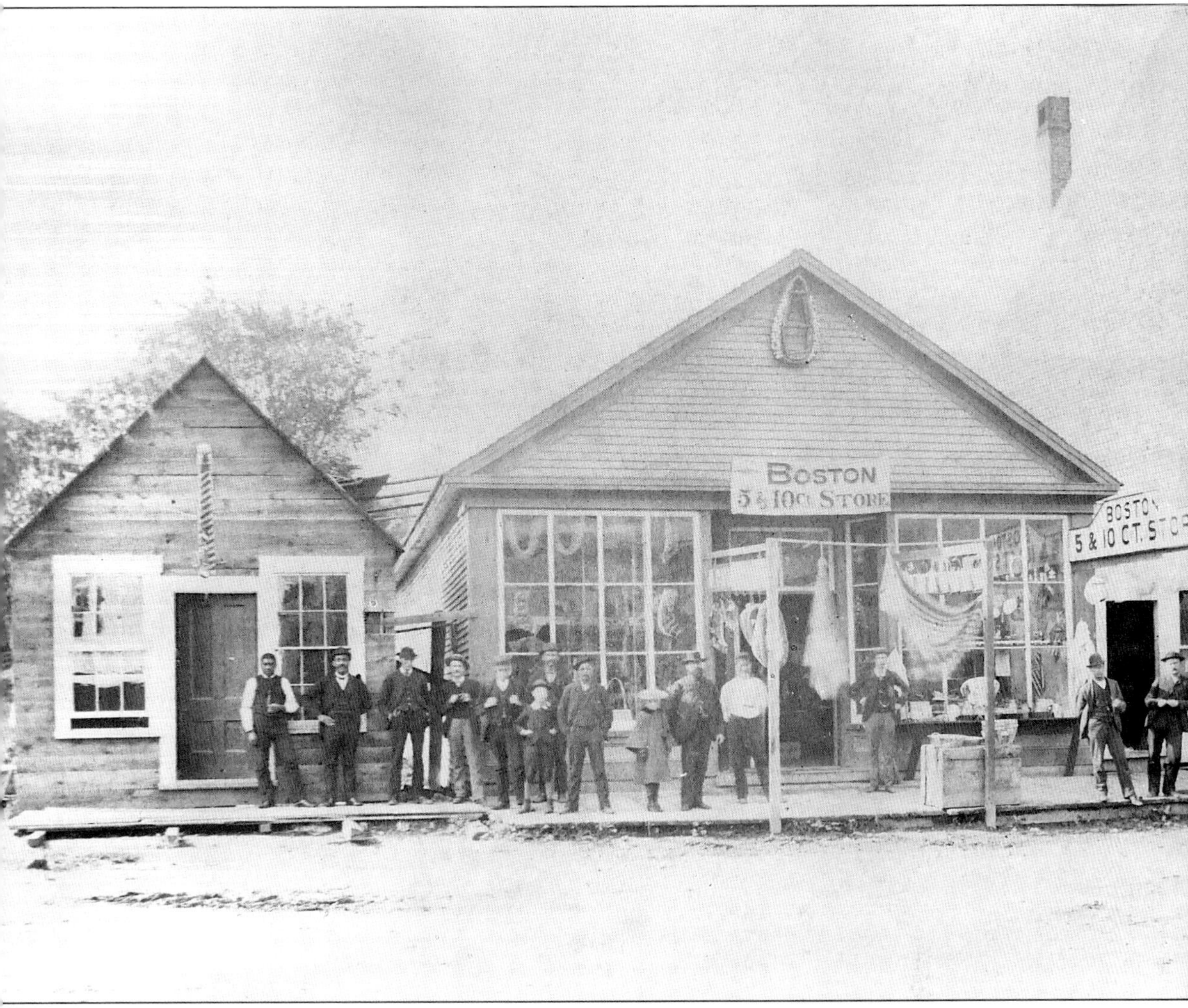

Here's the site of the Dunn Block in 1889, complete with Boston 5 & 10 Cent Store. Once again, all businesses did not stay put, even in a relatively conservative Market Square.

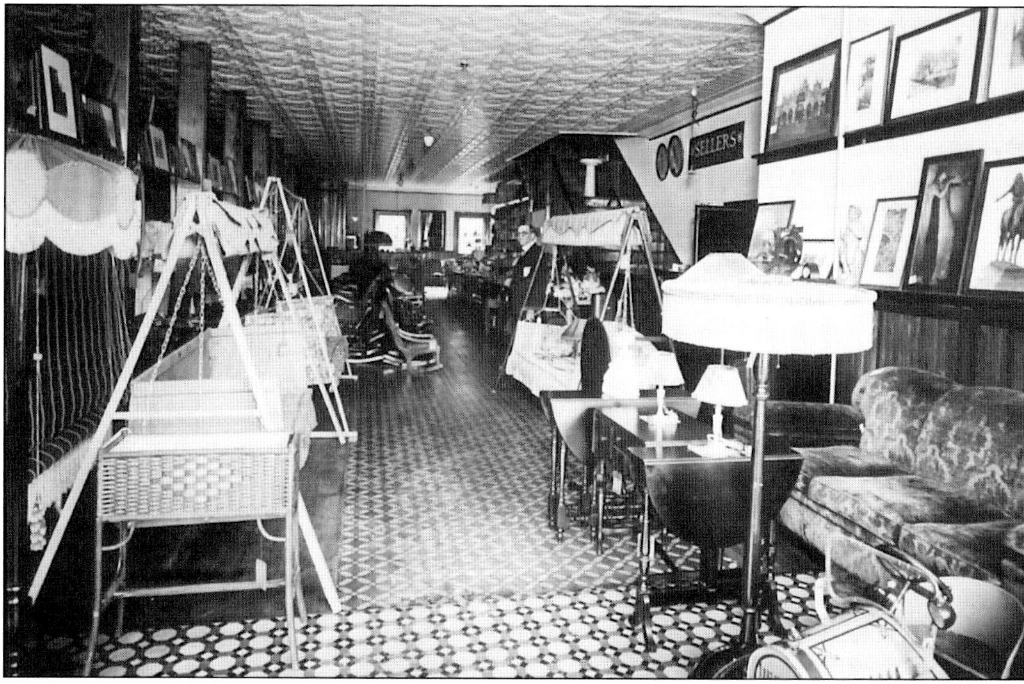

Frank Dunn stands in the Dunn Furniture Store after it opened in the Dunn Block on Main Street.

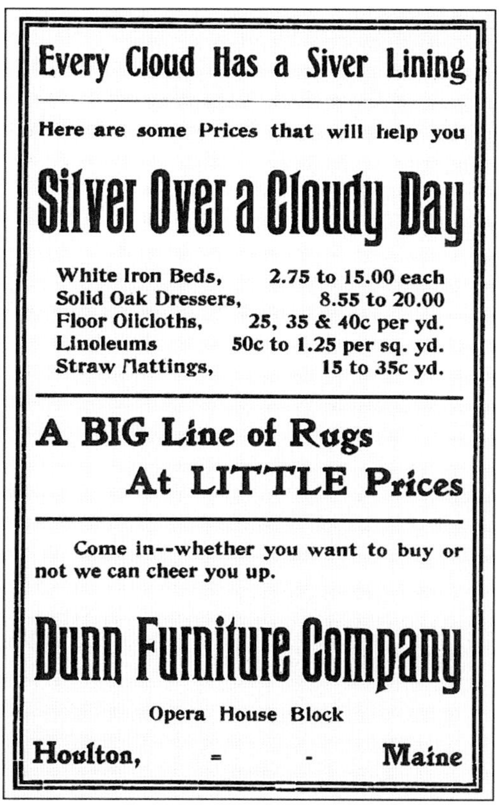

Look at the prices on the Dunn's advertisement! This advertisement appeared in the Monticello annual report for 1910.

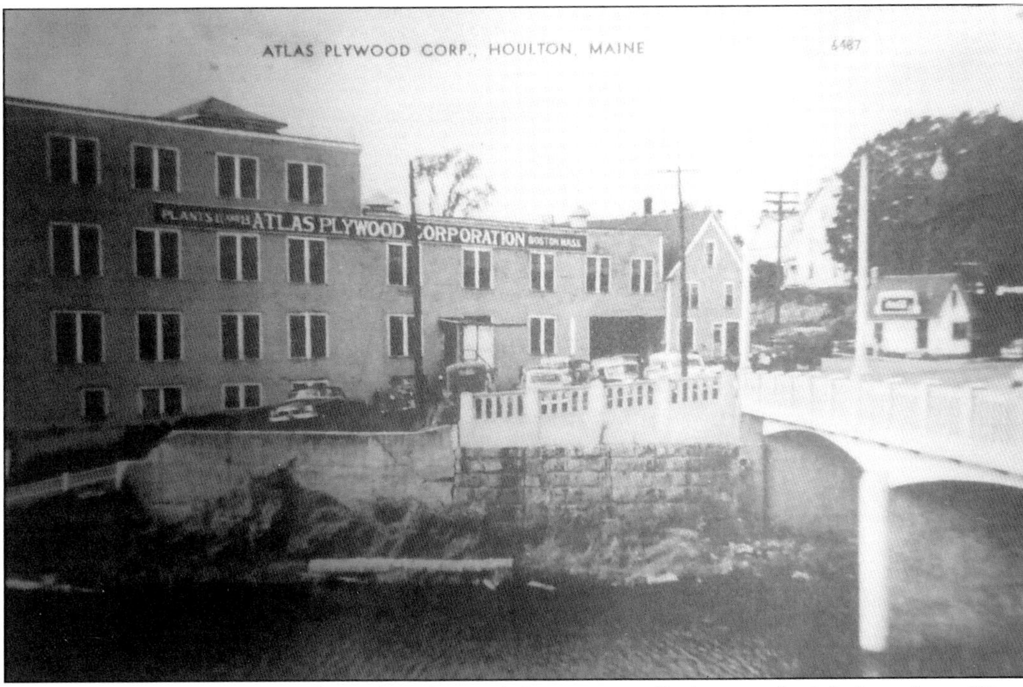

Of more modern vintage is the Atlas Plywood Company mill close to the Meduxnekeag River, photographed in 1954. The building had once been a woolen mill. It no longer operates.

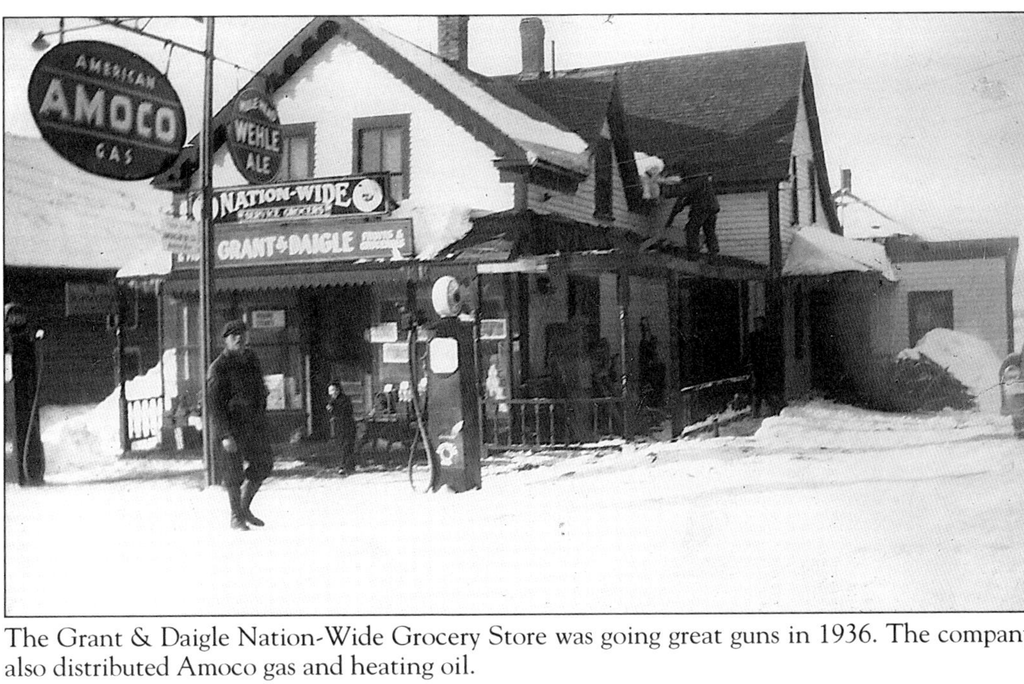

The Grant & Daigle Nation-Wide Grocery Store was going great guns in 1936. The company also distributed Amoco gas and heating oil.

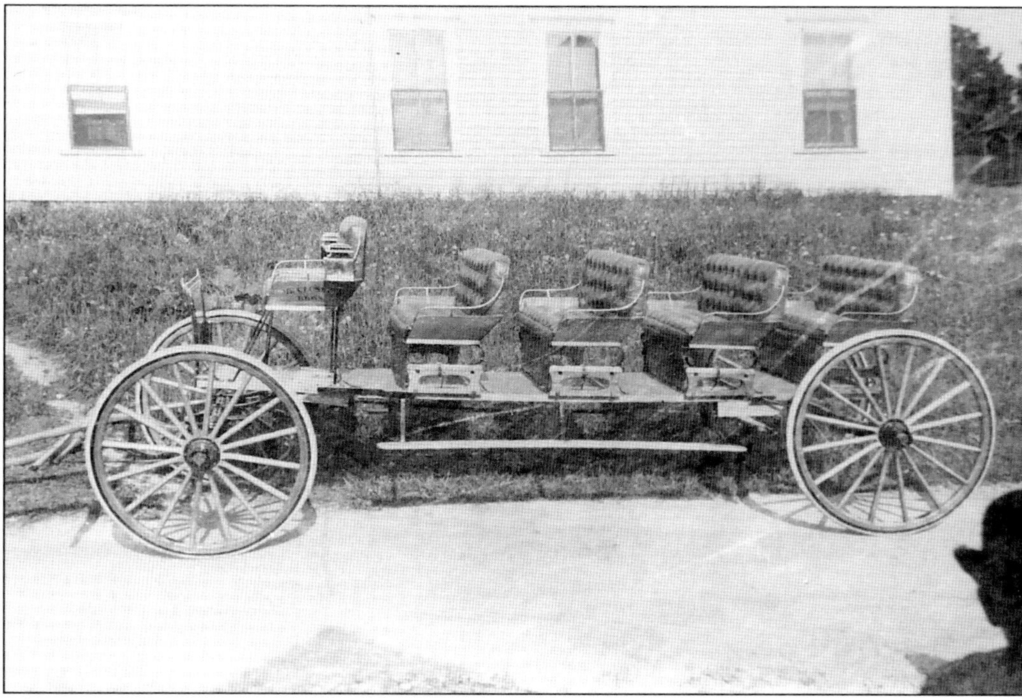

This buckboard was built by Silas G. Taber for the McCluskey Livery stable around 1898.

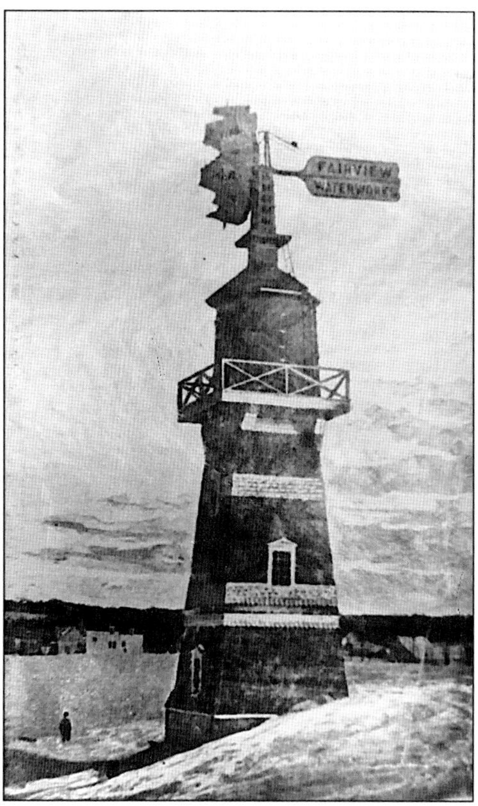

Fairview Water Works had this tower on High Street for a number of years in the later 1800s.

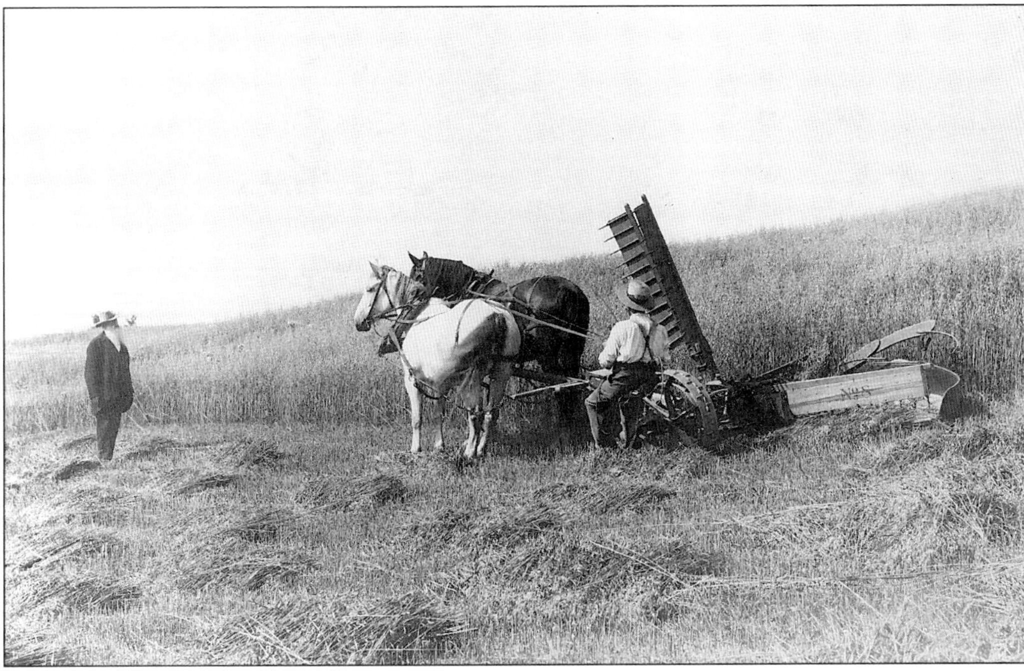

But where was farming in all this, the twin staple with logging before the potato became king in Houlton? Doing quite well, thank you! O.F. French observes as Fred Cox operates the McCormick Reaper at the French Farm on Bangor Road.

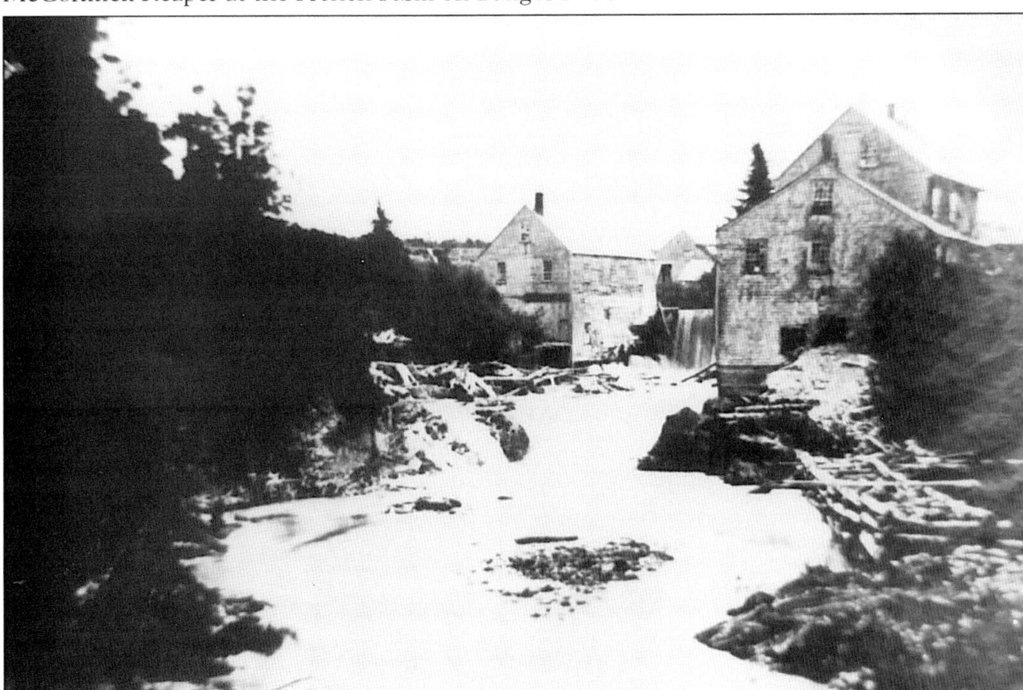

Wheat and other forms of grain were grown in quantity. The harvested grain was taken to mills like Cary's Grist Mill at Cary's Mills on Bangor Road. That mill was founded by Shepard Cary, for whom the area was named.

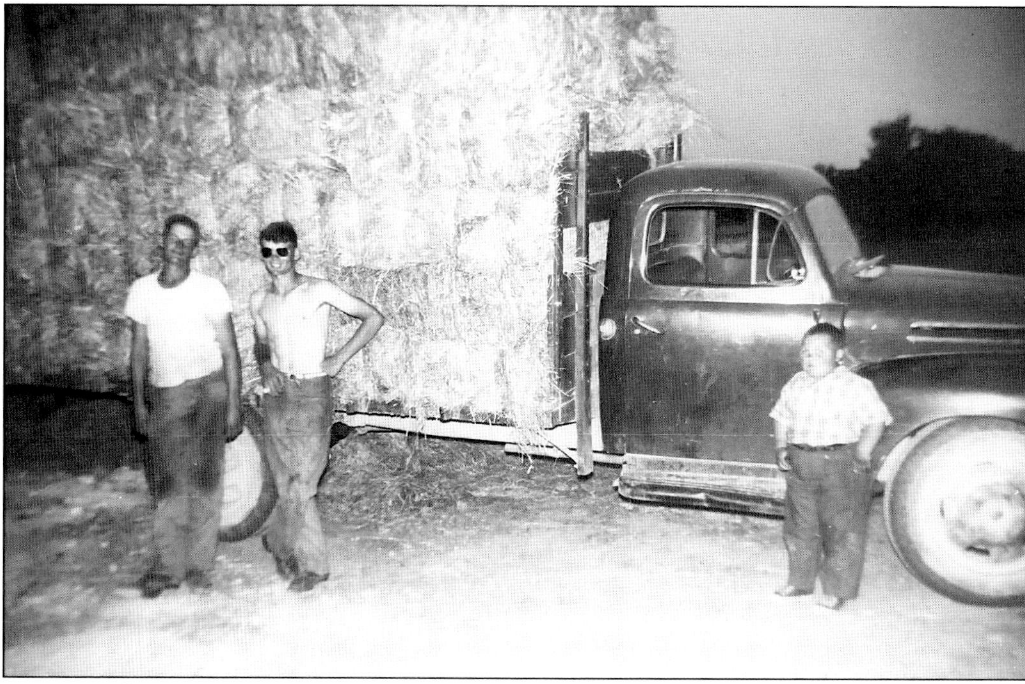

Farming, of course, has endured. Donald Fitzpatrick, Alan Harris and Charlie Currie are haying in 1954 on the Fitzpatrick farm in Houlton.

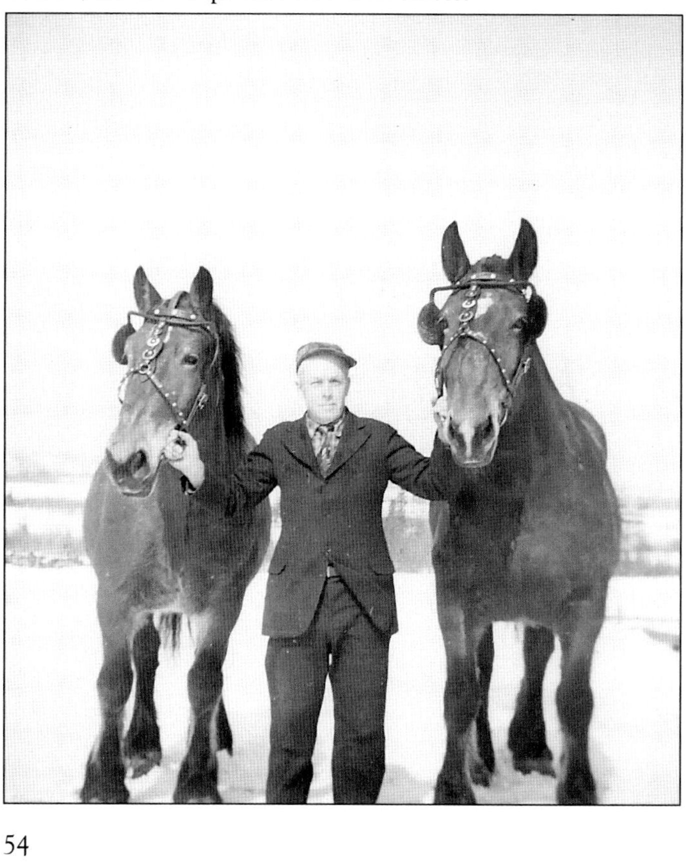

James R. Haley stands with Babe and Queen in 1944.

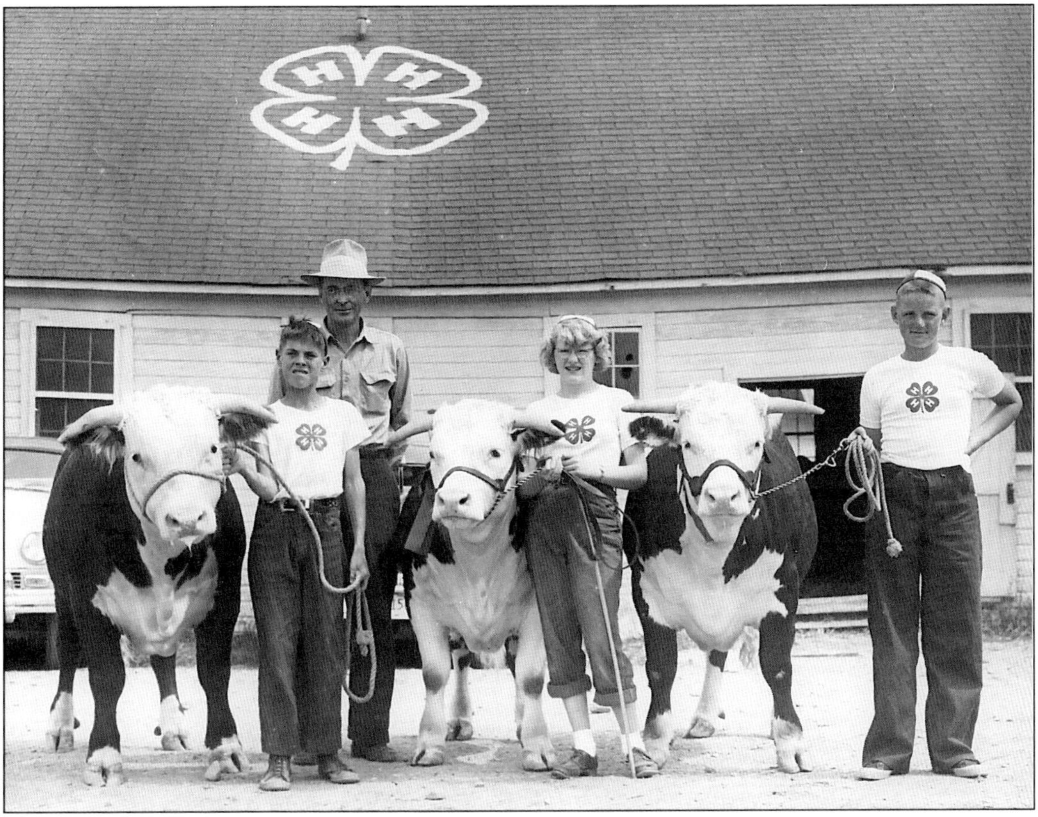

Prize-winning steers are shown off in a 1950 4-H contest at the Houlton Fair Grounds. Left to right are Ronnie London, who came in third; Barbara Berce, first; and Donald Fitzpatrick, aged twelve, second. Hudson Berce, contest leader, is in the rear. Fitzpatrick saved his prize money and used it as a deposit on the farm he purchased in January, 1958.

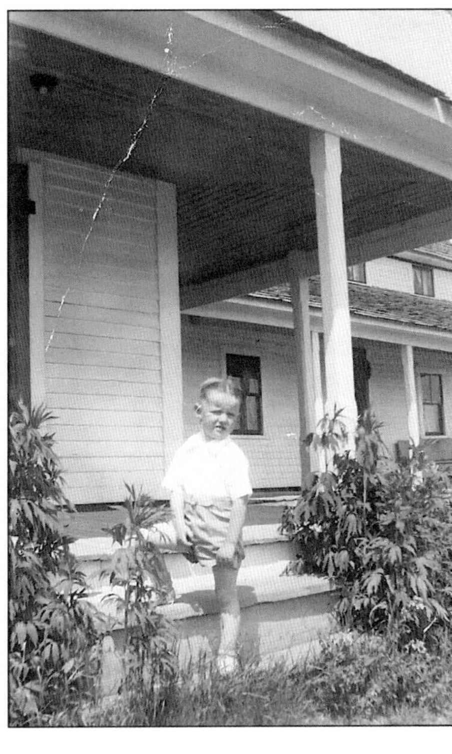

Donald Fitzpatrick, about four years old, in 1942 at the Fitzpatrick's B Road farm. Farms, as always, were ideal places to bring up children.

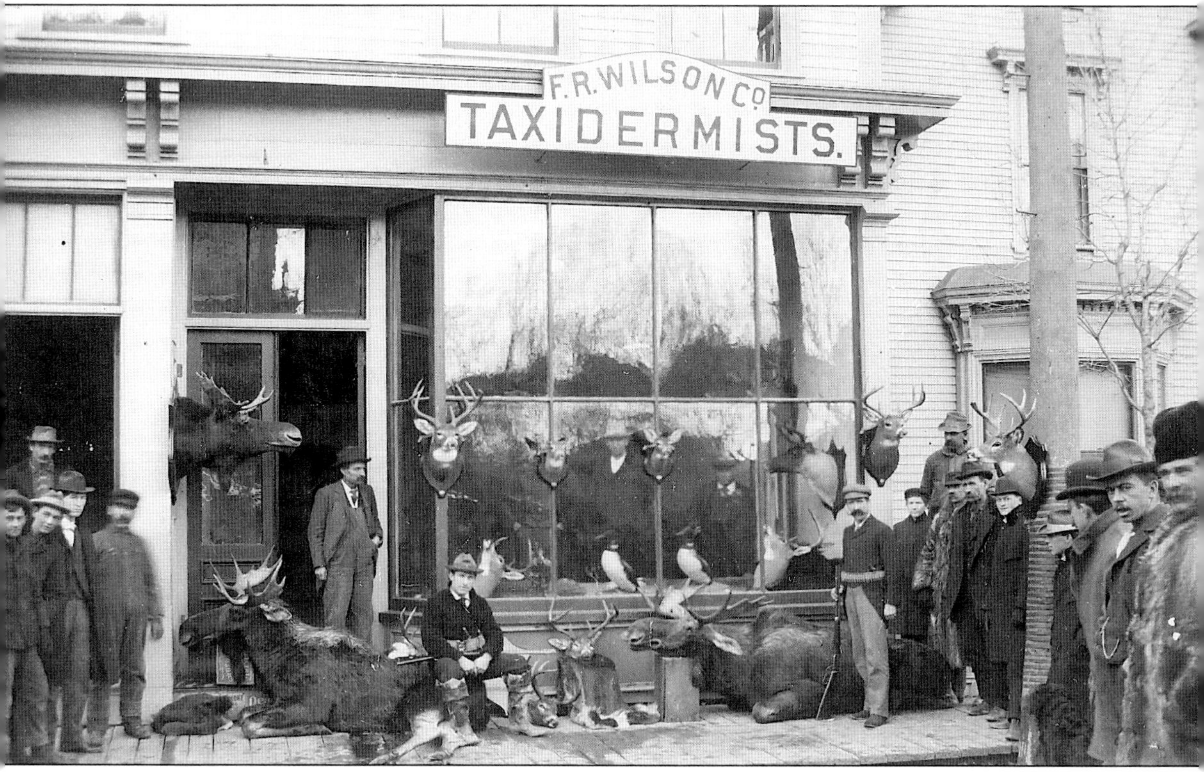

Business and recreation came together in front of F. (for Frank) R. Wilson Co., Taxidermists. Note the moose and deer heads and the ducks. Wilson developed quite a reputation with sportsmen all over the East for his efficient taxidermy work. This was a time when, with the coming of the railroad, sportsmen came to Houlton and Aroostook from all over the world for the hunting and fishing.

Three

Houlton Is Potatoes

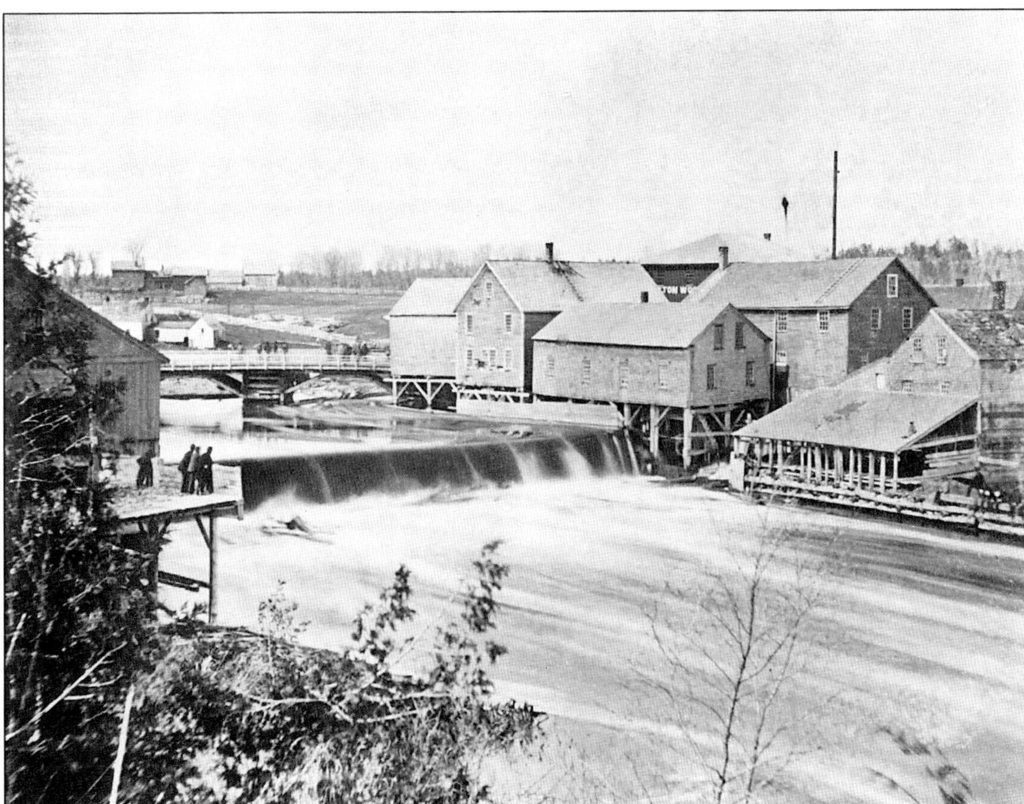

This may have been Aroostook County's first potato starch factory on the Meduxnekeag River. Starch was made from waste potatoes and had a variety of uses. Eventually, there were similar plants all over the county. The expansion of potato farming with the coming of the railroad brought an economic boom to Houlton.

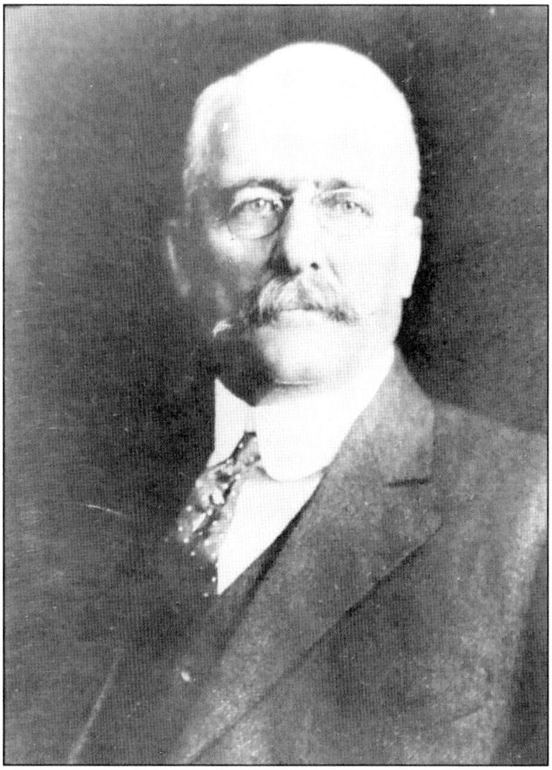

Edward L. Cleveland of Houlton was known as the potato king of Aroostook County. His operations eventually extended to the potato growing areas of the West.

Here is the E.L. Cleveland Co. of Houlton in working status. The potato shipper had storehouses in New Limerick, Easton, Mars Hill, Fort Kent, Houlton, Pierre, South Dakota, Woodstock, New Brunswick, Frenchville, Dyer Brook, Soldier Pond and Sherman.

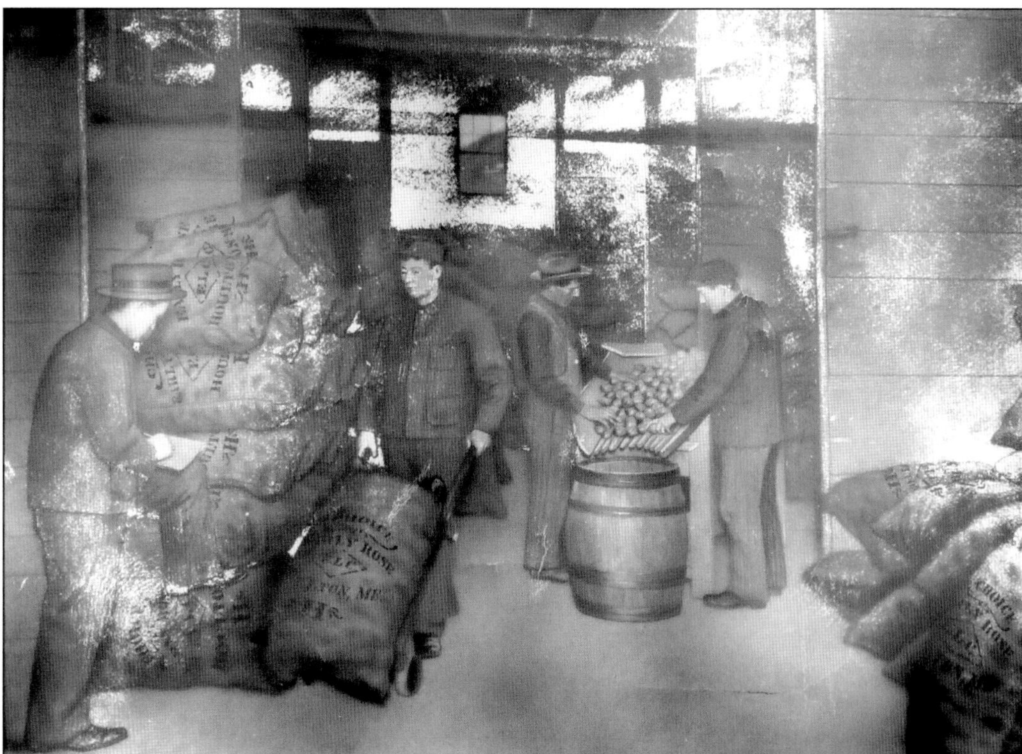

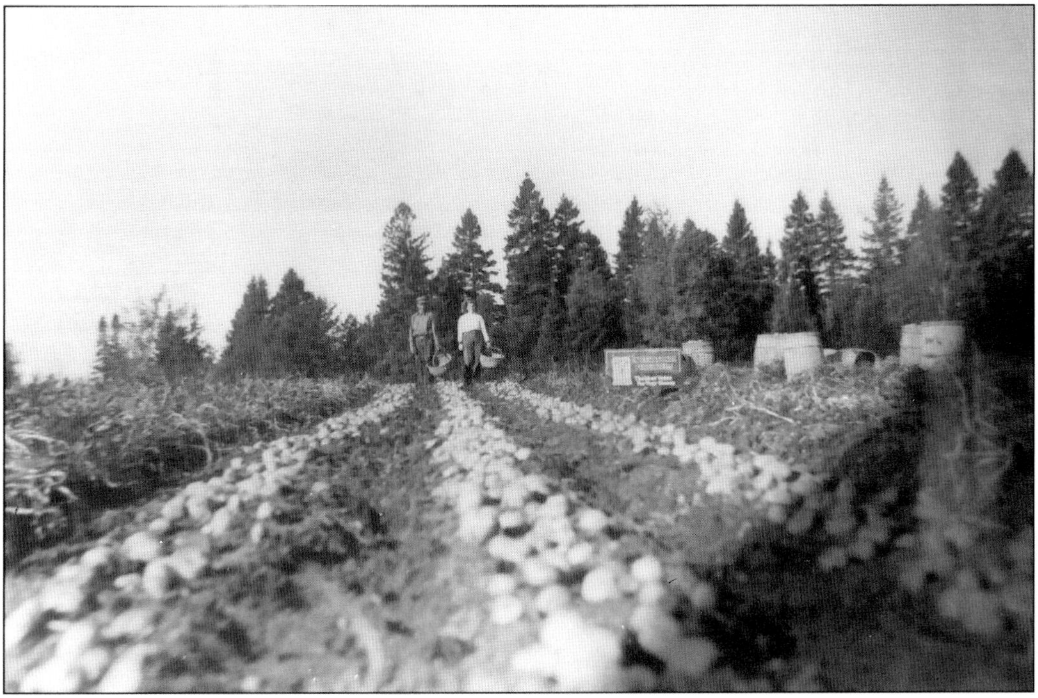

Potatoes sprouted all over Aroostook. Farmers around Houlton reaped a bonanza. The soil and the short growing season were just right for "spuds." This is a field at the W.A. Lowery Farm in New Limerick.

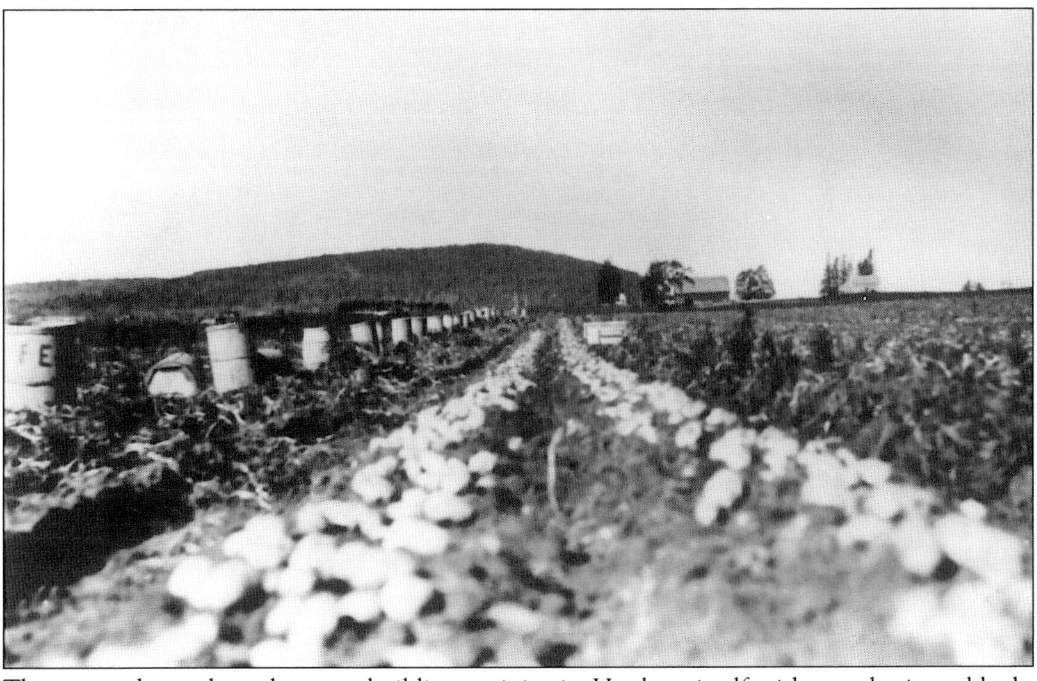

The potato boom brought great building activity in Houlton itself with new business blocks rising. Those that survived the Great Fire of 1902 in Houlton are still in the downtown and more outlying areas of the shiretown. The Frank C. Estabrook Farm shown here was in Linneus.

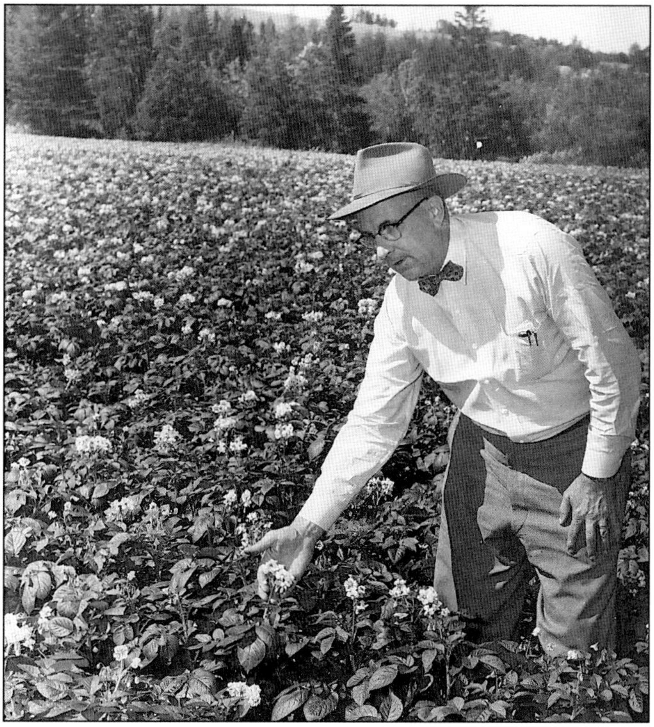

Fred C. Greaves in a Hodgdon potato field in 1952. This is an unused photograph taken for a February, 1953 *Saturday Evening Post* article which said that Greaves probably held more government posts than anyone in America. At that time, he was town manager of seven communities around Houlton. He was later a president of the Maine Municipal Association and a member of the Houlton Town Council.

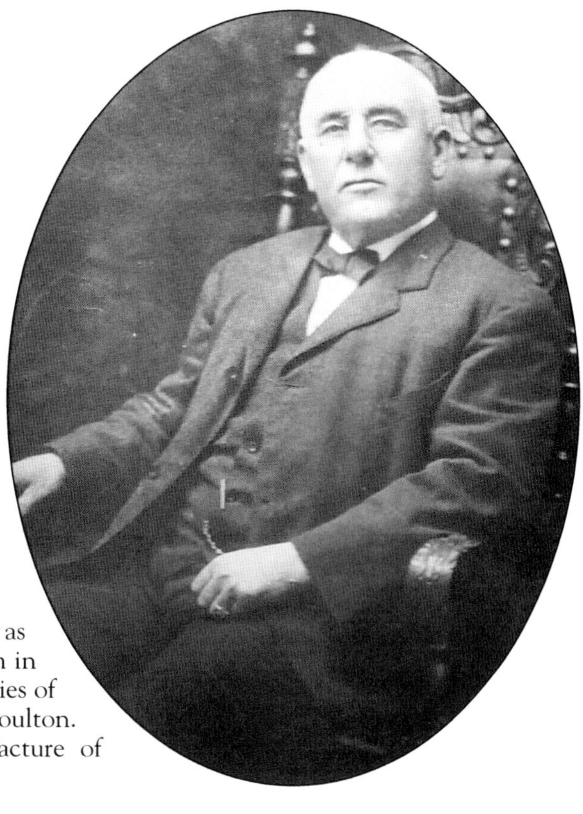

John H. Watson originally made his money as a hardware merchant. But, with the boom in potatoes, Watson built and operated a series of potato starch factories including one in Houlton. He also branched out into the manufacture of carriages, sleighs and pungs.

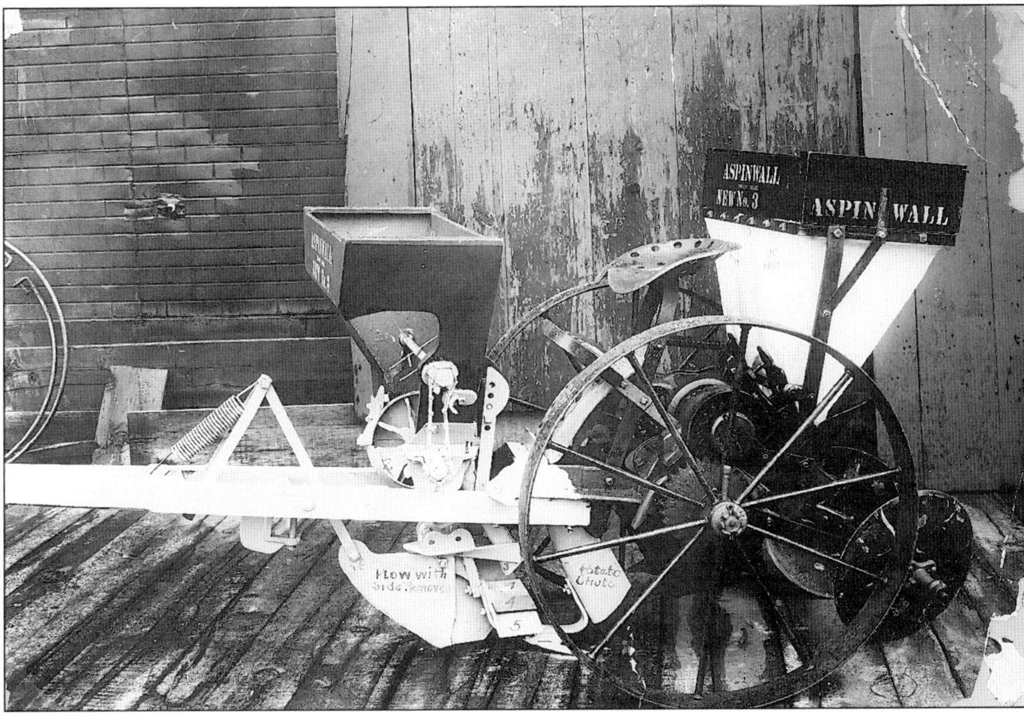

The Aspinwall potato digger was made in Houlton and Guelph, Ontario, Canada. Some reports say it was invented in Houlton.

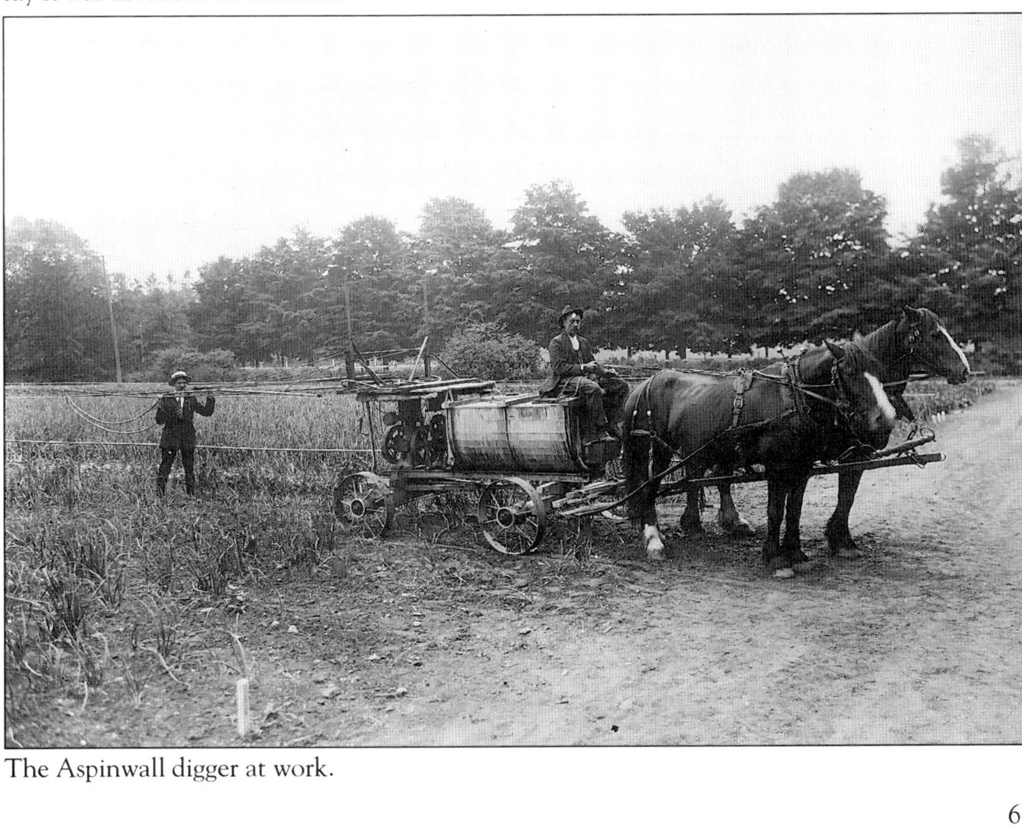
The Aspinwall digger at work.

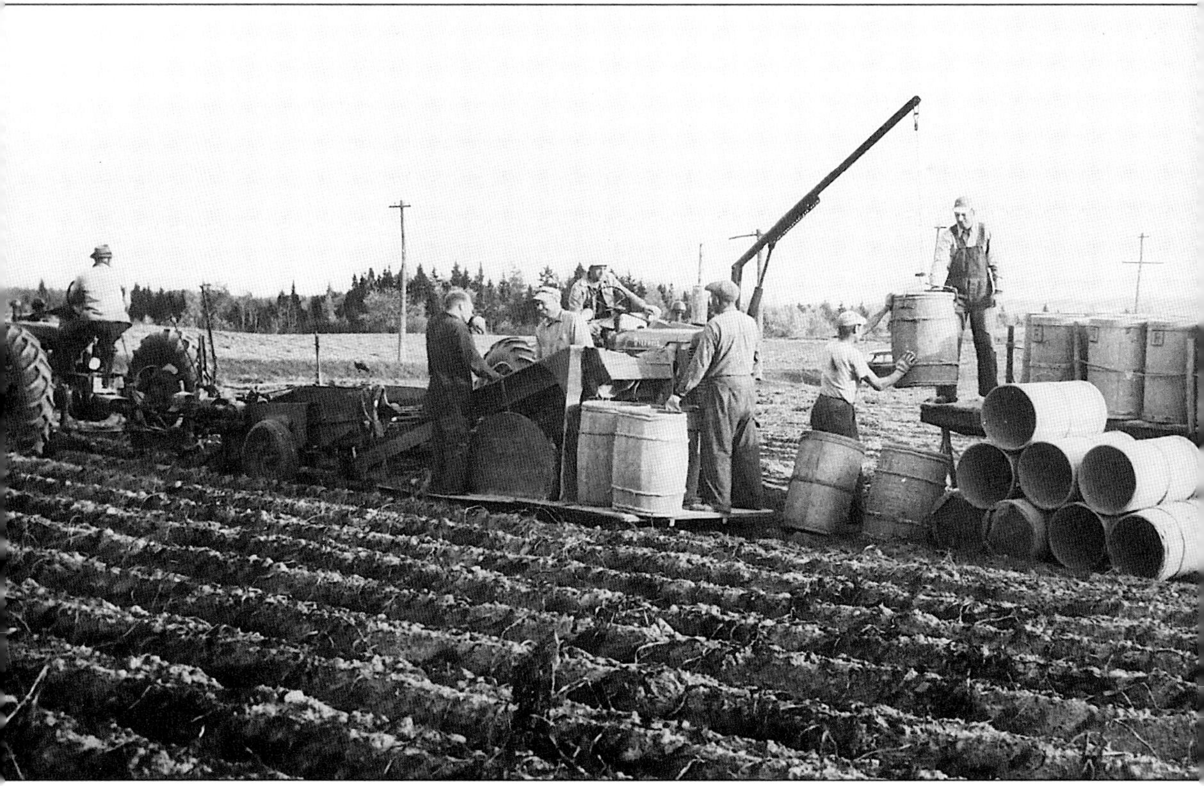

The first barrel harvester for potatoes in Maine was put into operation at what is now the Rhoda Farm on the Walker Road in Cary's Mills during 1943.

Four

Houlton Is Fun and Recreation

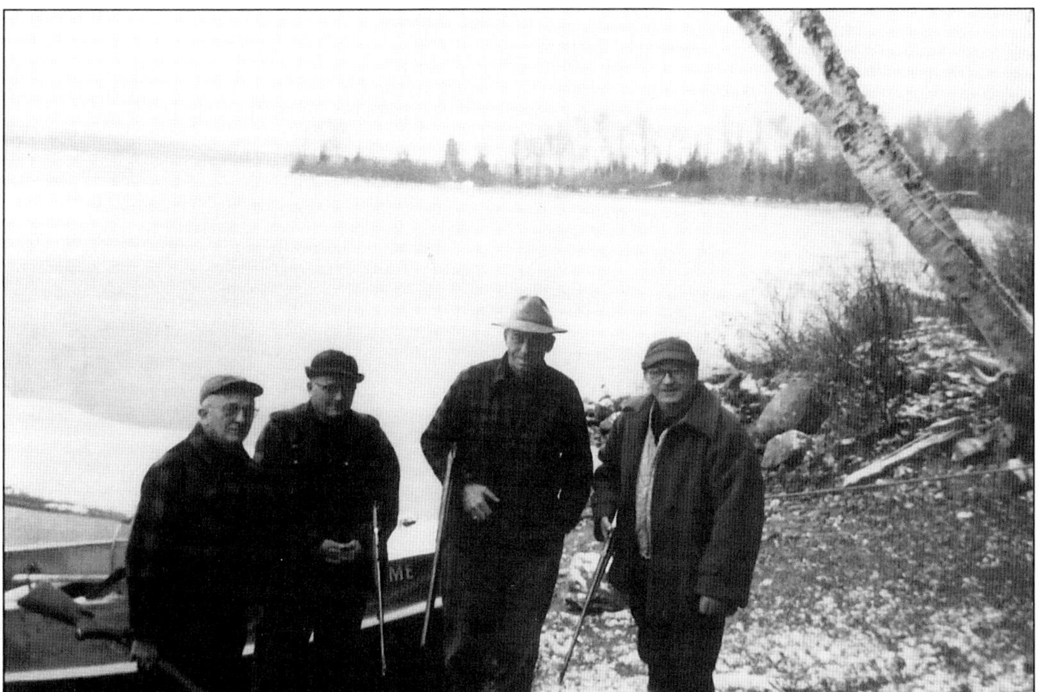

Hunting was, is and always has been big in Aroostook and the Houlton area. In the early 1950s, Donald H. Dunn, Ralph Sullivan, James Gardiner and Arnold Peabody were doing the honors at Meduxnekeag (Drew's) Lake.

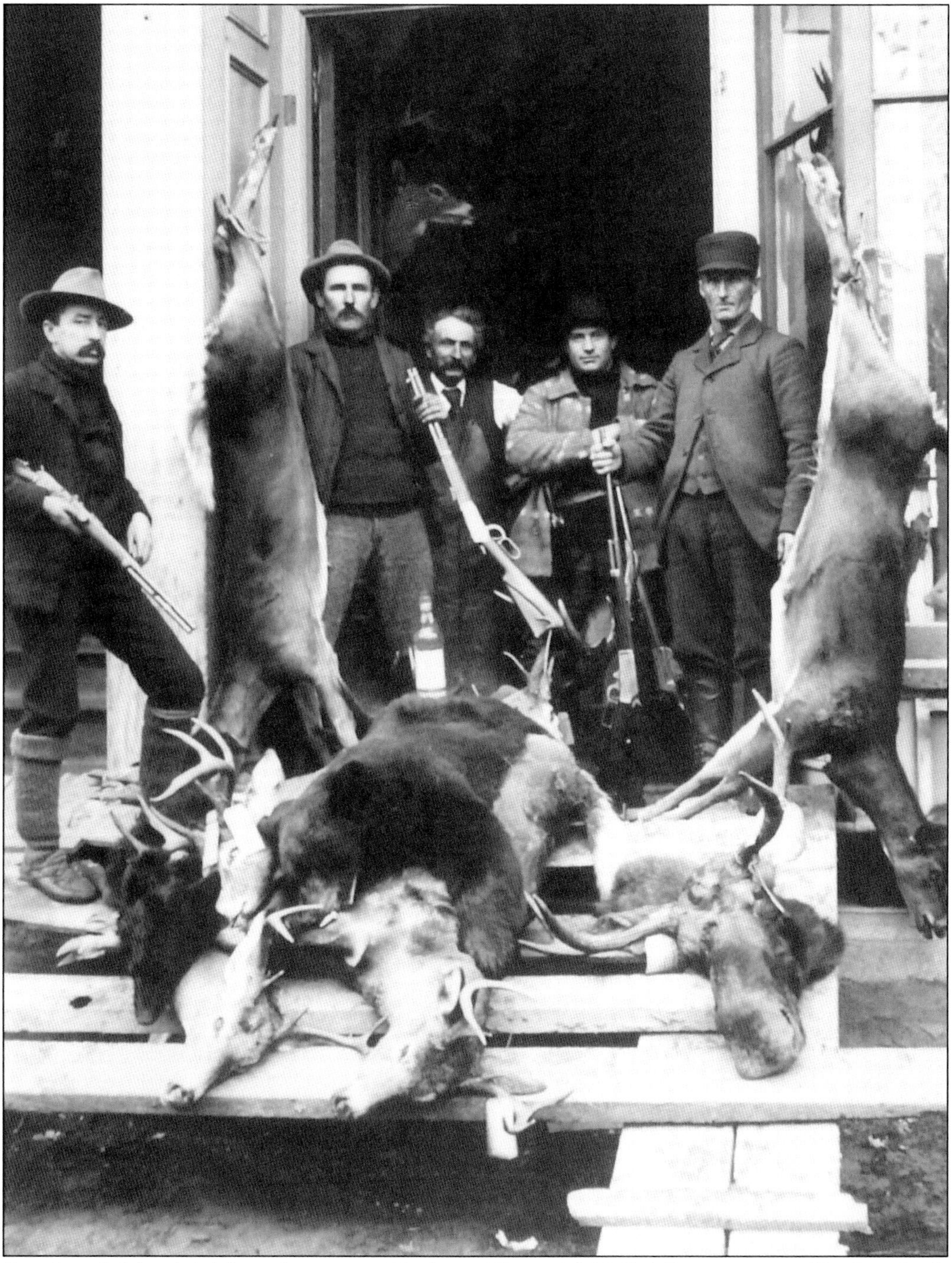

Yes, they did (and do) have hunters in Houlton. This is McNally's Restaurant in Houlton back around the turn of the century. The man in the center is Robert McNally. We see bear, deer and moose. The hunting is not quite that good anymore but plenty of hunters still are out. "Not so good" is comparatively speaking: at the turn of the century, it was possible to shoot something at nearly the drop of a bullet as moose were still plentiful. Now, moose are plentiful once more and, in fact, may be limiting the deer population in the area.

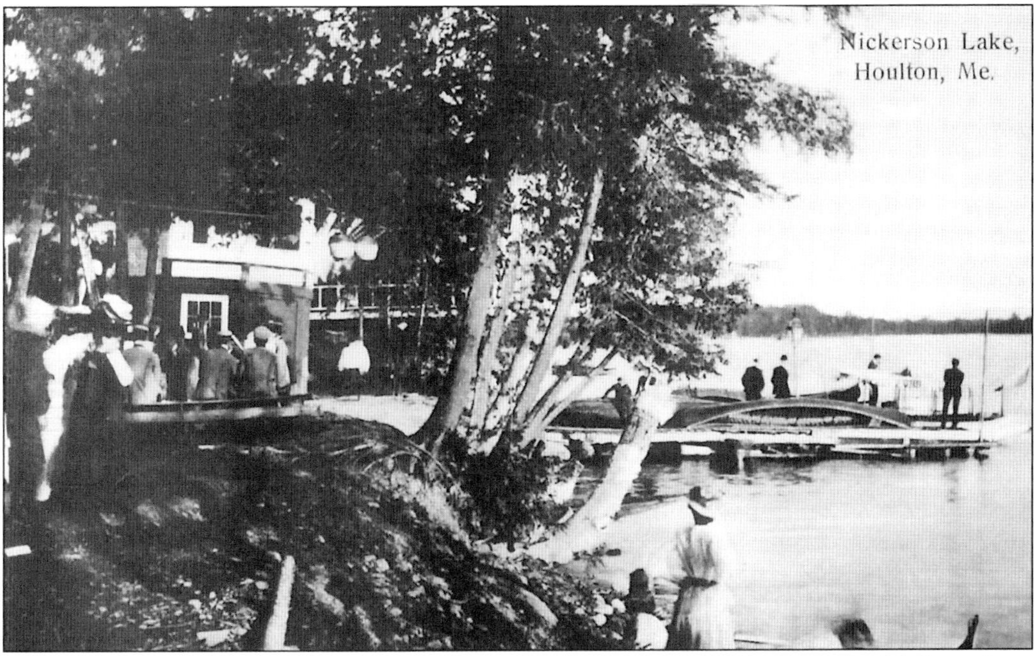

The cottage culture in the Houlton area centered on three lakes—Nickerson Lake, Meduxnekeag (Drew's) Lake in New Limerick and Grand Lake and East Grand Lake in the Danforth area. These were largely small, utilitarian cottages, not like the mansion-cottages of Bar Harbor. Other facilities grew up around them. One was the Pavilion at Nickerson Lake, also known as Lakewood, where the steamers landed. It was eventually purchased by the French family for use as a cottage.

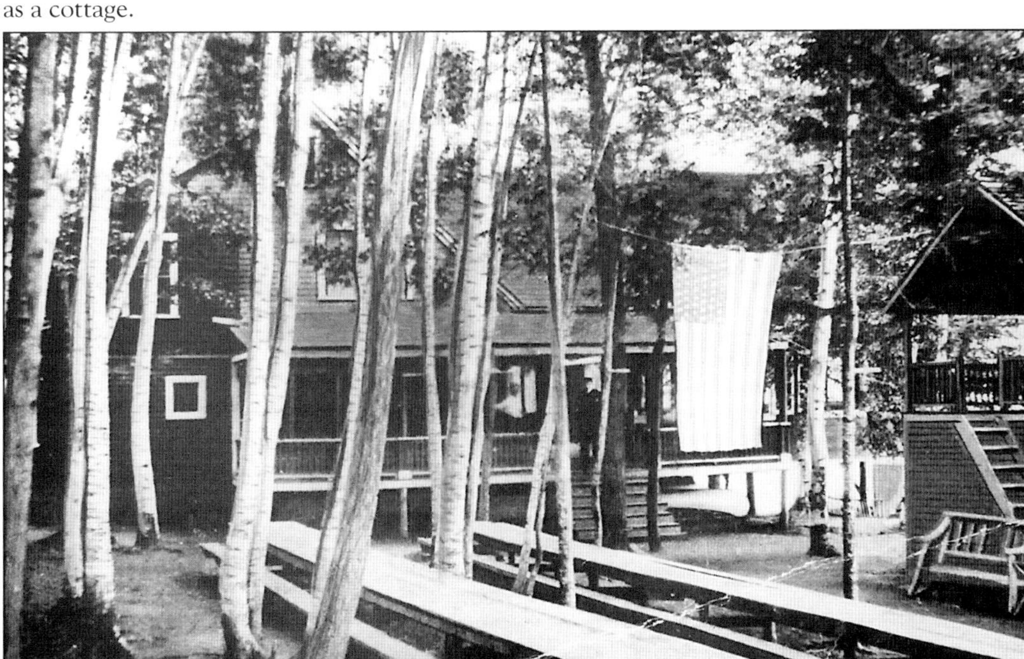

Crescent Beach became the dance hall and playland for Nickerson Lake. The forty-eight stars in the flag date this as sometime in the 1940s.

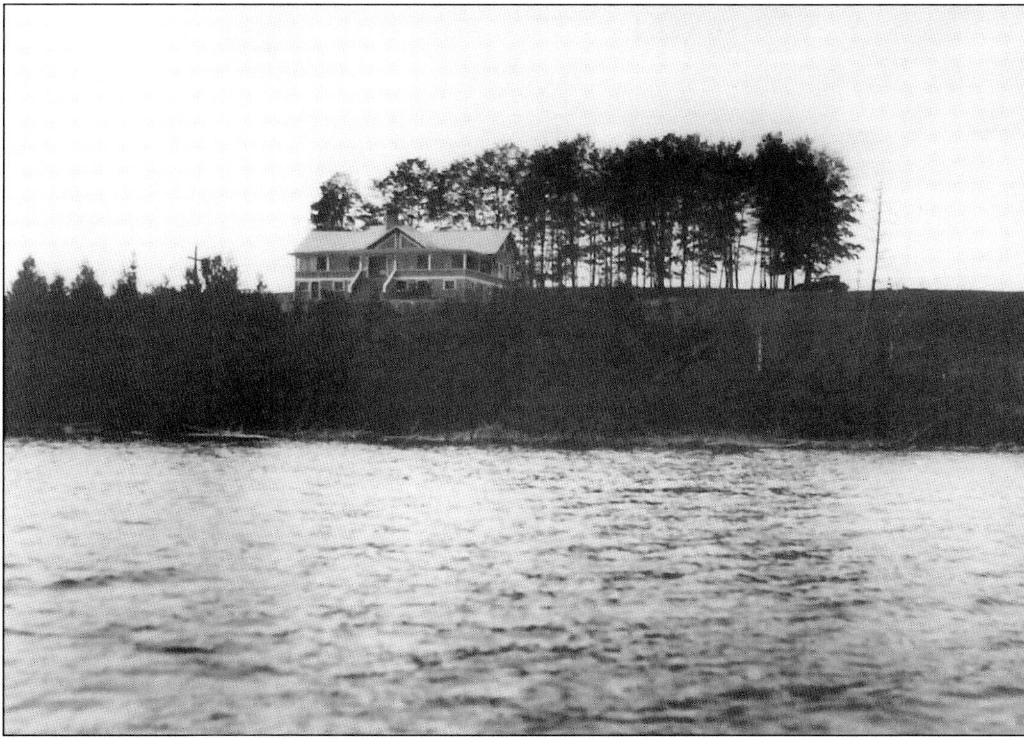

Further along the Nickerson Lake shore was the Houlton Country Club, shown here in 1932. It stood on a high hill overlooking the lake and running down to it. Some of the golf course is on the side of that hill.

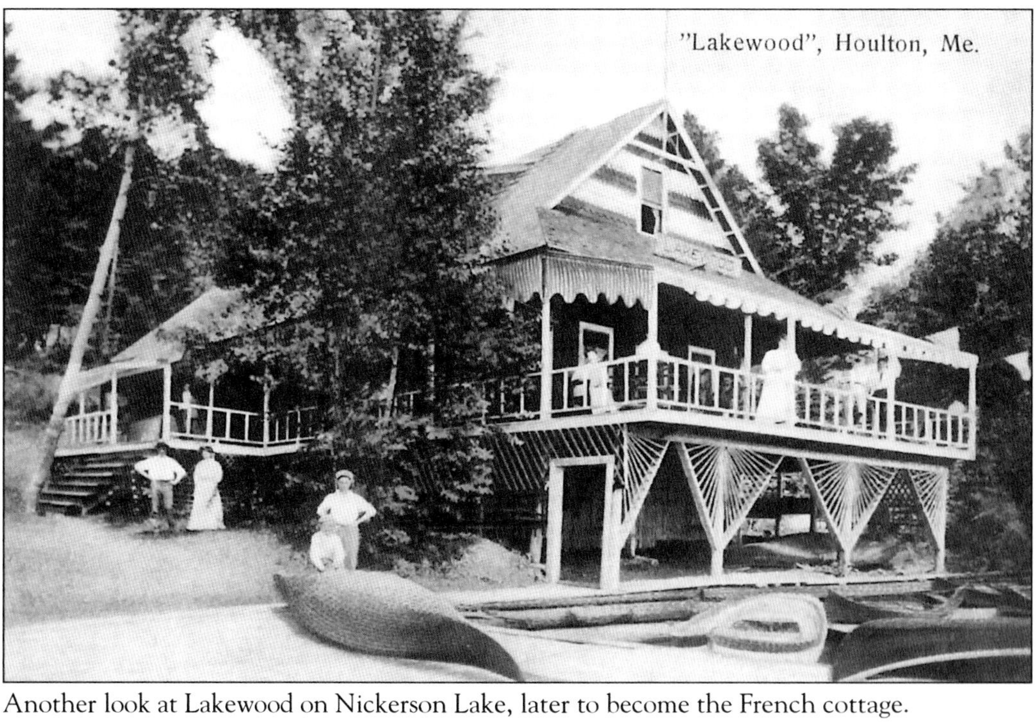

Another look at Lakewood on Nickerson Lake, later to become the French cottage.

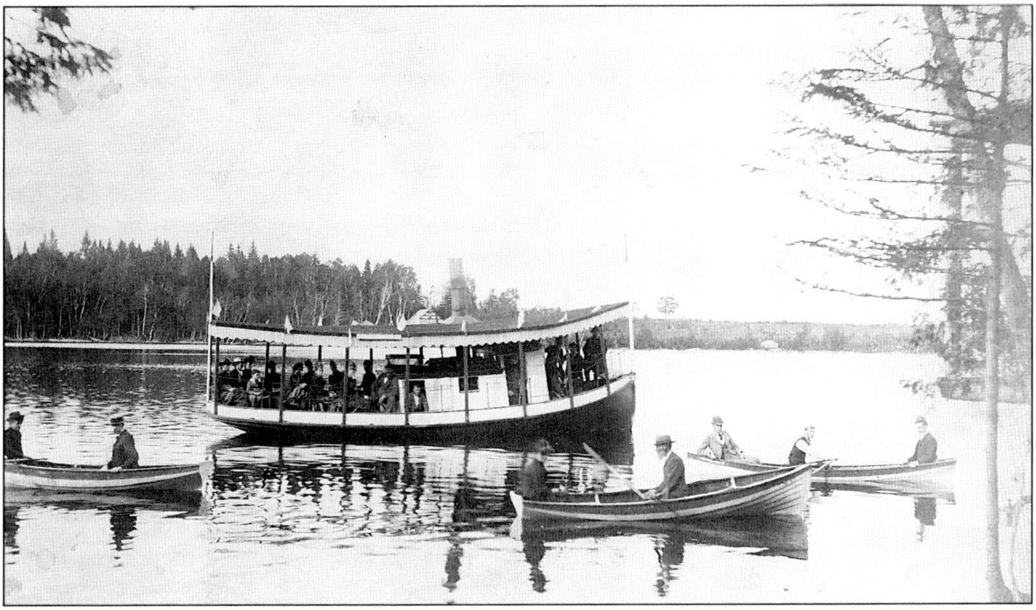

The steamer *Mabel* on Nickerson Lake in 1875. The steamers brought added enjoyment for those at the lake. However, motor boats eventually made them uneconomic as times changed.

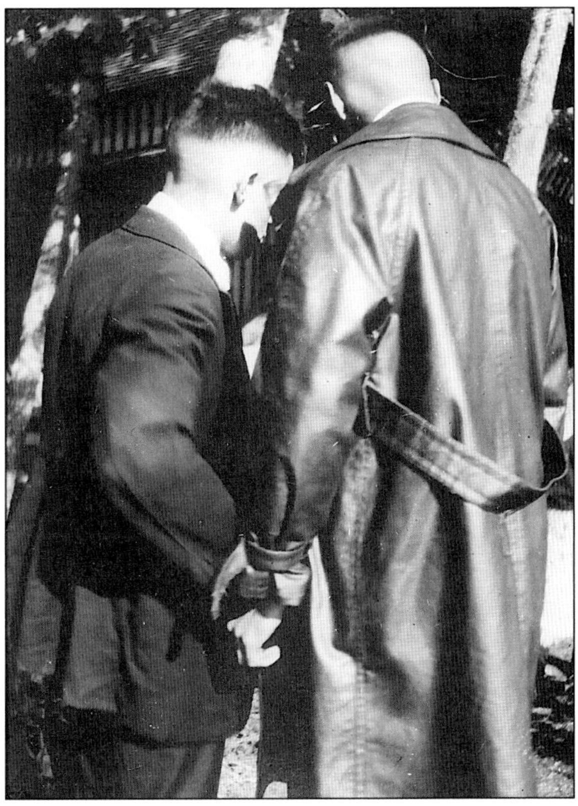

Dr. Francis H. Sleeper, left, and Harold Cates sport haircuts of the 1920s at Nickerson Lake.

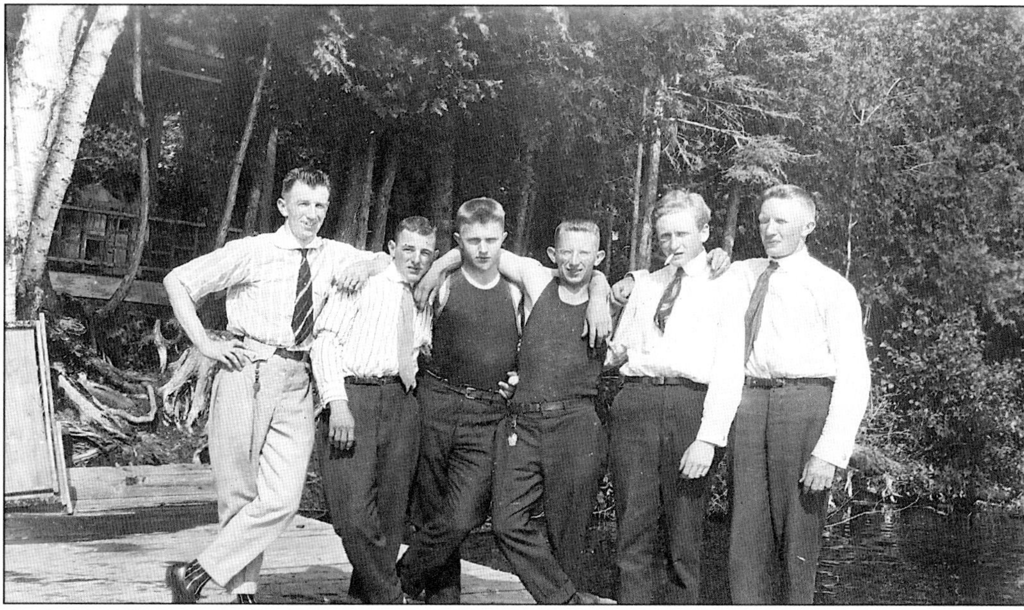

And then there were the house parties at Nickerson Lake. This took place at the Nickerson Cottage and lasted from Saturday through Monday in the summer of 1917. Left to right: "Daddy" Carroll, "Twinie" Caswell, Chandler Farley, Ervin "Mike" Putnam, "Reddy" Everett and Forrest Bradstreet.

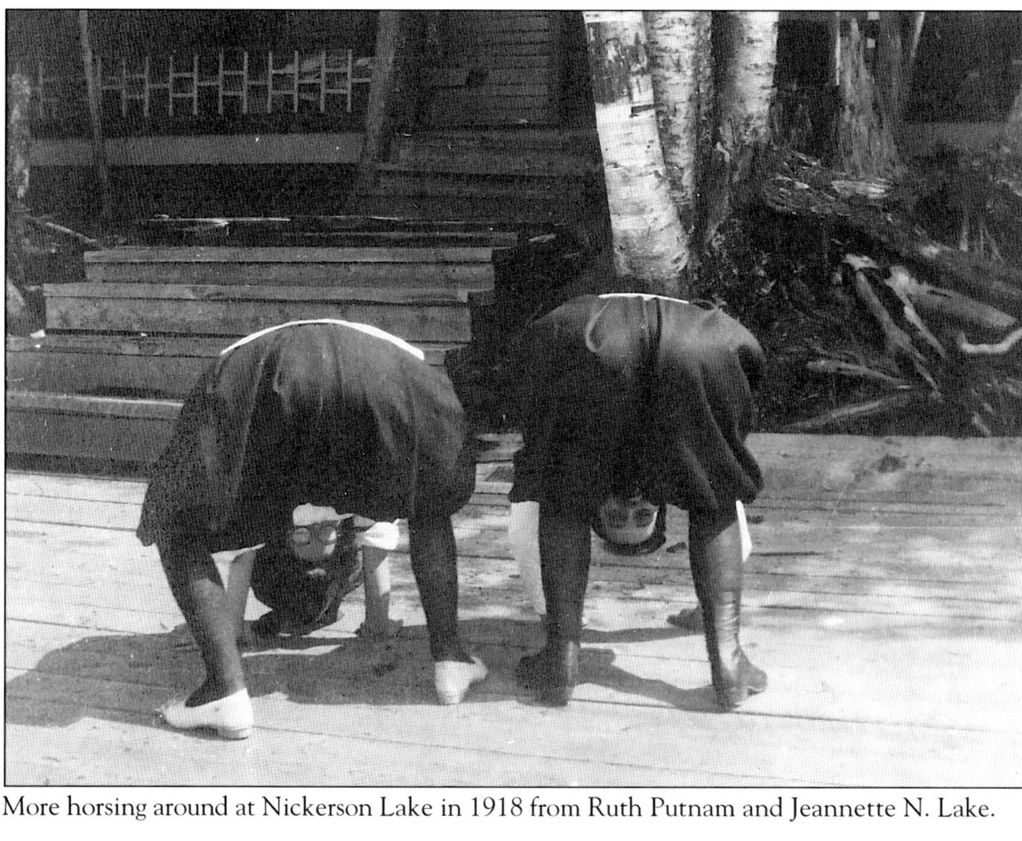

More horsing around at Nickerson Lake in 1918 from Ruth Putnam and Jeannette N. Lake.

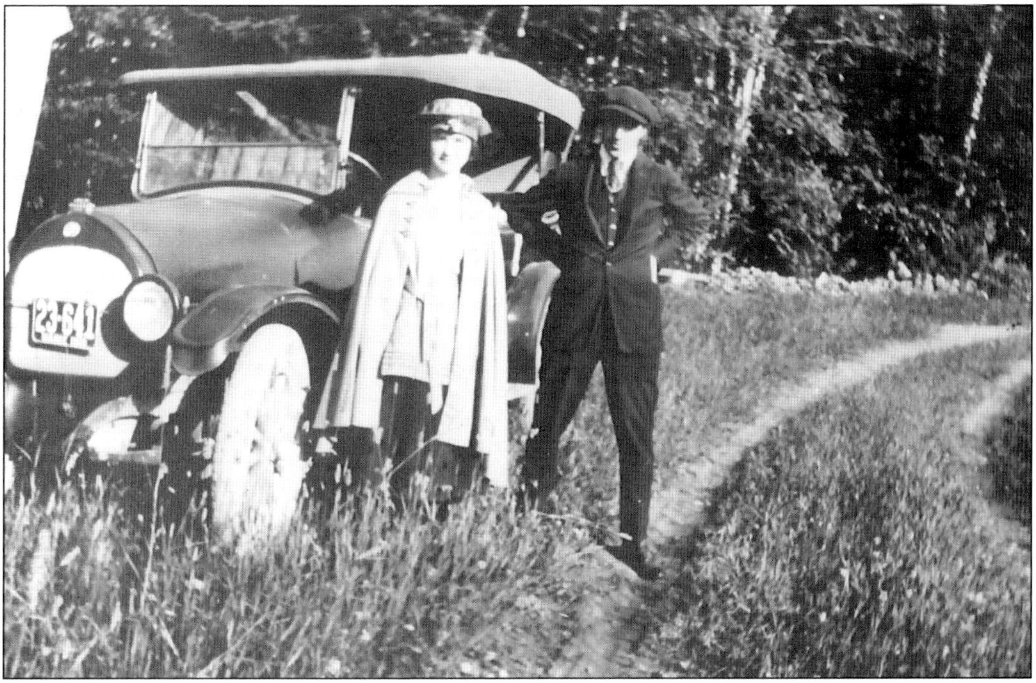

The Houlton High School Class of 1917 held its house party at Nickerson Lake in 1919. Lucy Chamberlain and Vernon Saunders attended.

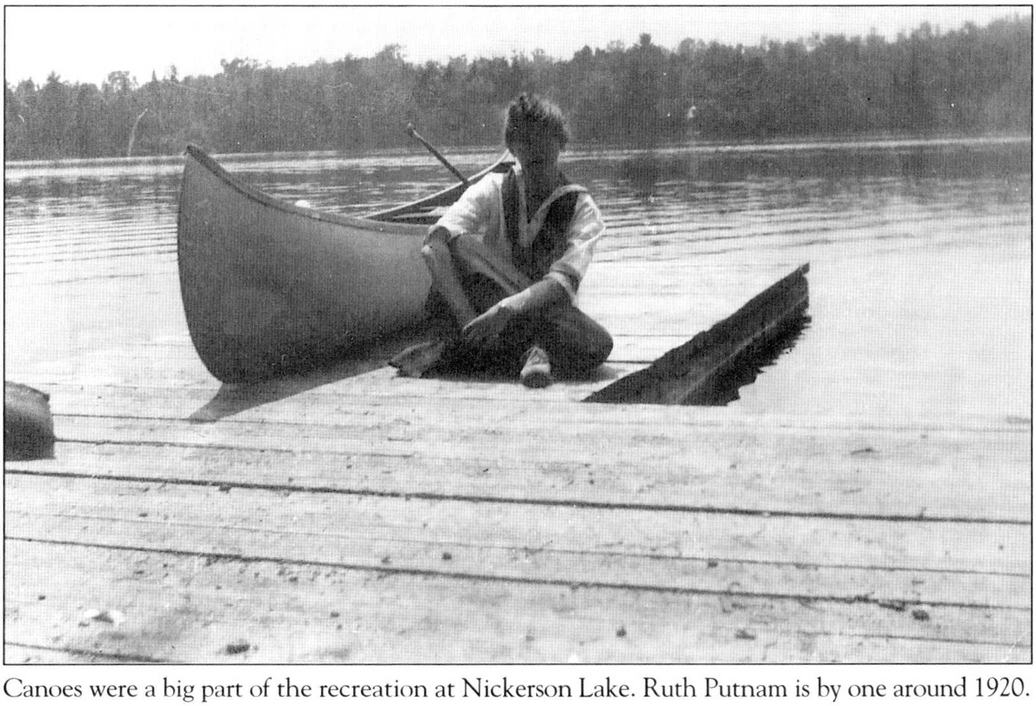

Canoes were a big part of the recreation at Nickerson Lake. Ruth Putnam is by one around 1920.

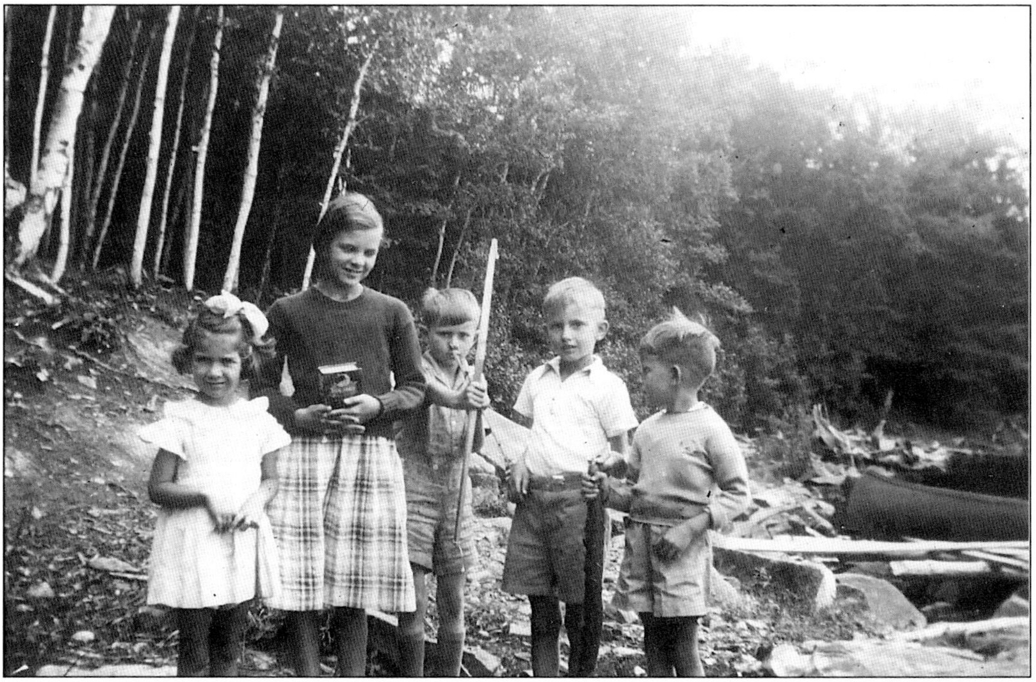

It was usually a bit more sedate at Drew's Lake in New Limerick, 9 miles from Houlton. In this 1936 photograph a group of cousins is lined up on a rock in front of the Putnam Cottage. Left to right: Jeannette Cates (now Vosburgh), Frances Ann Cates, Frank (Buster) Sleeper, Stanley Greaves and Joe Greaves.

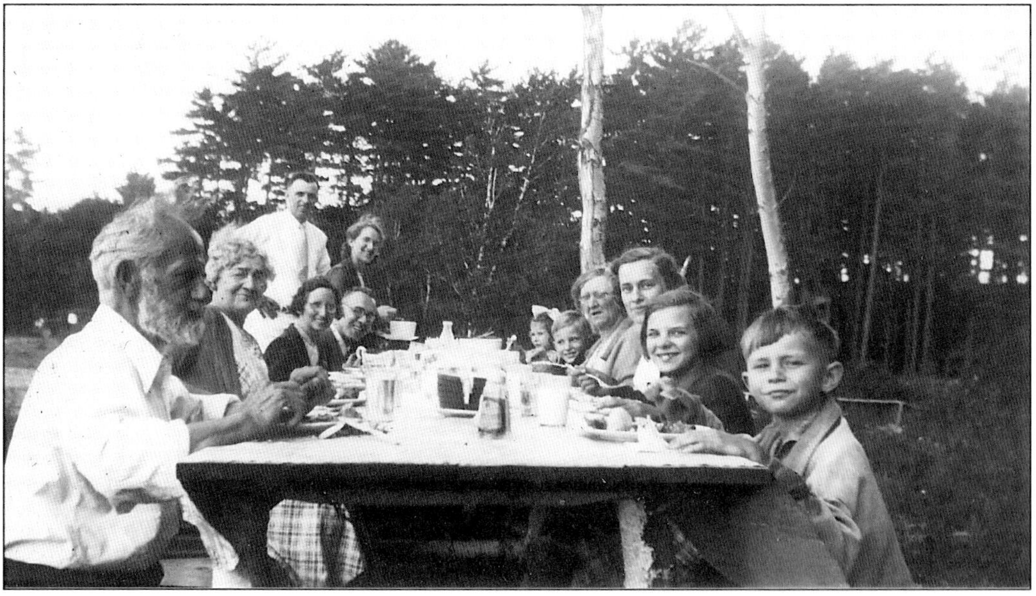

Talk about good times! Around the table at the Putnam Cottage on Drew's Lake, were, left to right: Amos Putnam, Mrs. Harry (Dee) Cates, Margaret Greaves, Harold Cates, Fred Greaves, Harriette Cates, Jeannette Cates, Stan Greaves, Cora Putnam, Mary Doganitis, Frances Ann Cates and Frank Sleeper. The Putnam Cottage was the first built on Drew's Lake. It was constructed by Allie Hutchinson and moved years ago down the lake to its present location.

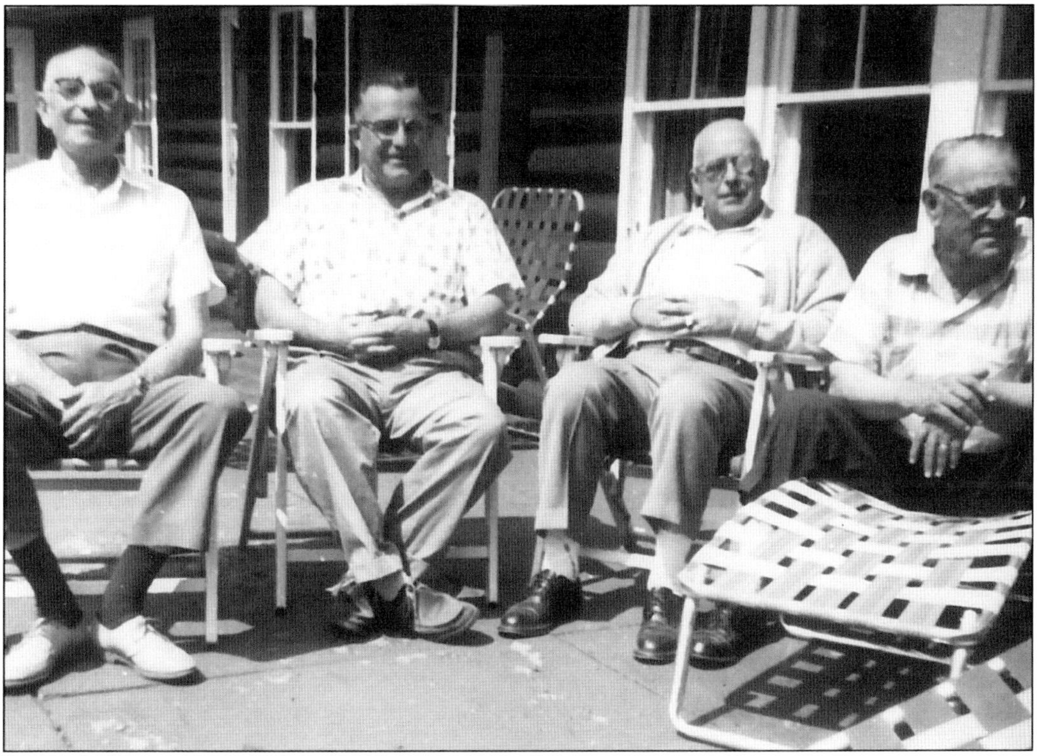

The third lake in the Houlton cottage game plan was Grand Lake. At the MacNair Cottage in June, 1962, were, left to right: Emmons Robinson, Leonard MacNair, Dana Nickerson and Ernest Whited. MacNair had purchased the former Sunset Park area at Grand Lake and the property is still in his family.

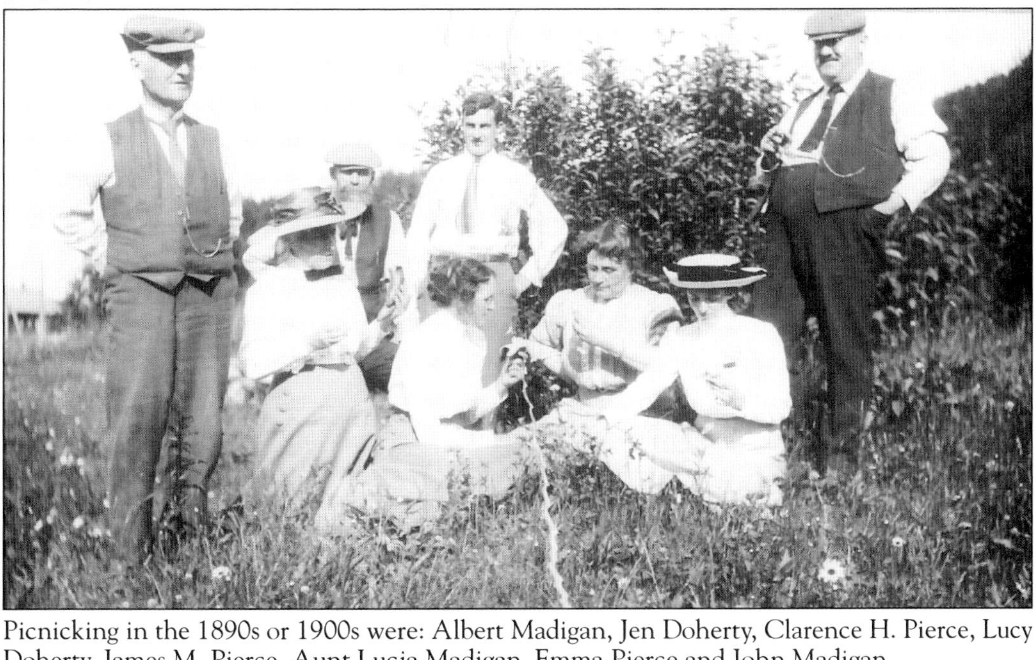

Picnicking in the 1890s or 1900s were: Albert Madigan, Jen Doherty, Clarence H. Pierce, Lucy Doherty, James M. Pierce, Aunt Lucia Madigan, Emma Pierce and John Madigan.

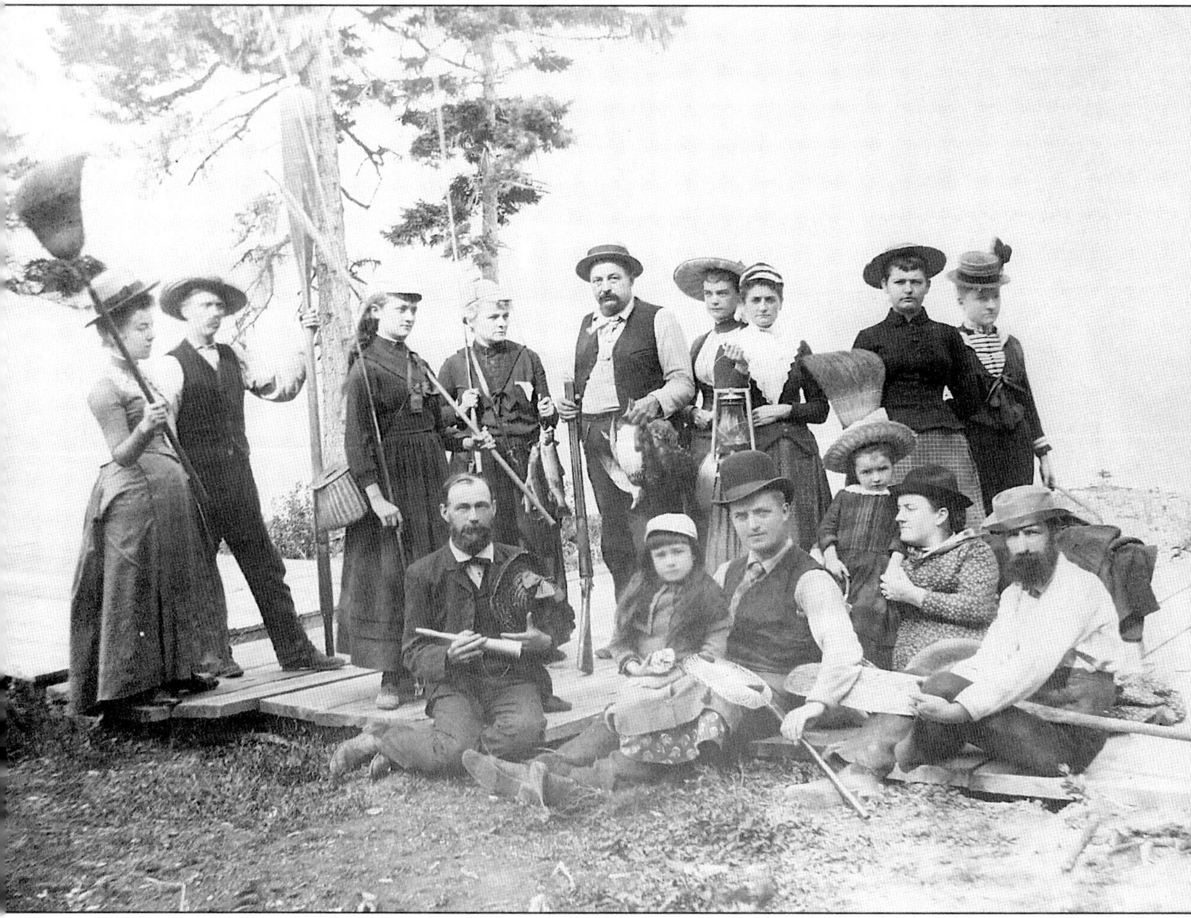

In 1892 at Grand Lake were (front row, left to right) Frank Pierce, Lottie Pierce, Albert Madigan, Molly Pierce, Frances Pierce and Clarence Pierce. Grand Lake was ideal for picnicking.

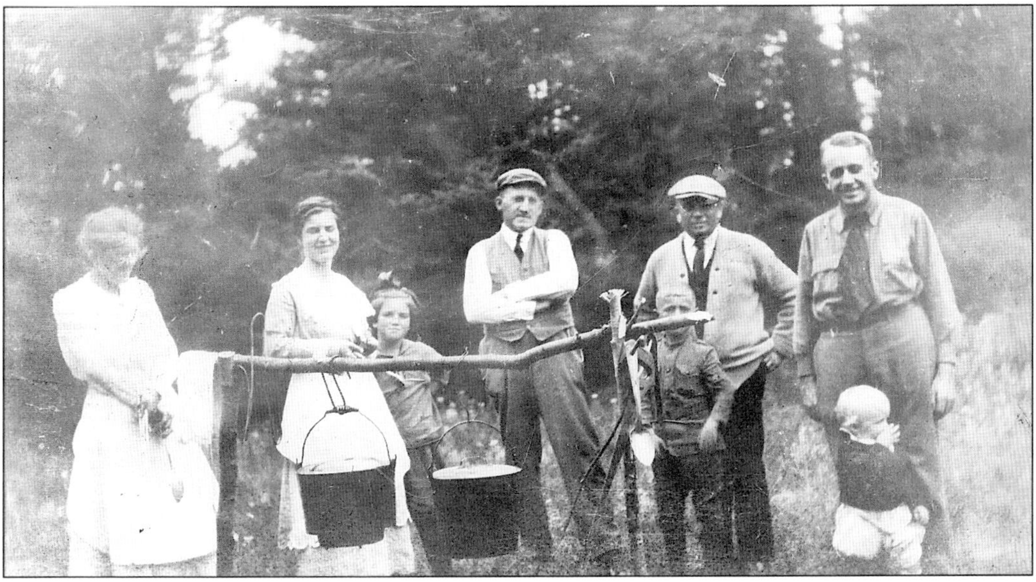

Two of Houlton's most influential natives having an excellent time at a picnic in Houlton. The last man on the left is Leonard A. Pierce who left his Houlton law practice to join Maine's largest law firm, Pierce, Atwood and Scribner, and who was also lawyer for Central Maine Power Co., Maine's largest utility, for many years. Next to Pierce is Fred L. Putnam, a large potato shipper and director of the Bangor and Aroostook Railroad. From left to right are Alice Putnam, Molly Putnam, Cordelia Putnam, Justin C. Rose, Albert Putnam, Fred L. Putnam, Leonard A. Pierce and Jotham D. Pierce.

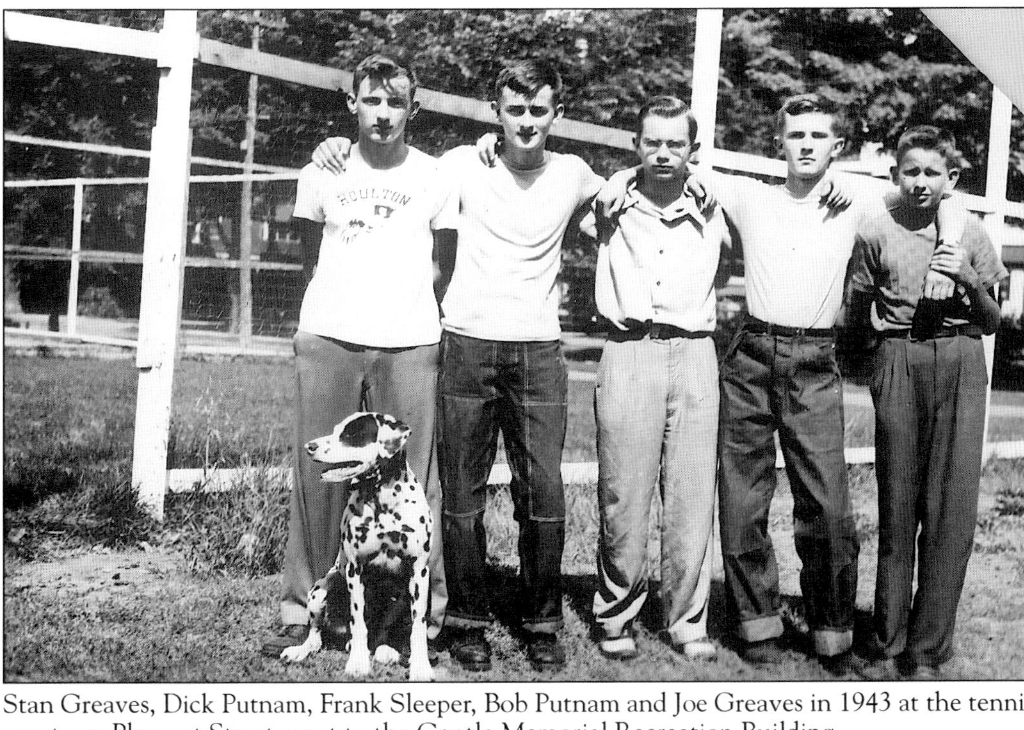

Stan Greaves, Dick Putnam, Frank Sleeper, Bob Putnam and Joe Greaves in 1943 at the tennis courts on Pleasant Street, next to the Gentle Memorial Recreation Building.

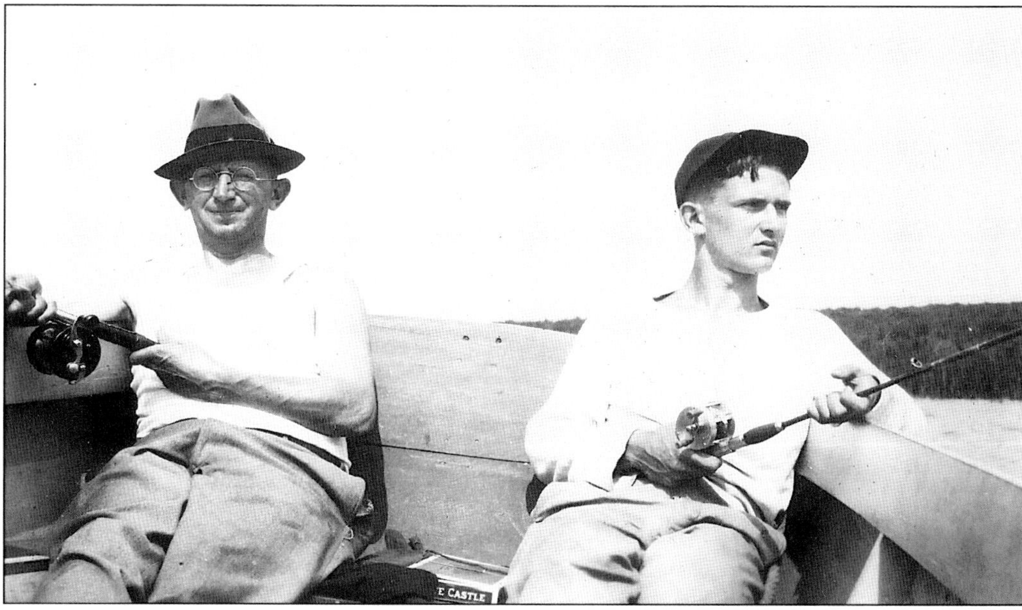

Ervin E. "Mike" Putnam and his son, Bob, are trolling for salmon and trout.

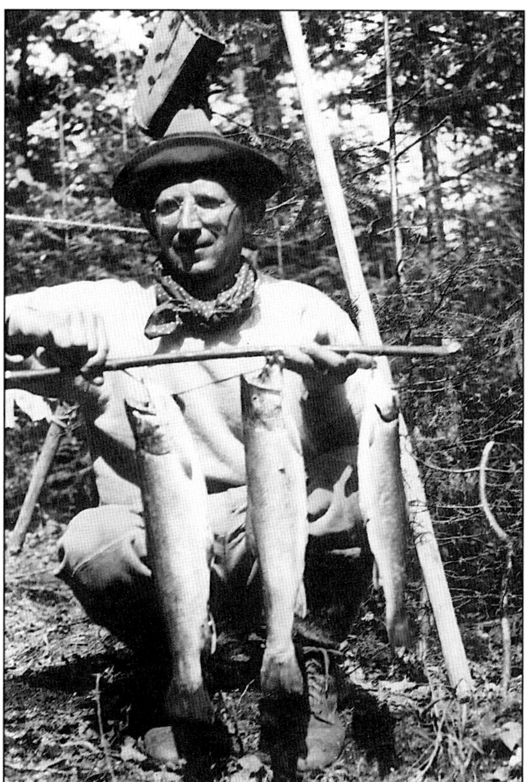

"A Fisherman's Dreams Come True." Ervin E. "Mike" Putnam, a Houlton native who guided doctors around the Allagash, shows the results of one day's good fishing.

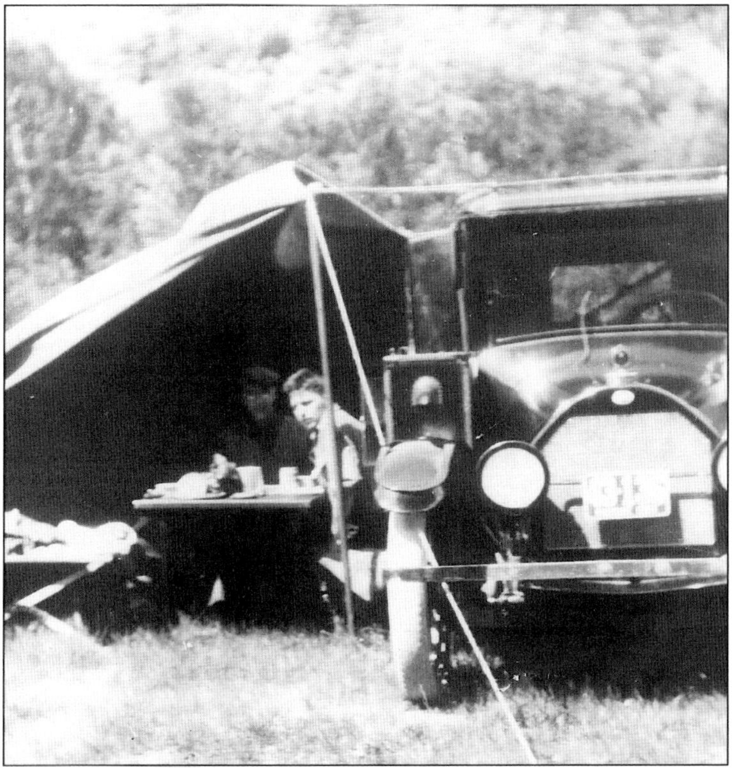

Harold Cates and Dr. Francis H. Sleeper camped with a Model T Ford in the early 1920s.

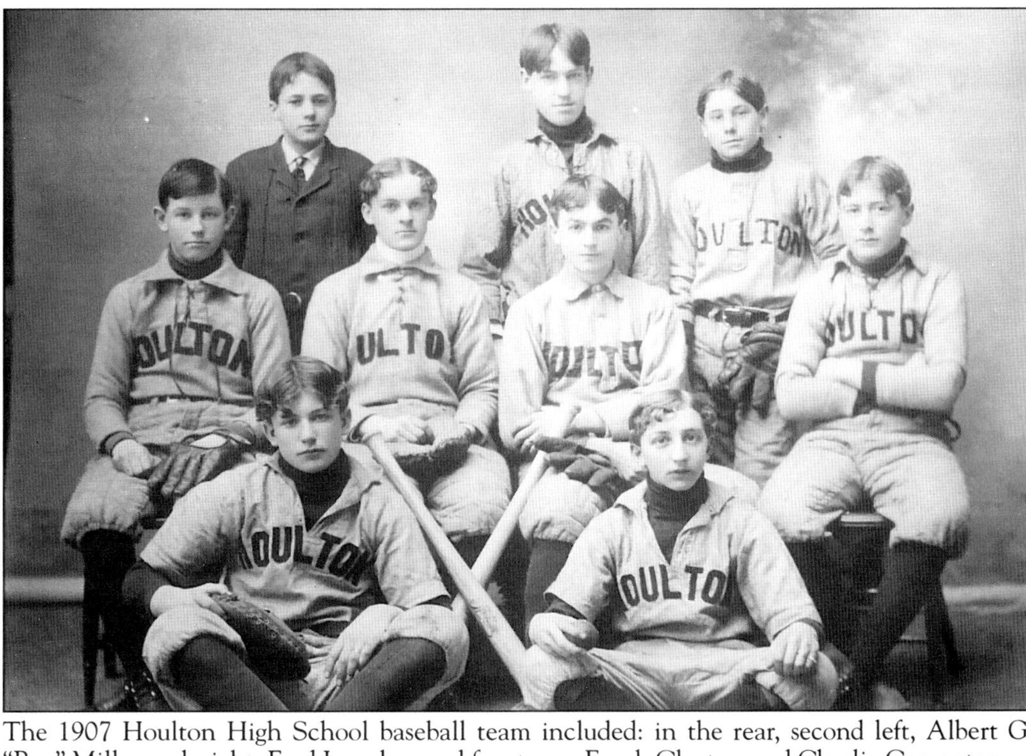

The 1907 Houlton High School baseball team included: in the rear, second left, Albert G. "Bug" Millar and, right, Fred Larrabee and front row, Frank Clayton and Charlie Carpenter.

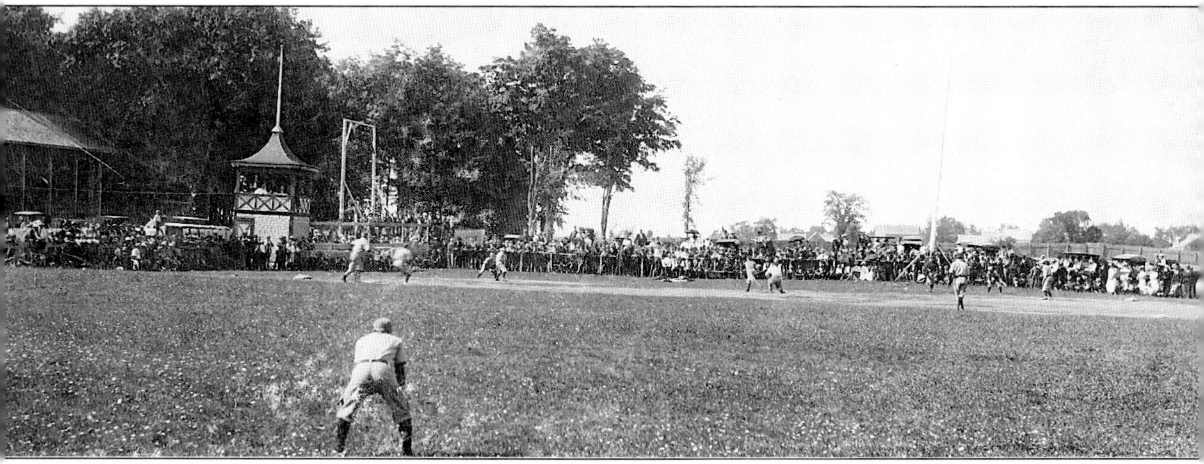

There has always been deep interest in baseball throughout Houlton. As early as 1885, players were out on the diamond at the North Street Park. All sorts of semi-pro teams flourished over the years. There were games at every Fourth of July celebration. Cross border competition with Woodstock and other Canadian teams was frequent.

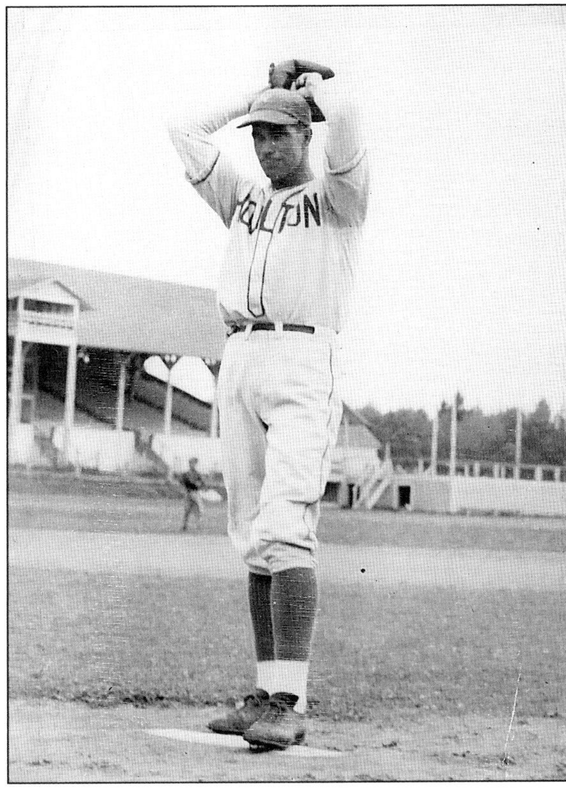

Just after the Second World War, the Houlton Collegians semi-pro baseball team won thirty-two straight games in 1947/8. Graden Swett was the team's leading pitcher. His pitching skill was picked up at Ricker College and by watching others. The Collegians were finally defeated by the Augusta Millionaires in Augusta, a team that featured future Boston Red Sox player Ted Lepcio. Swett, however, didn't pitch that game; Jim DeFrederico did. Swett worked for years for the Bangor and Aroostook Railroad, retiring as superintendent of tracks.

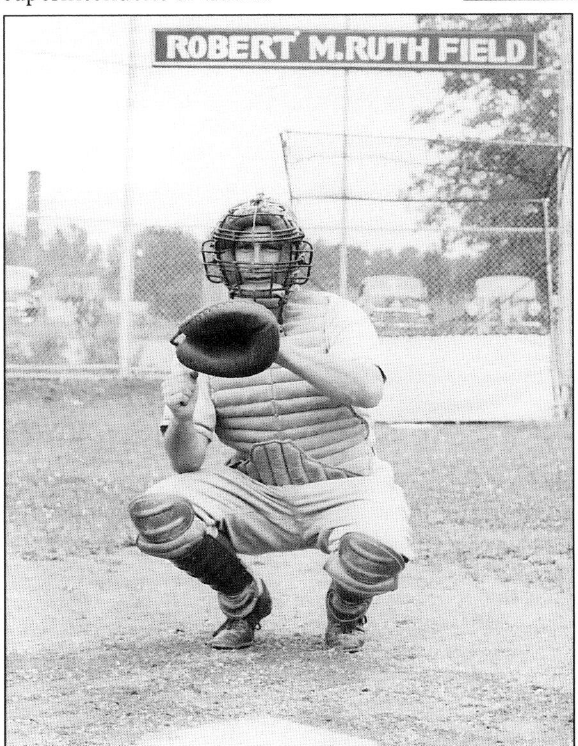

Clifford McQuarrie was the Collegians catcher for that 1947/8 run. Here he is shown at Robert M. Ruth Field, Community Park. A star catcher and athlete at Houlton High School, Ruth was killed in the Second World War. McQuarrie picked up a good measure of his catching skills while performing for service teams during the Second World War.

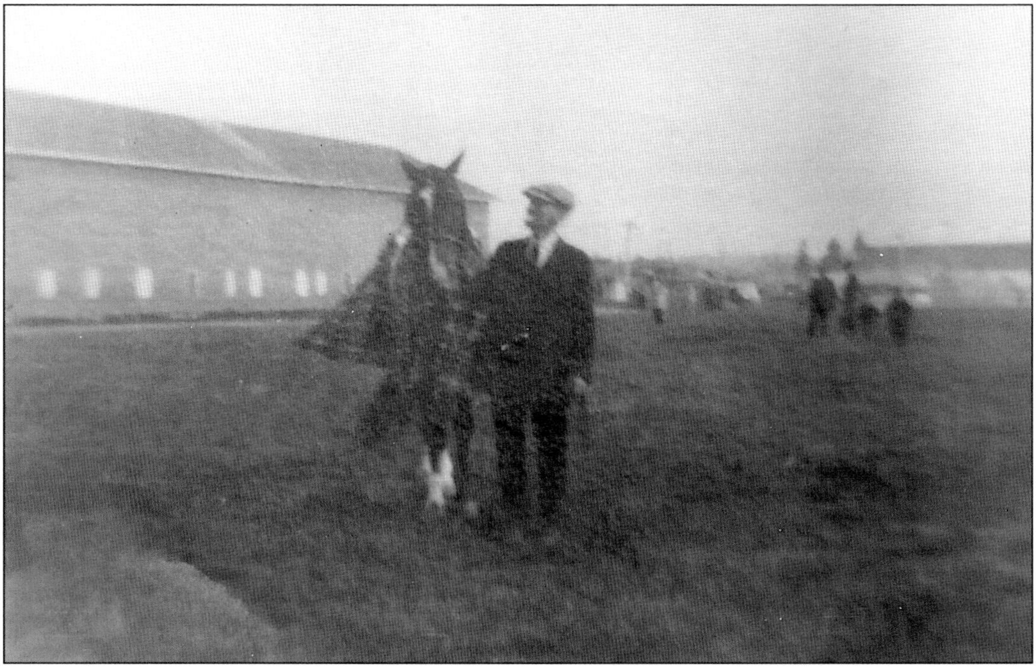

Another sport looming large on the Houlton scene was harness horse racing. This is Jackson Grattan, the horse Houlton purchased to do battle with John R. Braden, Presque Isle's almost undefeated horse. Jackson Grattan never did beat the Presque Isle horse.

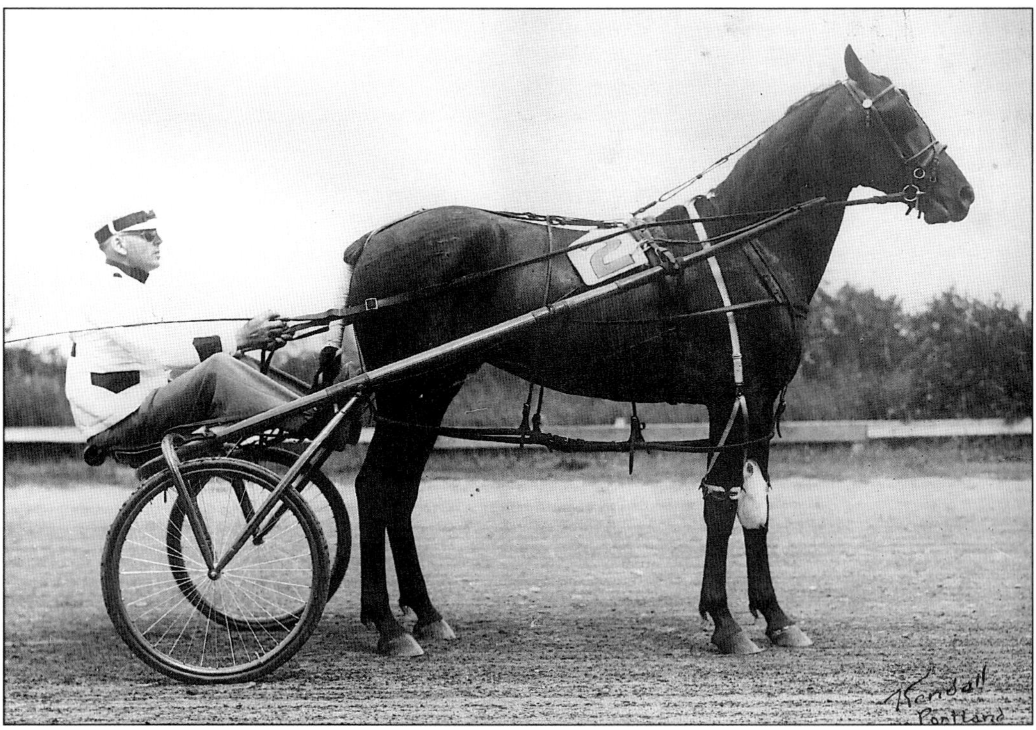

Thomas "Vic" Holdaway was one of Houlton's best-known harness race horse owners and drivers. He is here with "Hal O." Appropriately enough, Holdaway operated a meat business.

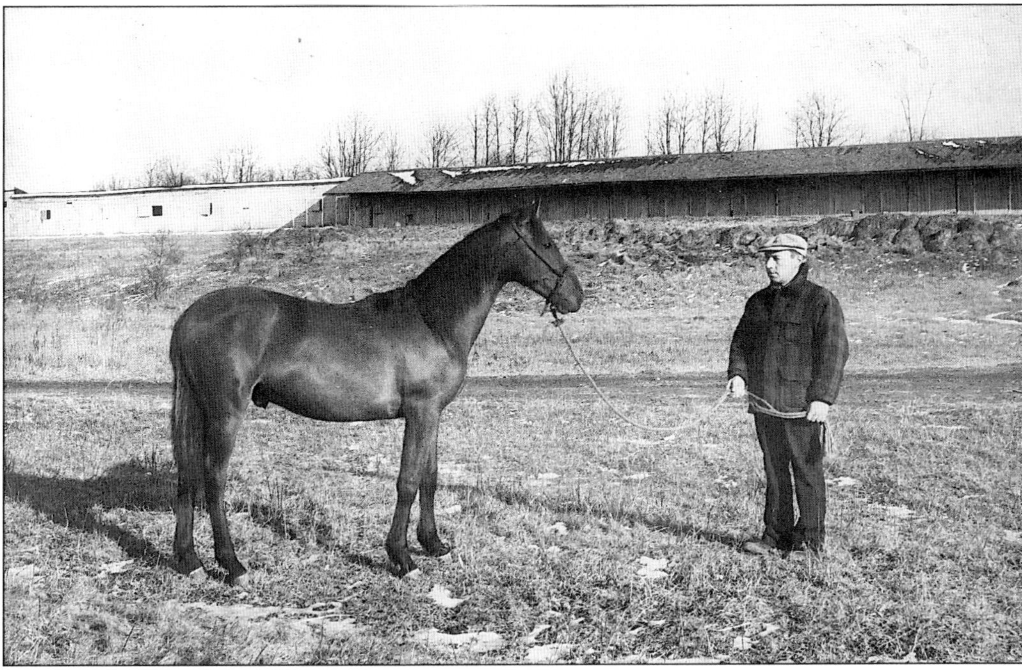

Phil Daigle, owner of the Grant & Daigle grocery store, is seen with Marcia Clegg, one of his harness racing horses.

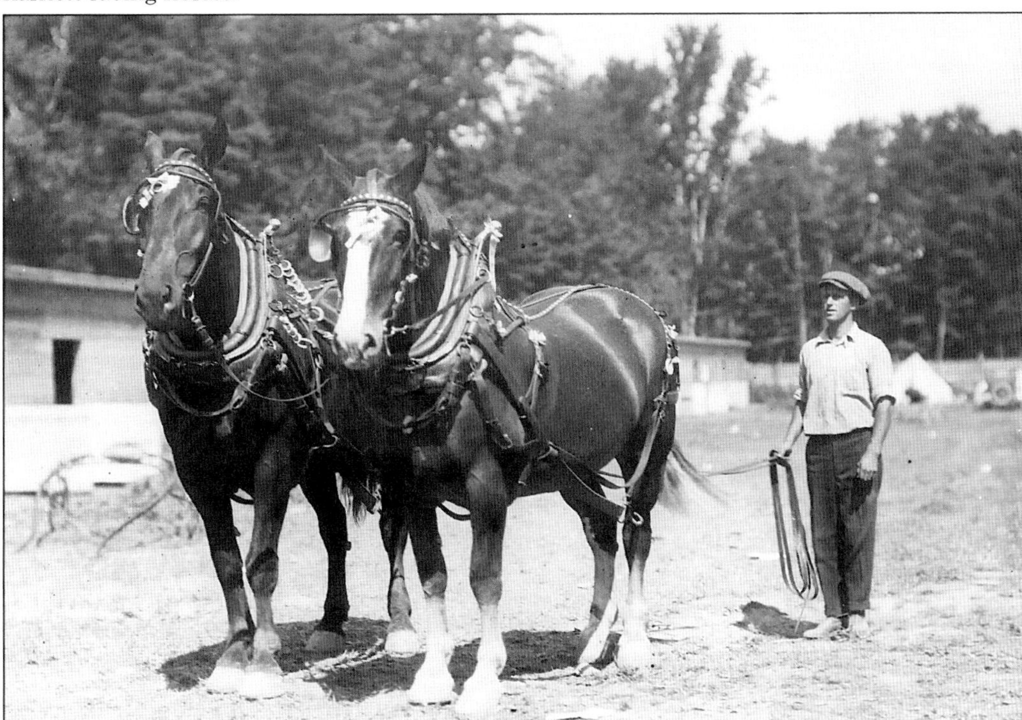

And there was also horse pulling. Here is the champion horse pulling team of Elrod and Perley, owned by the Rhoda family and driven by Earl Rhoda.

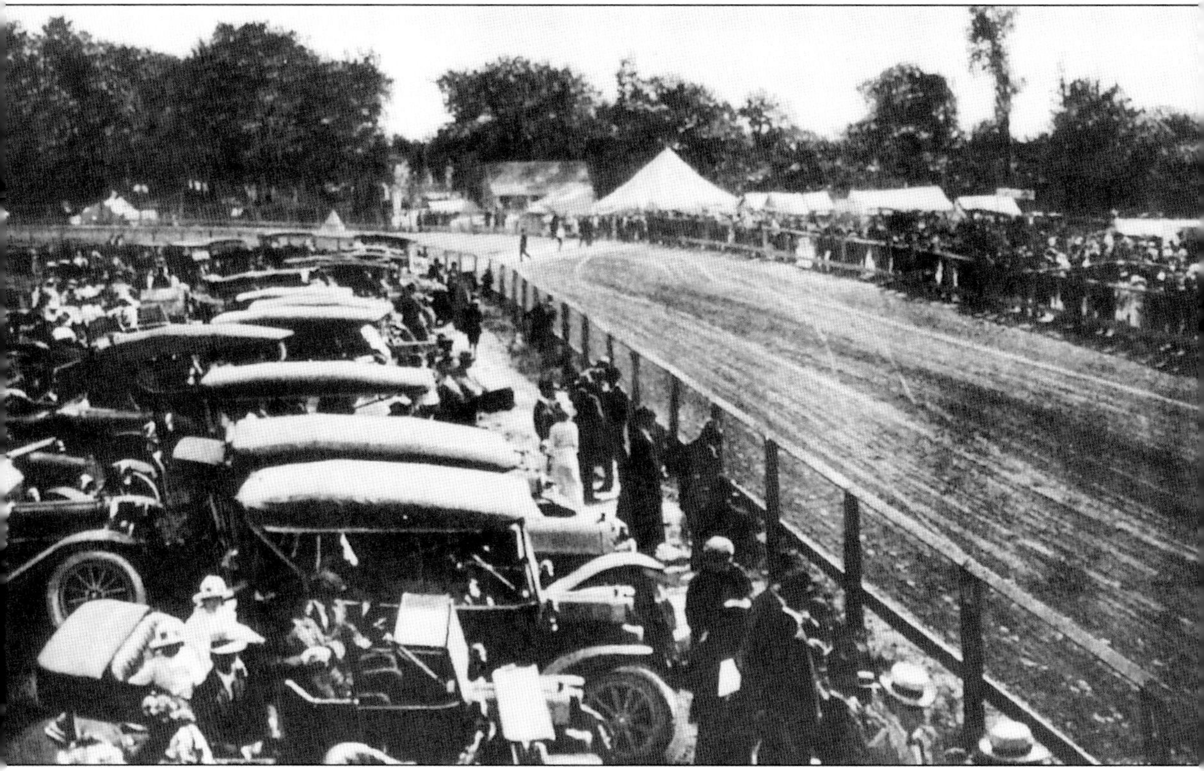

The annual Houlton Fair was the focus for harness racing and baseball since its start. It drew huge crowds for its midway and other attractions and is still going strong. It has, over the years, also stressed the agricultural side of Houlton's economy with many farm exhibits and contests. This scene in the 1920s is typical. The Houlton Fair was, from the crowd viewpoint, much like Market Square on Saturdays—only it lasted several days.

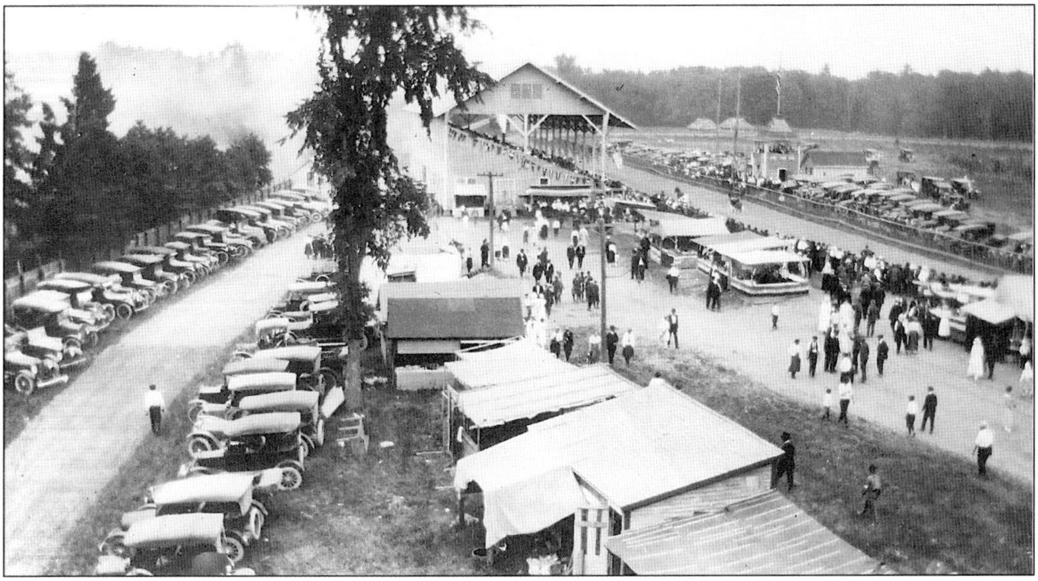

And here is another view of the fair, this time on 3 July, 1919.

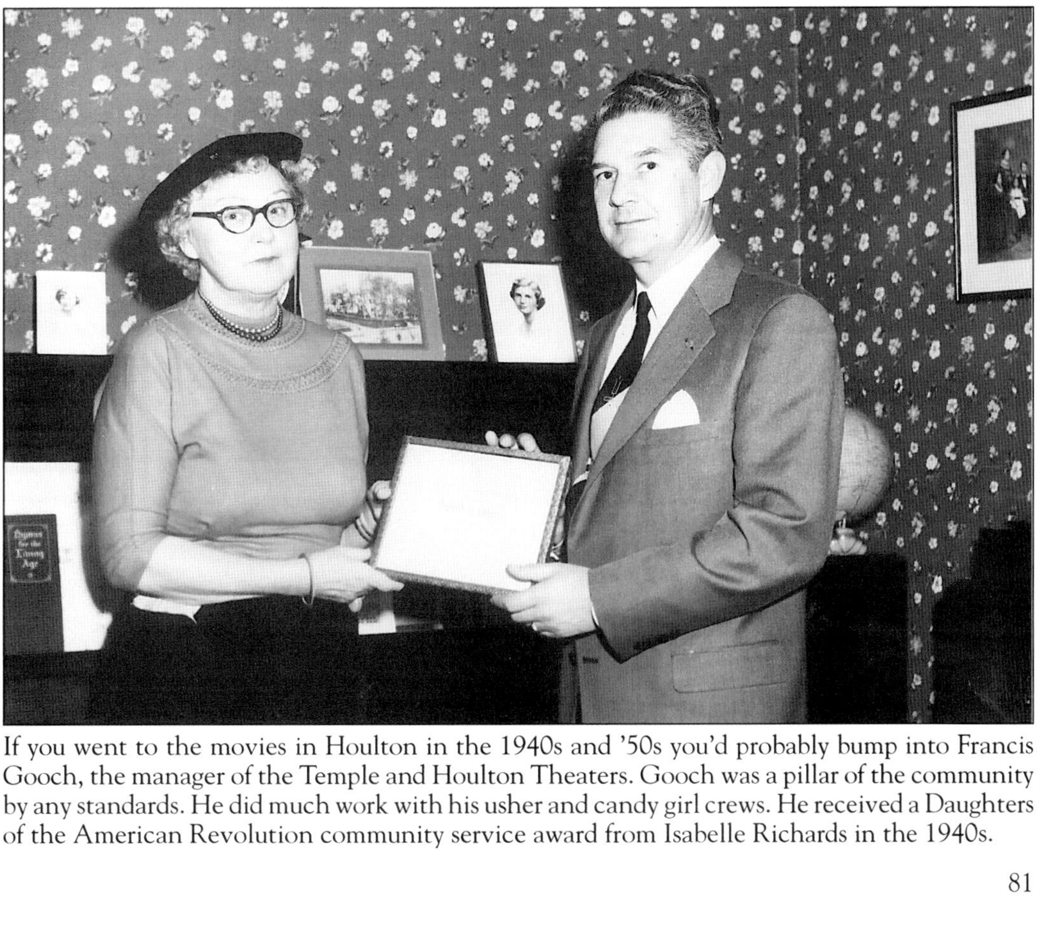

If you went to the movies in Houlton in the 1940s and '50s you'd probably bump into Francis Gooch, the manager of the Temple and Houlton Theaters. Gooch was a pillar of the community by any standards. He did much work with his usher and candy girl crews. He received a Daughters of the American Revolution community service award from Isabelle Richards in the 1940s.

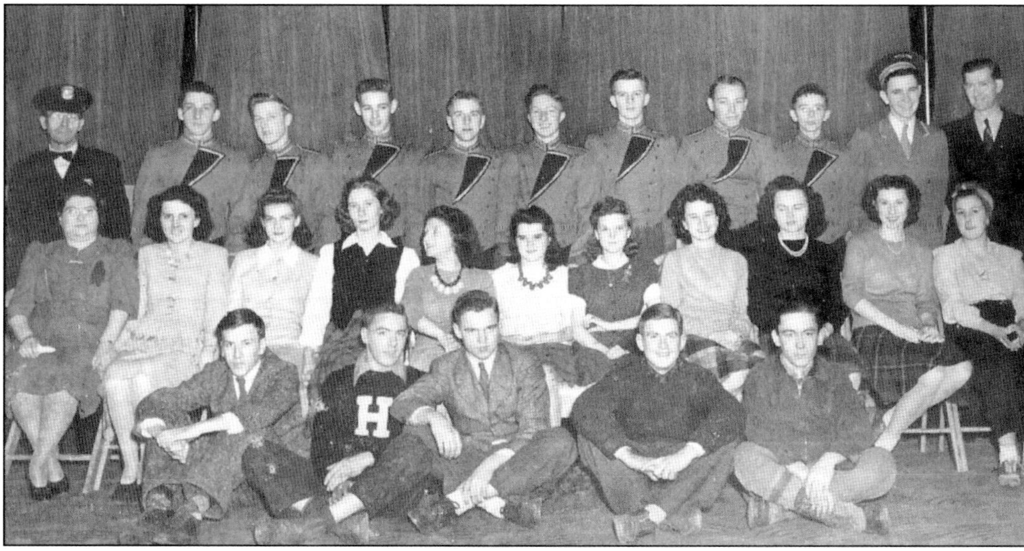

Ushers and candy girls from the Houlton Theater in 1944 lined up for a Christmas card photograph. They were Frank McNally, Bob McCormack, Billy Rush, Hank Skehan, Larry Reece, George Pray, Bob MacNair, Don Philbrick, Phil Jenkins, Harold McNutt, Ralph Bickford, Geneva McKinney, Nina Callahan, Phyllis Hardy, Patricia O'Donnell, Ruth Ross, Ruth Currier, Theresa Plourde, Mary Stantial, Patty Russell, Harriette Watson, Bonnie Jones, Romey Clifford, Benny Cameron, Teddy Hawkins, Jack Conlogue and Walter Sibley. Not in the photograph were Stan Greaves, Ken and Alvean Ellis, Arthur McElwee, Don Roberts and Francis Gooch.

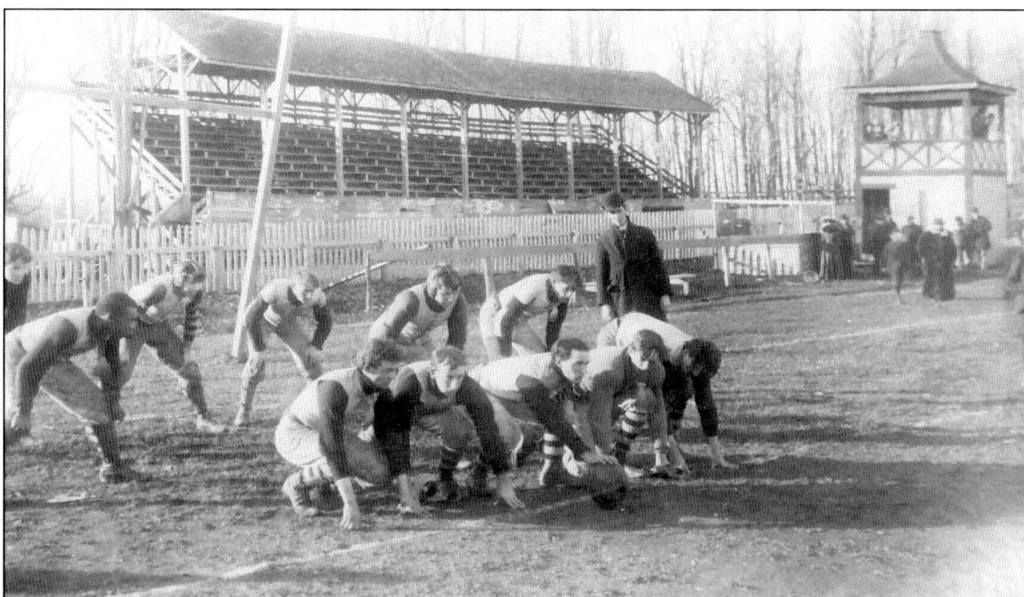

There was football, too, though in Houlton there no longer is a high school team. The 1900 Houlton High football team featured Augustus Clark, James Donnelly (coach), Allan Bird (coach), Frank Logan, John Donovan, Ludlow Cornelisson (a great athlete), F.W. Burrill, Harry Hallett, Kenney and Joe Donovan, Ralph Nelson, Murdock McKay, Arthur Putnam, Chester Davidson and Hamilton Flinton.

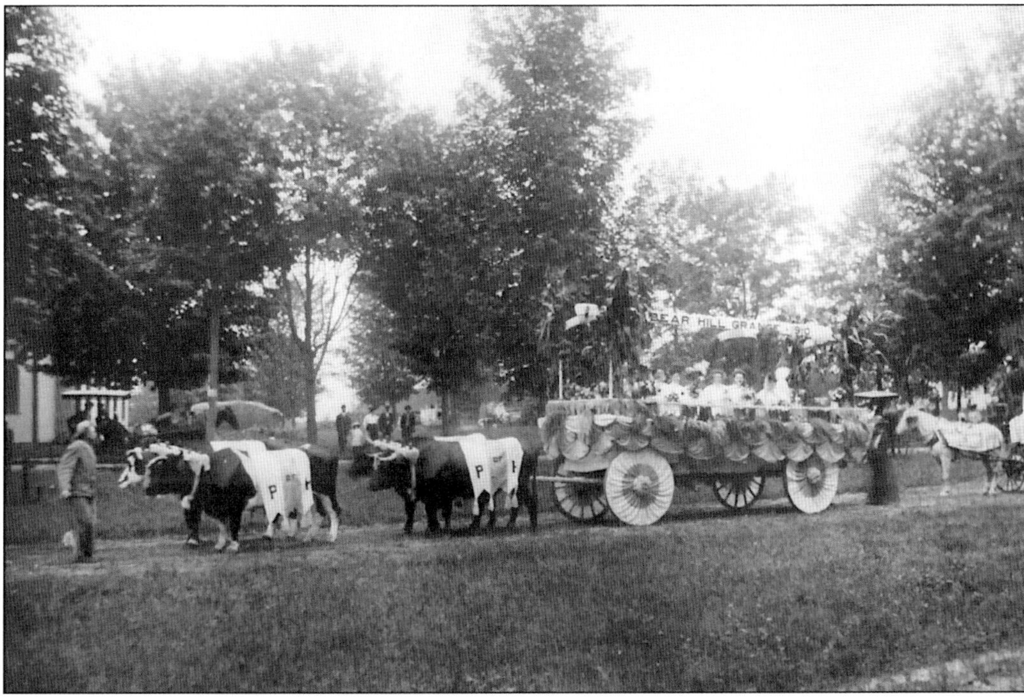

Parades have always been important in Houlton. In a 1910 parade, probably on the Fourth of July, this float from the Bear Hill Grange stood out.

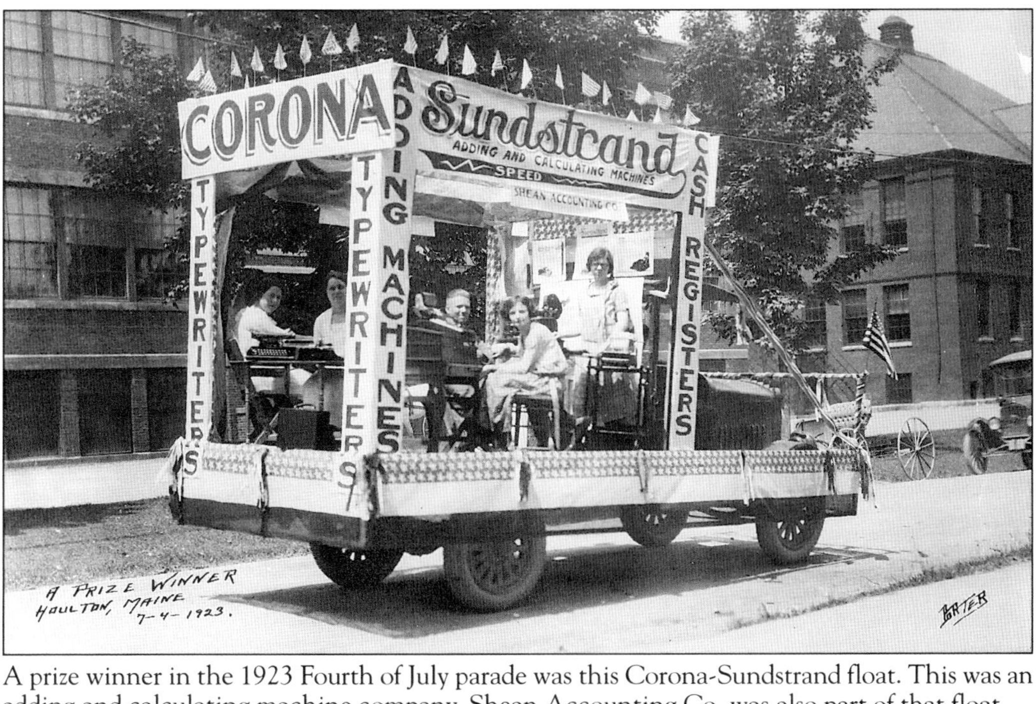

A prize winner in the 1923 Fourth of July parade was this Corona-Sundstrand float. This was an adding and calculating machine company. Shean Accounting Co. was also part of that float.

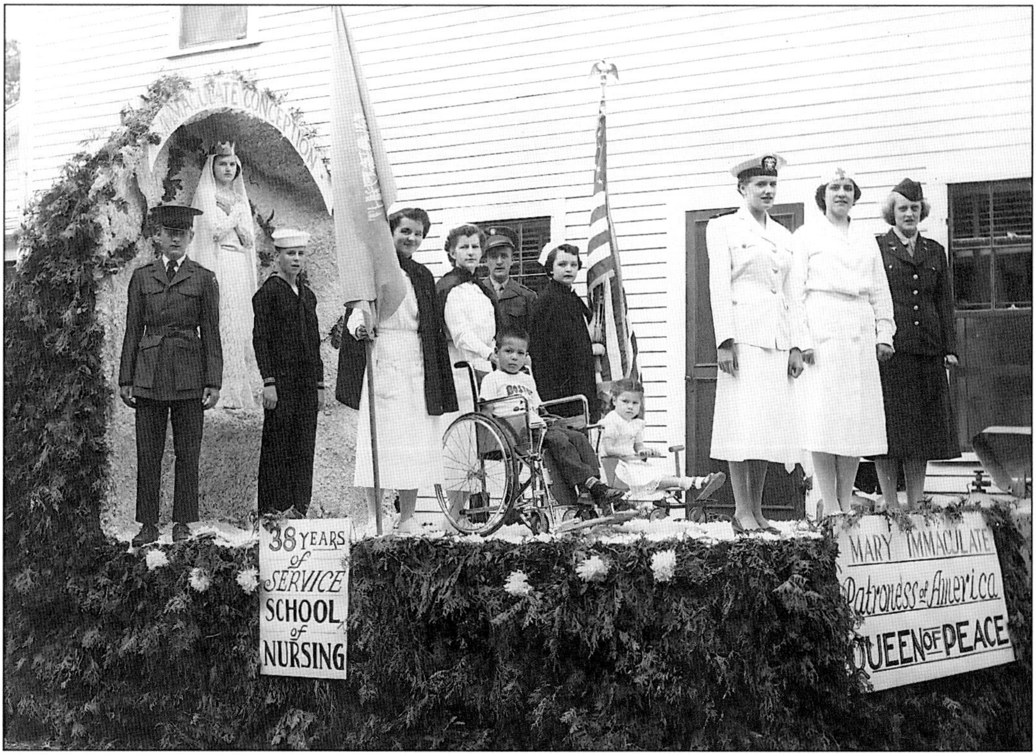

In the 1952 Fourth of July parade, the school of nursing, probably from Madigan Memorial Hospital, celebrated thirty-eight years of service.

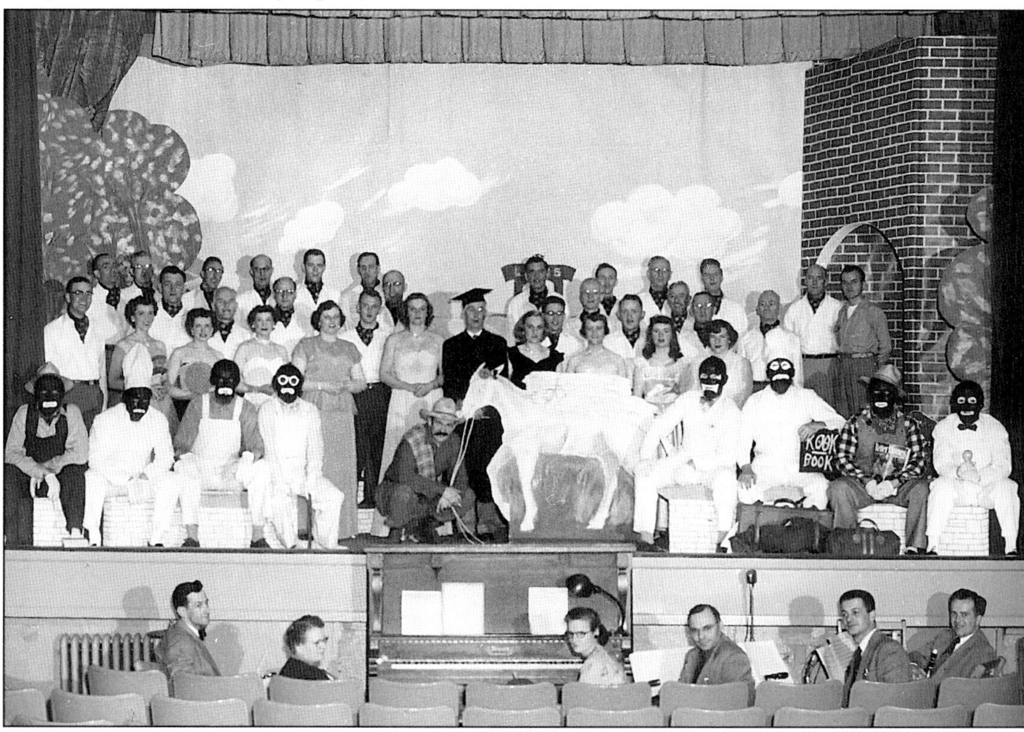

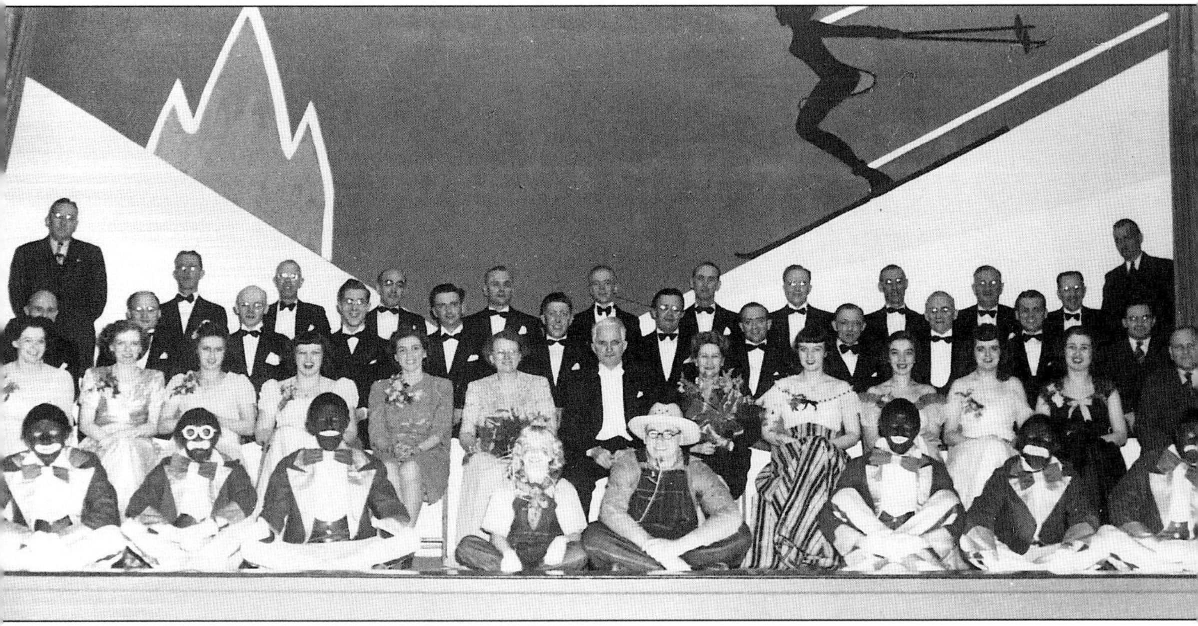

Here is the cast for the Lions Club Show in 1946 with, rear, left to right: Hillus Ingraham (manager), Gilfred Colbath, Fred Purington, Mike, Walter, Hump Flemington, Victor Totman, Don Ellis, Gerald Dunphy, Ned Joy and Lester Baker; second row: Norman Mullen (director), Carl Steiler, Ralph Dill, Harold Helms, John Hall, Leland Longstaff, Harry Baulch, Gordon Witney, Ralph Porter, Arthur Feeley, Ken Young (director) and Rod Palmer (lights); front row: Shirley Moreshead, Bernice Boynton, Patty Robichaud, Joyce Bell, Miss Maller, Marge, Tom Vose, Lila Gardiner, Shirley Hall, Joan Green, Frances Clark, Clara Gartley and Dode Robinson; and front, center: Janice Palmer and Lewis Potter. End men were: Newell Titcomb, Percy Campbell, Ralph Ellis, Fred Sylvester, Phil Churchill and George Barnes.

Opposite: They used to take children out of school to watch the Lions Club Minstrel Shows in the 1950s.

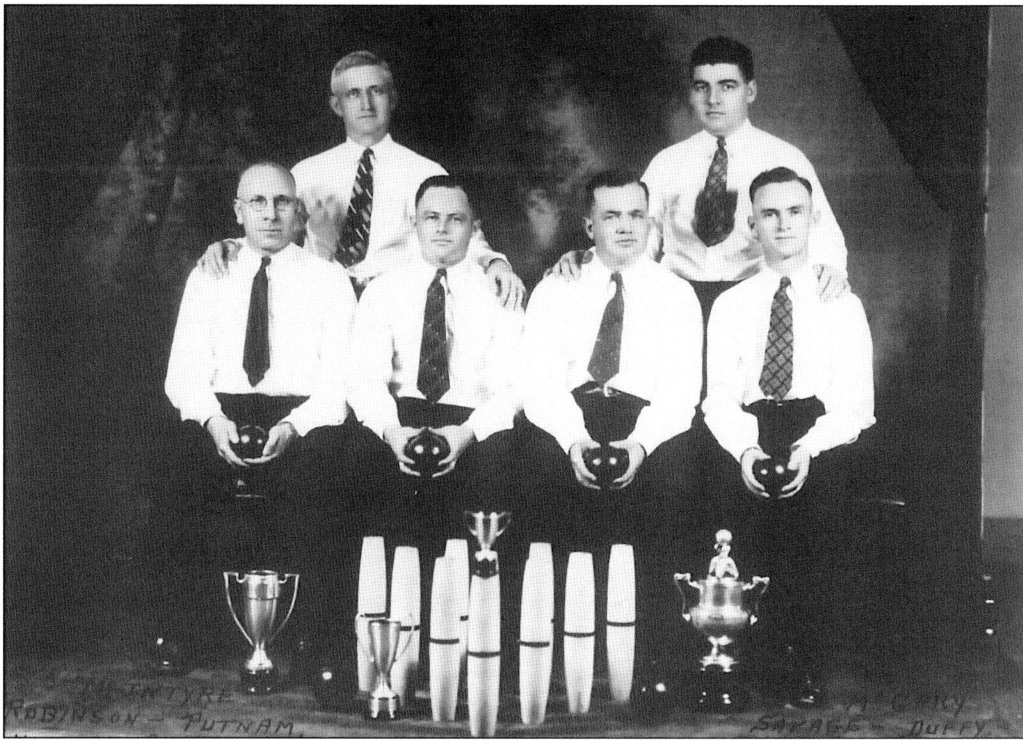

Bowling, especially of the candlepin variety, was always popular in Houlton. On the Elks 1936 Eastern Maine bowling championship team were left to right: Robinson, McIntyre, Putnam, Savage, McGary and Duffy.

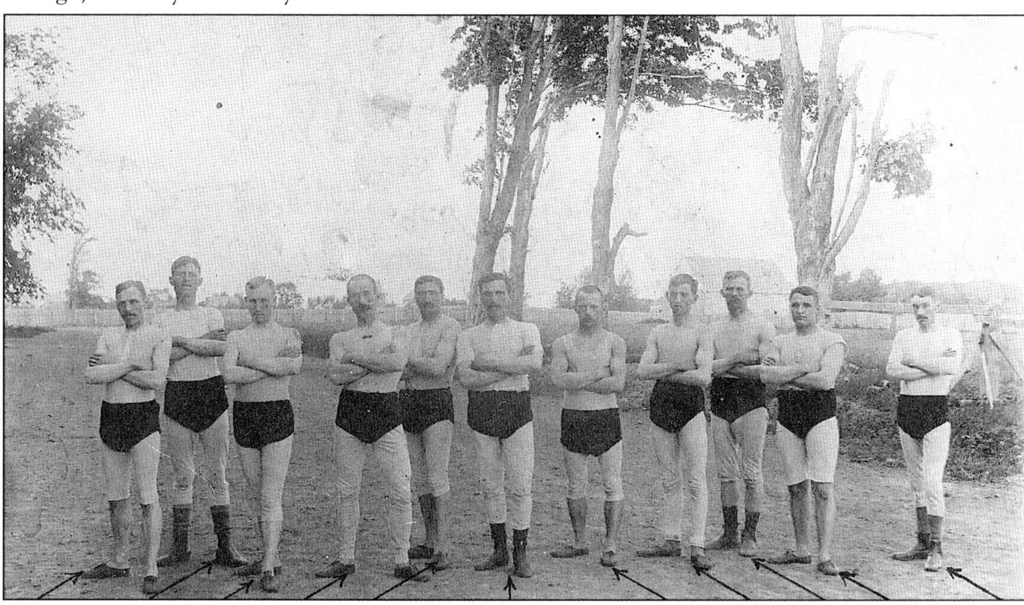

They didn't just fight fires. On the Houlton Fire Department running team in 1886–88 were, left to right: George Nickerson, George Small, Warren Inman, Samuel Webber, John Harrigan, Olin B. Buzzell, Amos Putnam, Robert Esters, Lowell Chandler, Wellie Buzzell and Leslie Bryant.

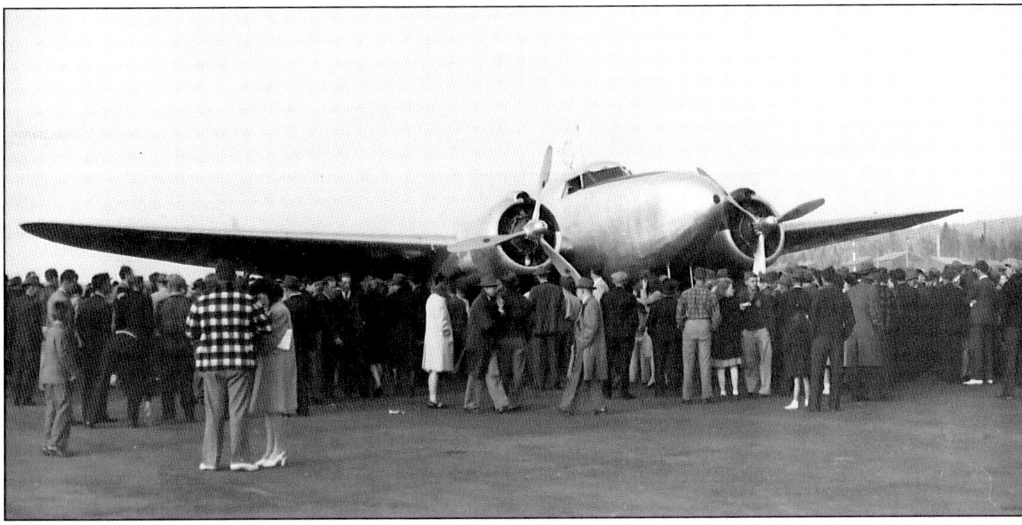

There were other forms of flight than running. Air shows like this one were a highlight each year at the Houlton Airport. Here a crowd surrounds a DC-3, either just before or after the Second World War.

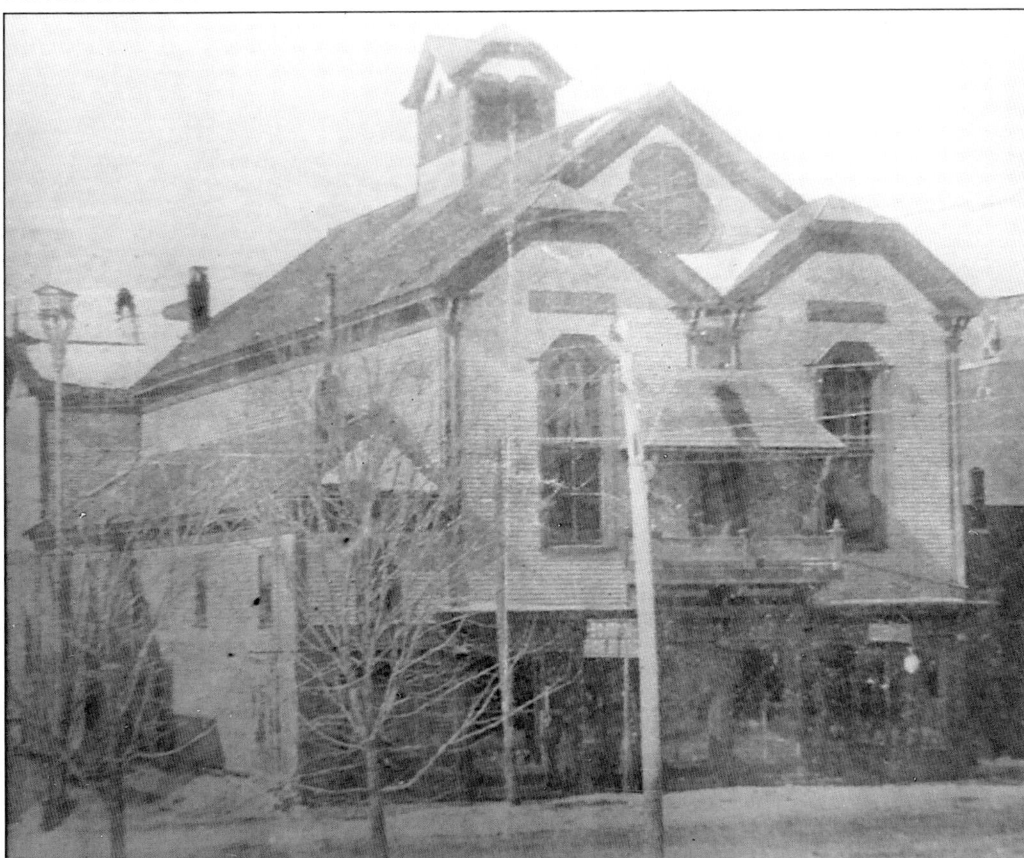

Houlton even had an Opera House. This photograph was taken in 1895. It was eventually converted to what is now the Heywood Apartments.

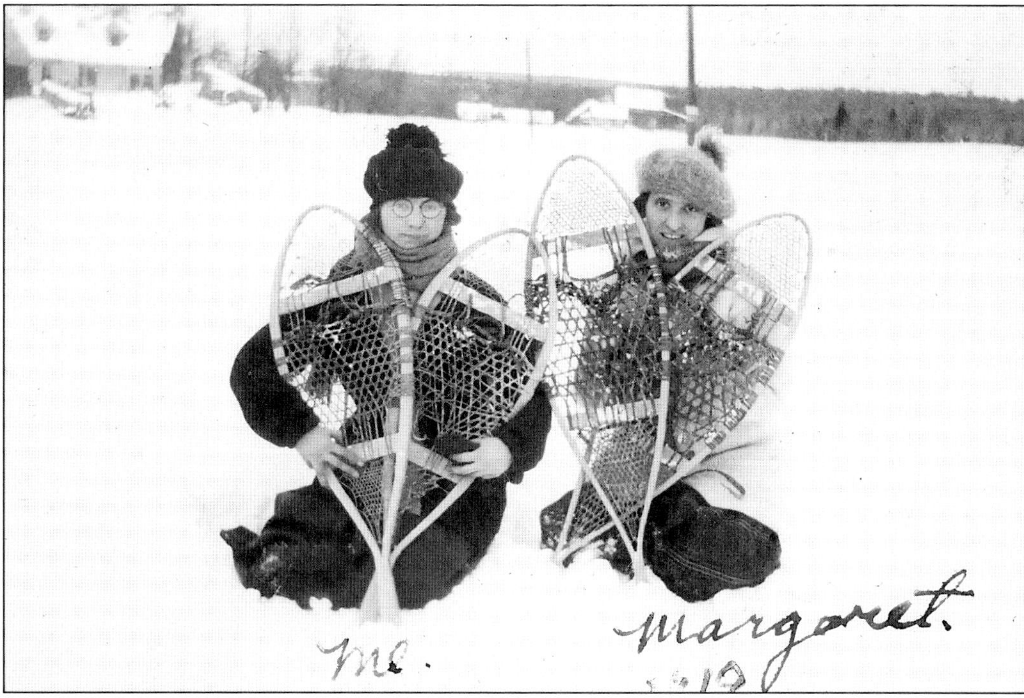

The winter in Houlton does have its uses: Ruth and Margaret Putnam horse around on snowshoes in 1919.

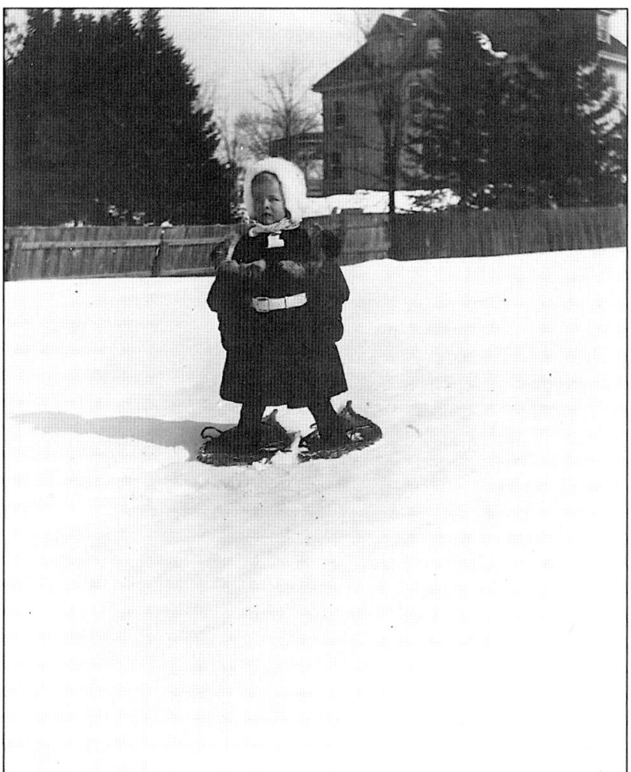

Nothing like starting out young in Houlton on snowshoes!

Five

Houlton Is the Town and Surroundings

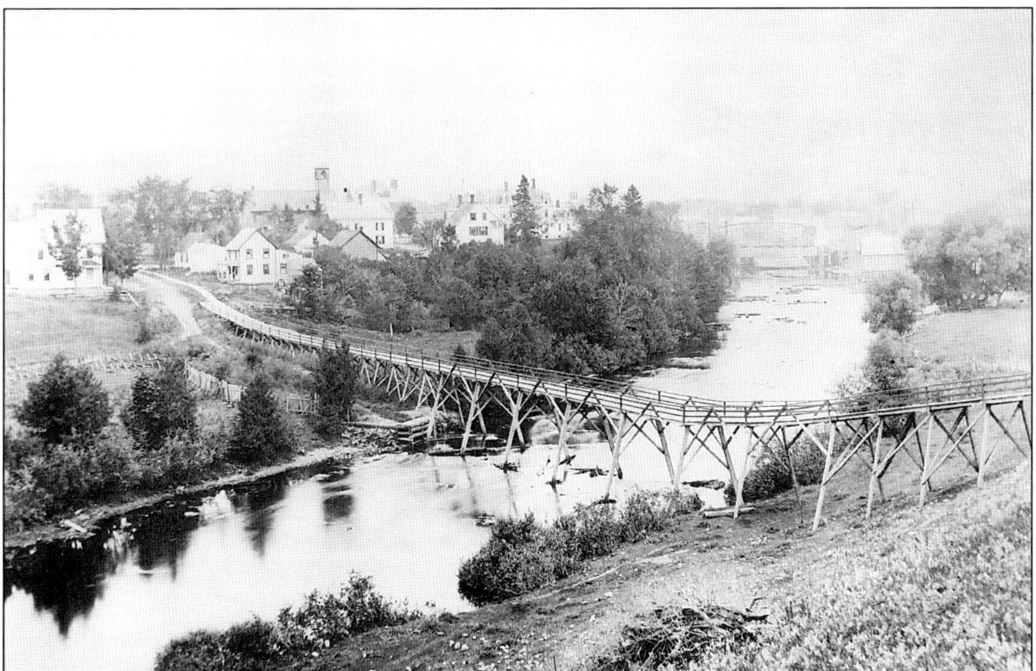

The footbridge over the Meduxnekeag River on Highland Avenue was picturesque in 1892.

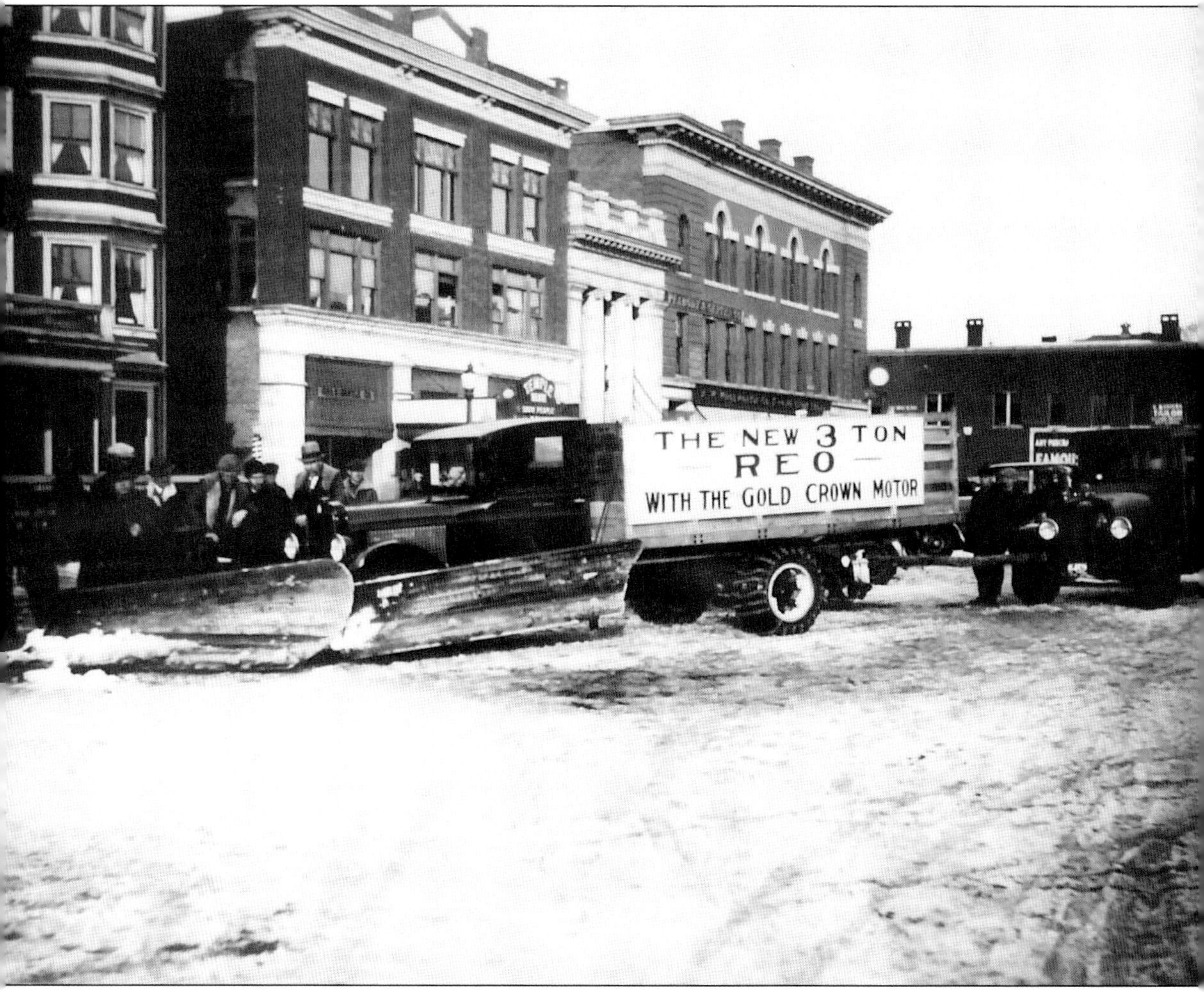

The first commercial snowplow of any size came to Houlton in the 1930s where it was put to good use. It was a three-ton Reo. Some of those with it are: Edward Dysart, Marshall Dysart, Dewey Webber, Gary Haskell, Harold Cole, Jaspar Harvey and Donald Dunn. Over the years, of course, Houlton has become expert in taking care of itself when there's plenty of snow. Most years, there is plenty. Allie Cole first plowed from Lincoln to Houlton in 1928/9. The Reo allowed Cole to plow all the way to Presque Isle.

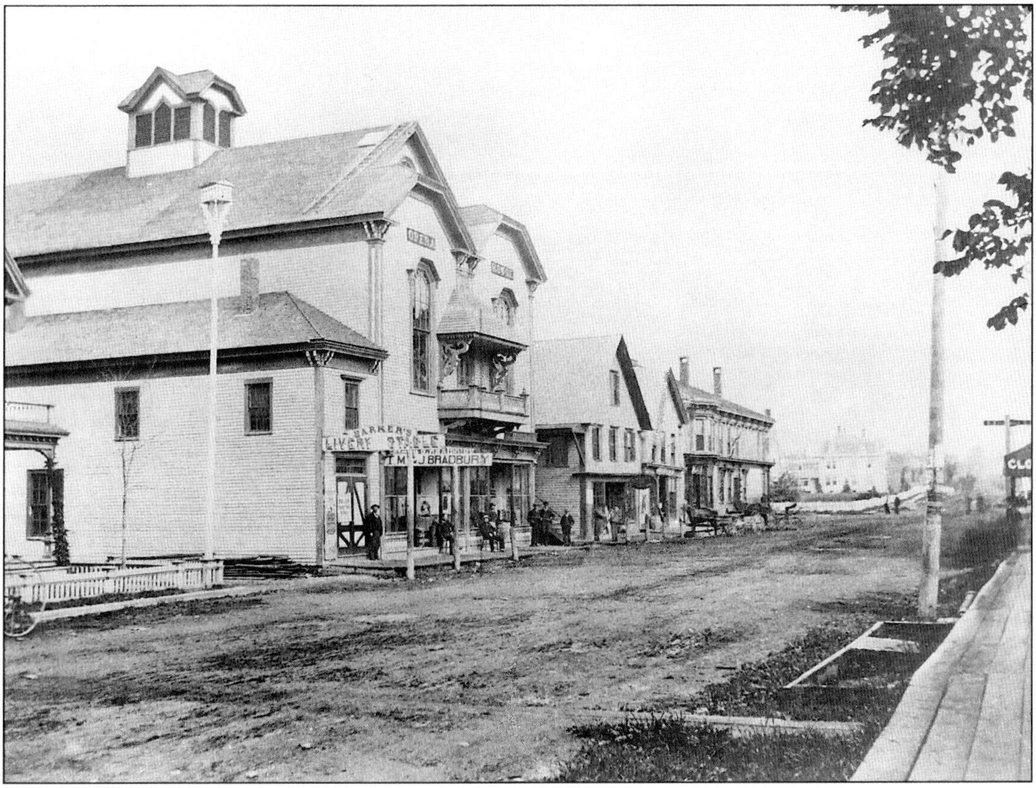

This is Court Street looking north with the building that is now the Heywood Apartments. This could have been as early as the 1860s.

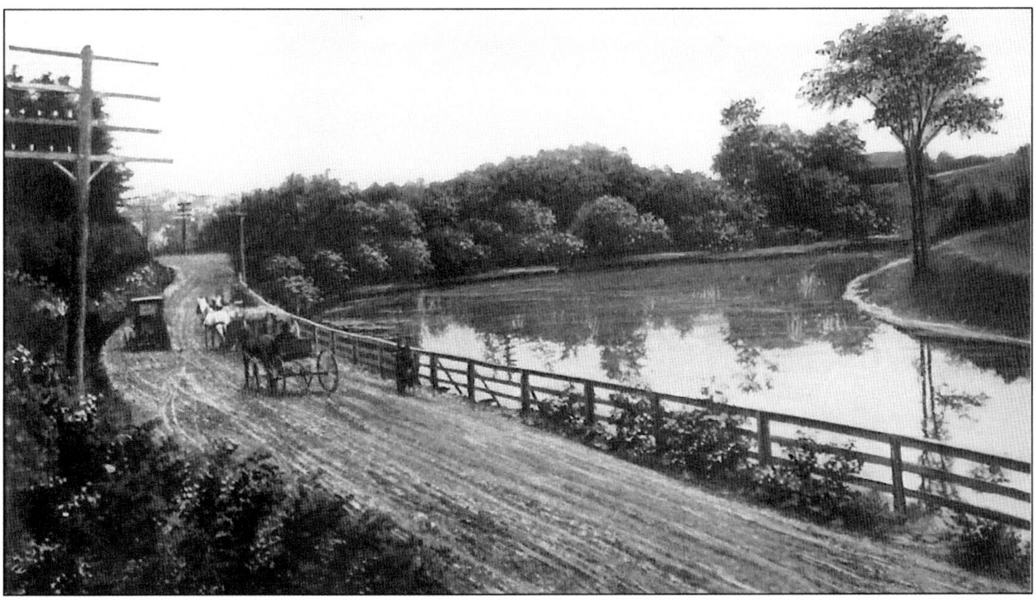

Bangor Road has both horse-drawn buggy and horseless carriage. The transition had started around 1915 or so.

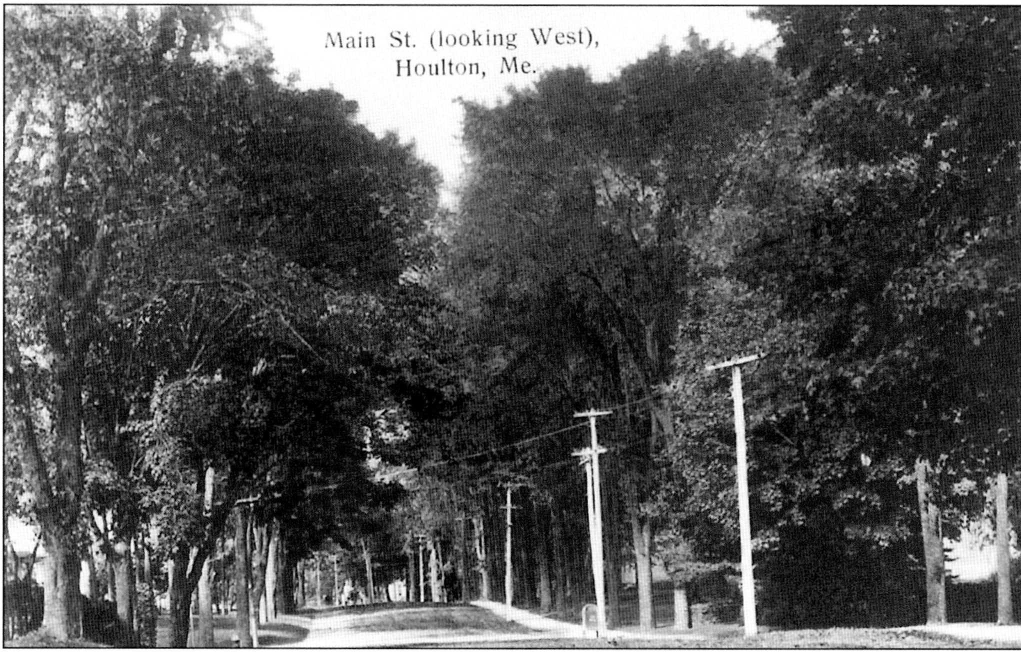

Main Street looking west while Houlton still had its beautiful elm trees was a joy to see. Dutch Elm disease and other causes brought the eventual elimination of all the elms.

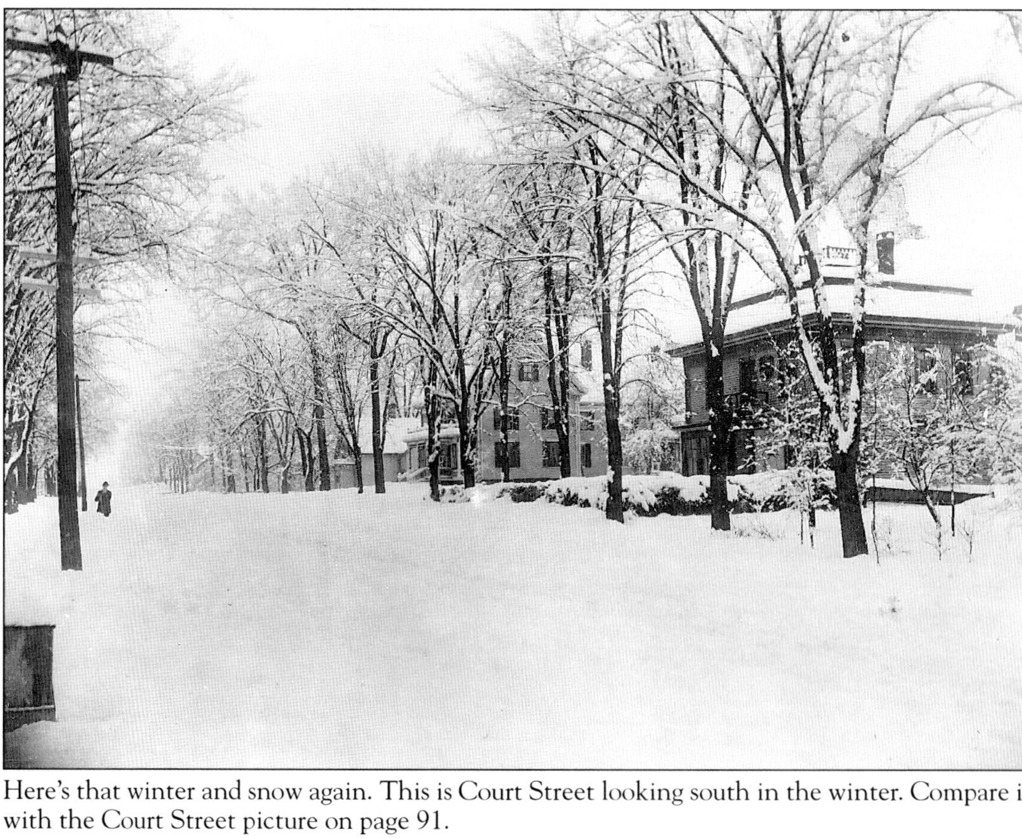

Here's that winter and snow again. This is Court Street looking south in the winter. Compare it with the Court Street picture on page 91.

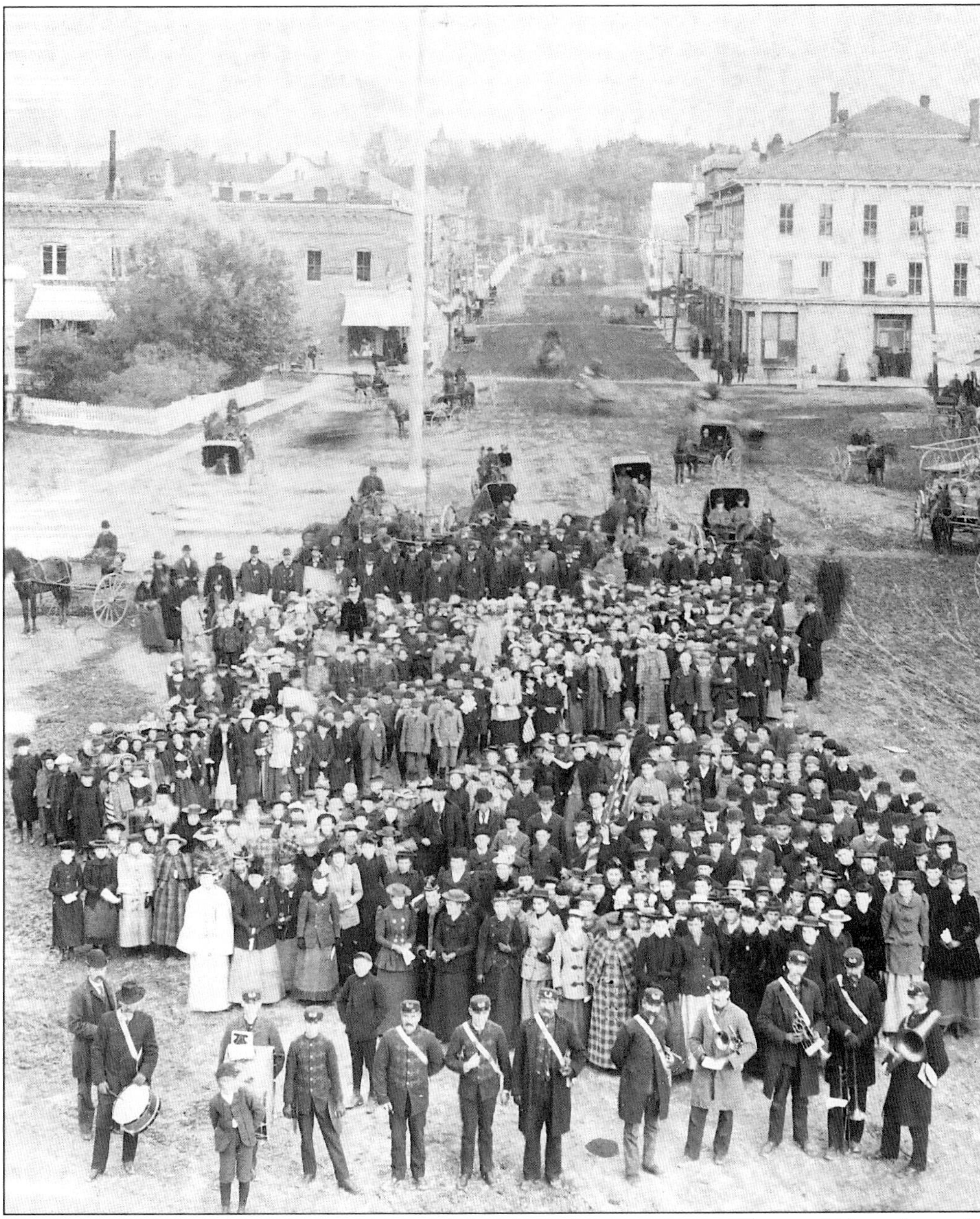

Market Square was not always crowded with carriages, buggies or cars. This could have been the end or the beginning of a parade. Note the soldiers in front. Market Square was always a focal point for activity in Houlton.

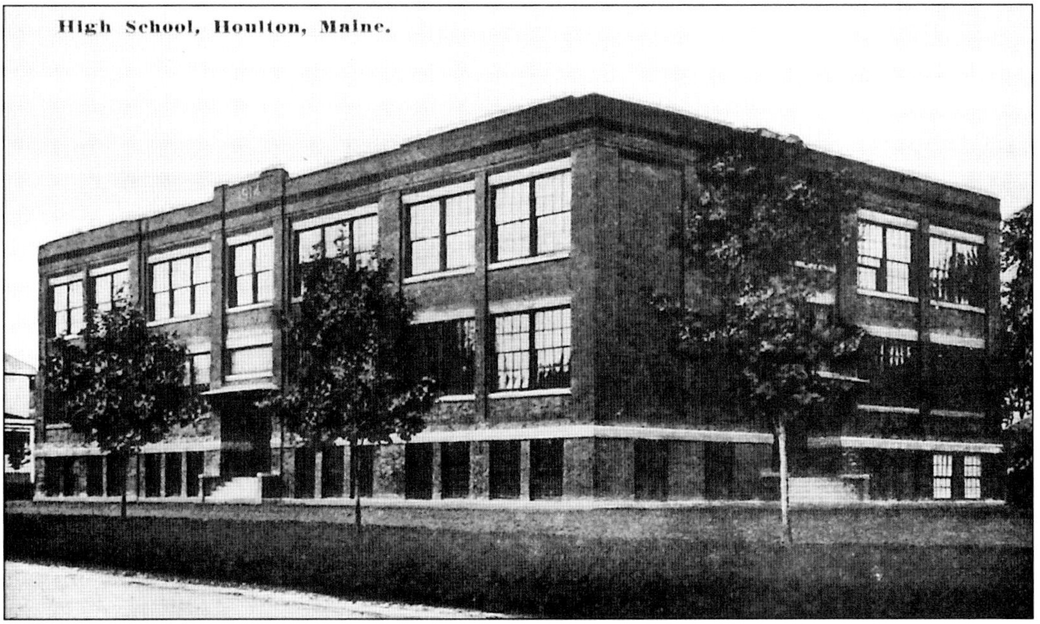

Houlton High School opened a new building in 1914, when this picture was taken. The building later became the Lambert School and was not closed until 1993.

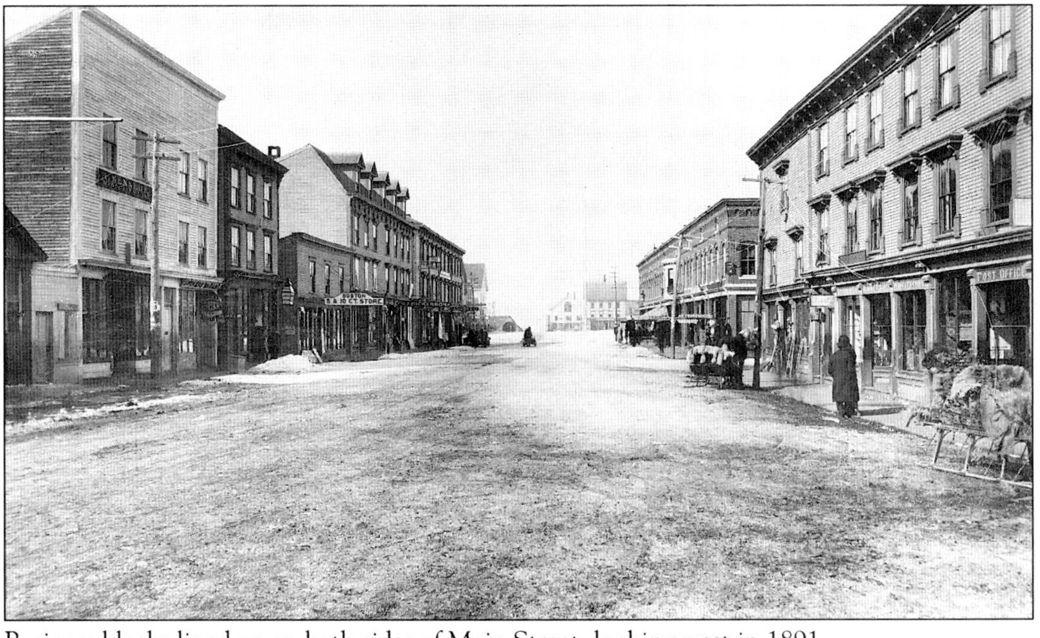

Business blocks lined up on both sides of Main Street, looking west in 1891.

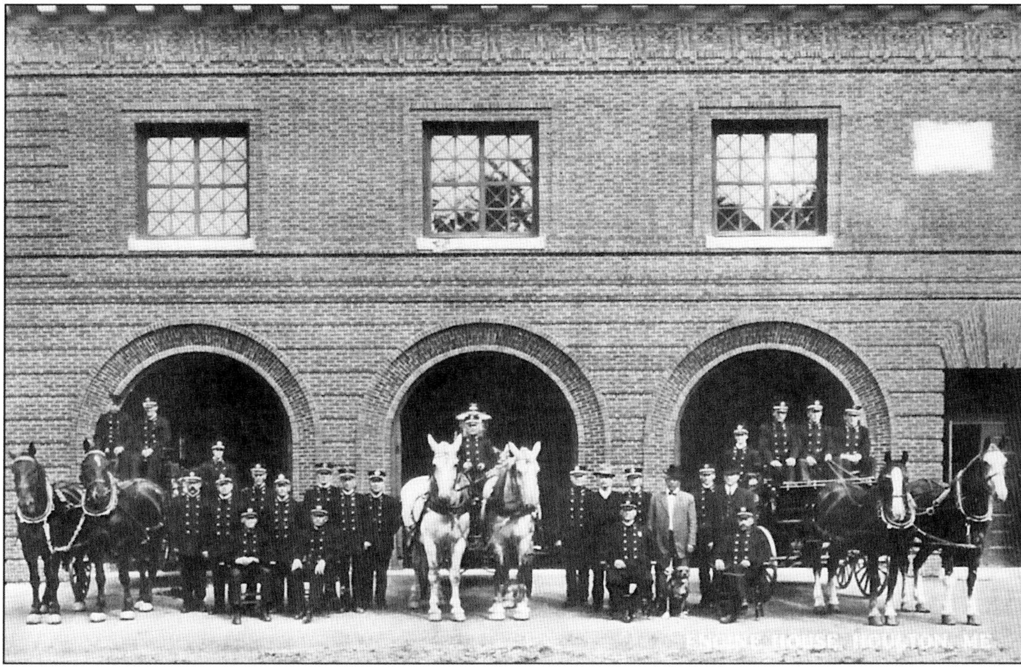

The Houlton Fire Department lined up before its headquarters in the days when it still used horses, probably early in the twentieth century.

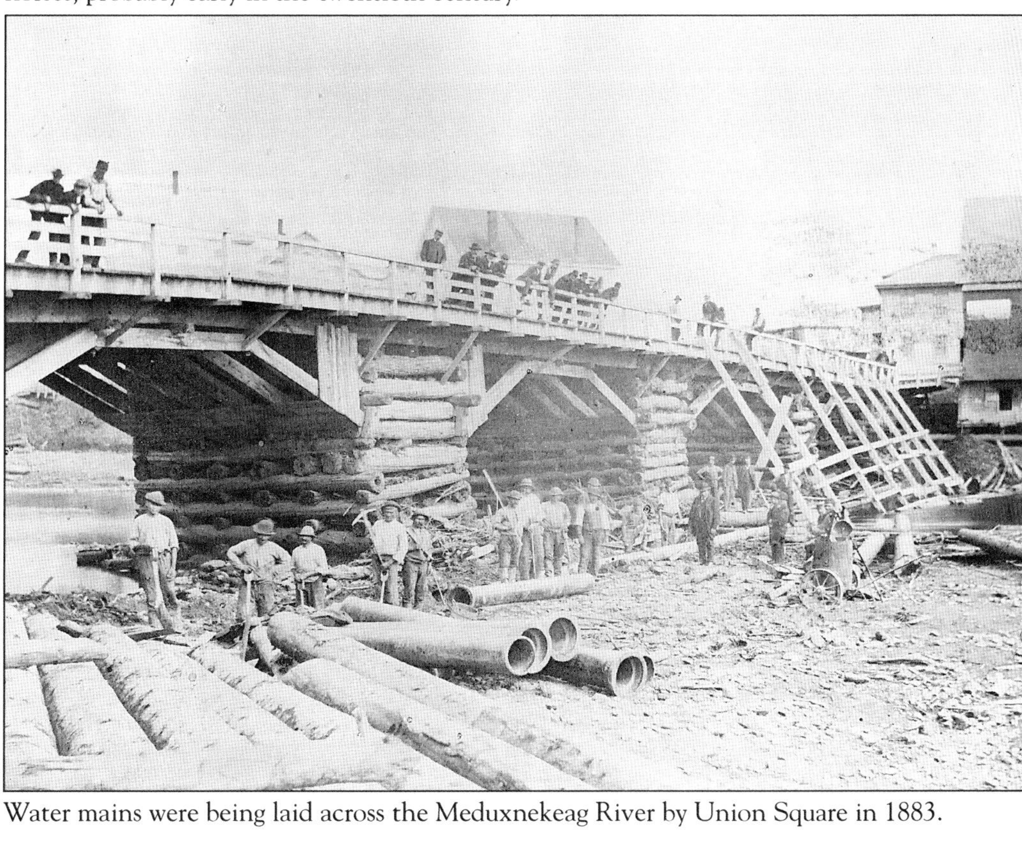

Water mains were being laid across the Meduxnekeag River by Union Square in 1883.

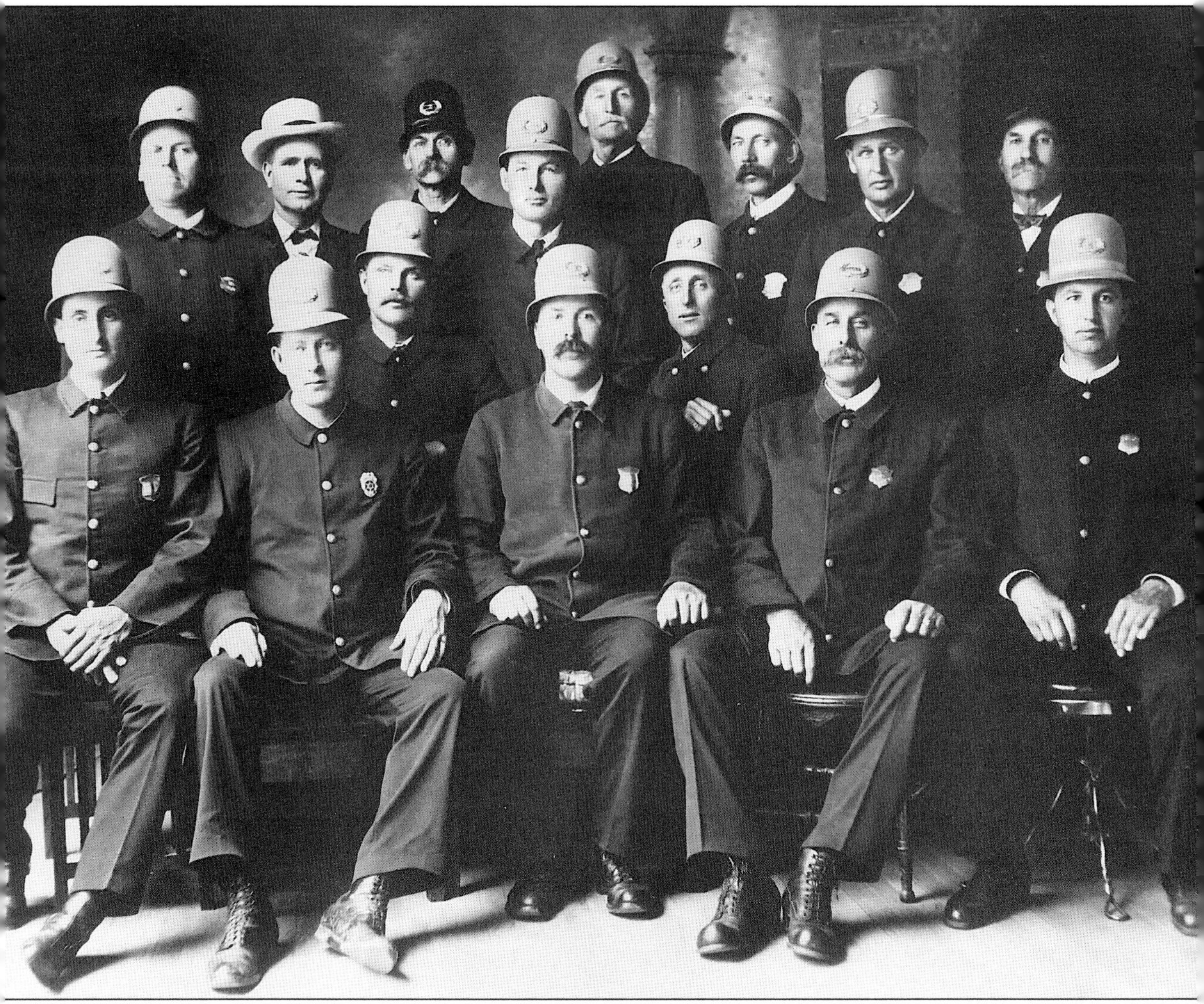

The Houlton Police Department was in good shape in 1913. Members included: Leon Ingraham, Frank Hogan, Ralph Whitney, Joe Anderson, Mel Whitney, Kendall Jackins, Al Howard, George Slipp, Del Atherton, George Reed, John McLaughlin, John Cosboom, Robert Peabody, George McNair and Mike Rideout.

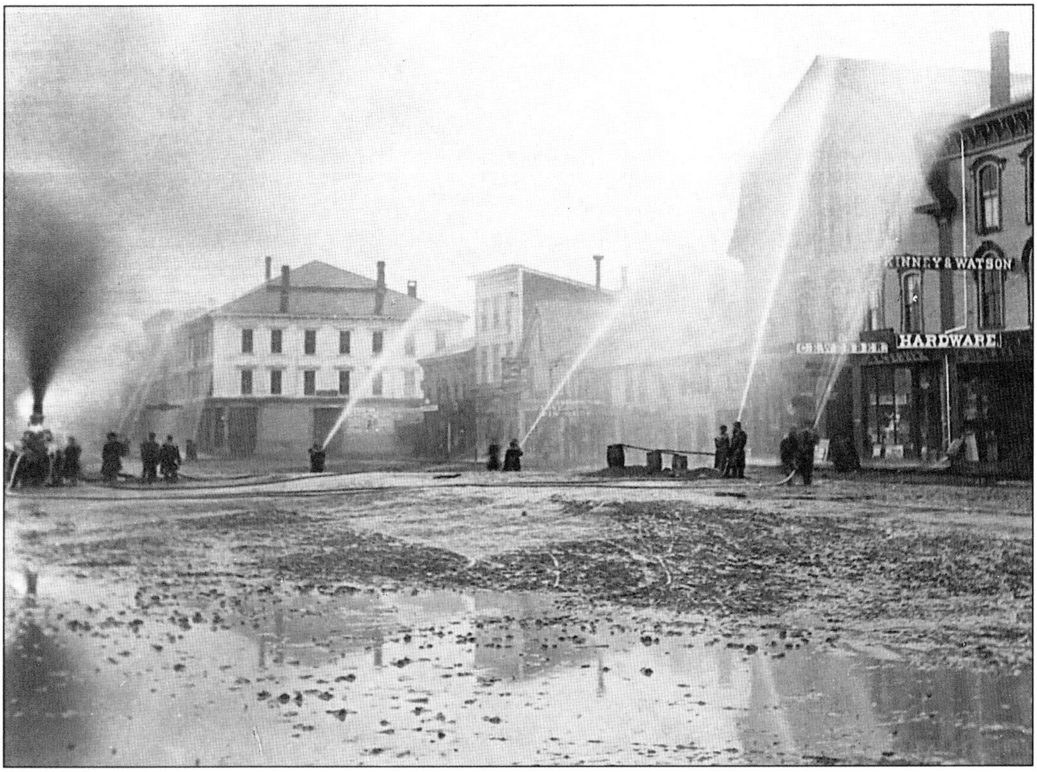

Houlton had its share of fires. This was an early demonstration of its steam fire engine, which was purchased in 1881.

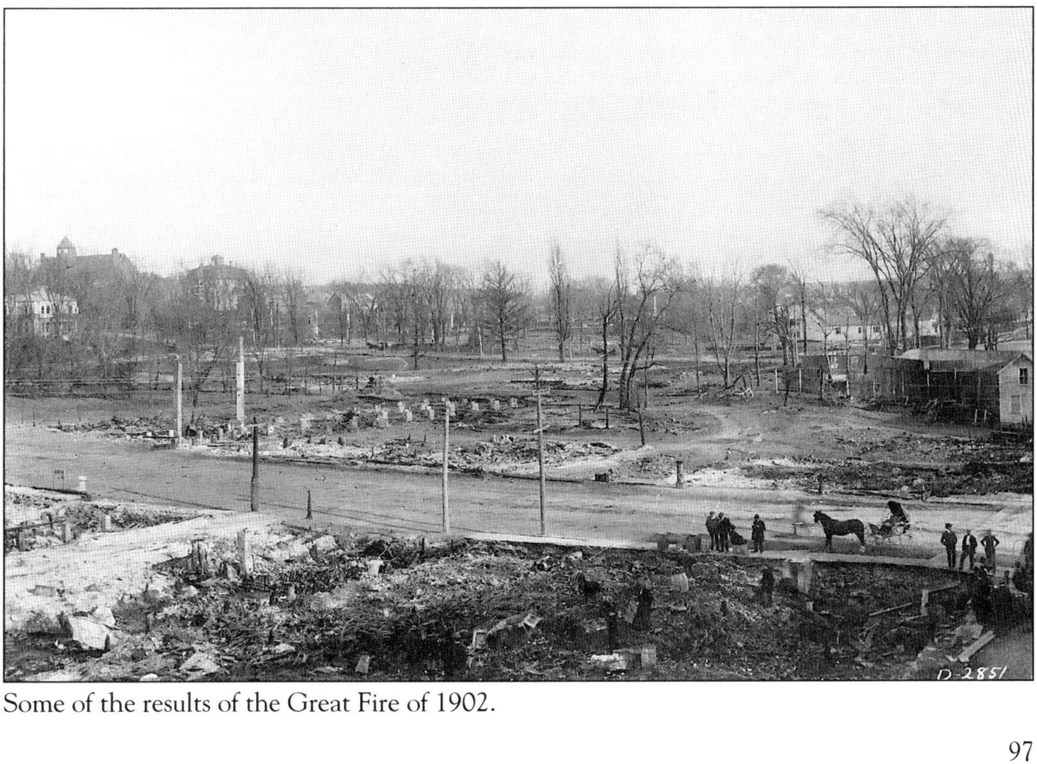

Some of the results of the Great Fire of 1902.

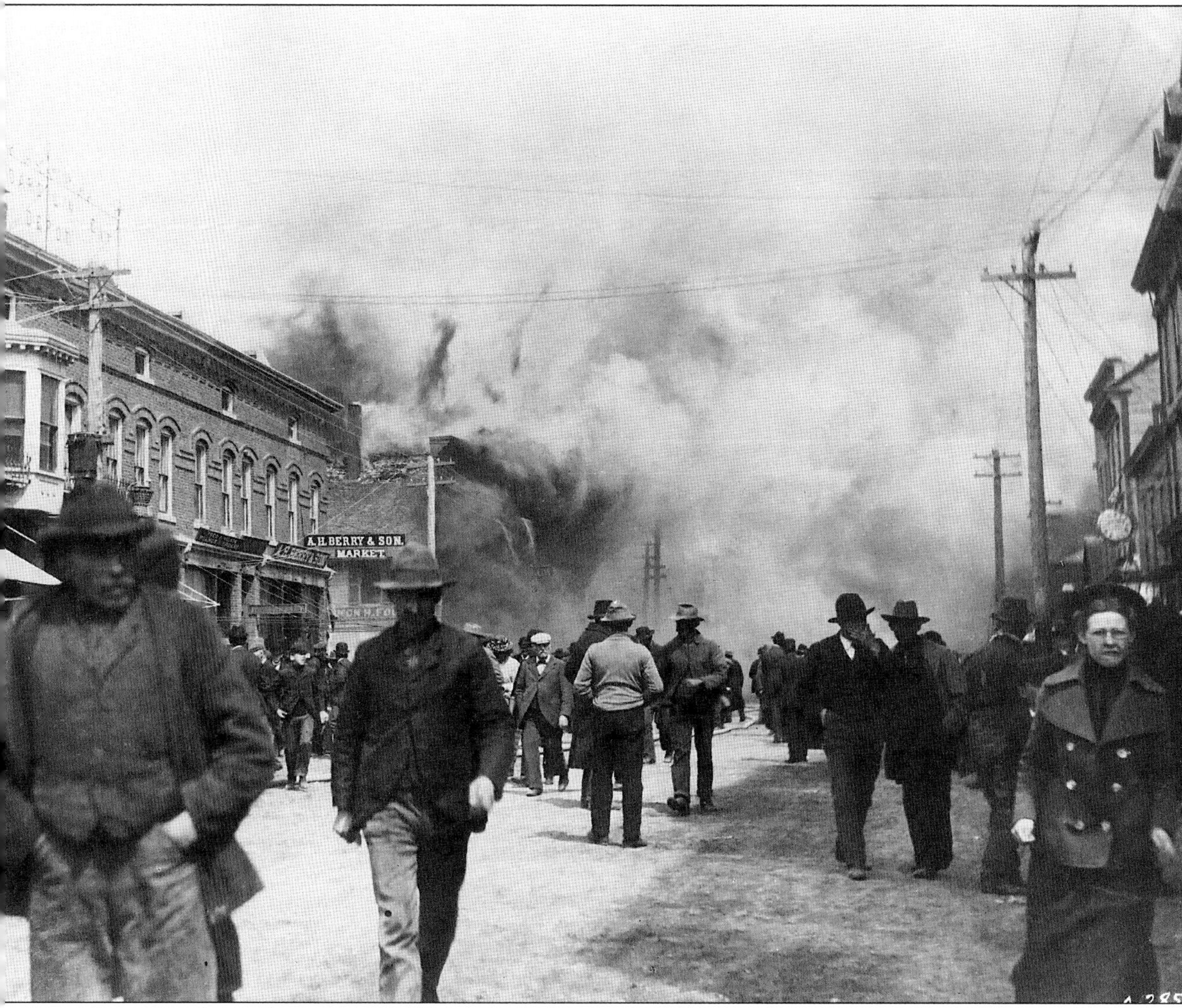

This was right at the start of the Great Fire of 1902. The man in the left foreground is Jim Pete. The blaze began on 17 May at 12:40 p.m., according to my grandmother's history of Houlton. It started in the rear of Dyer's Market in the Fogg Block on Main Street and rapidly went out of control in spite of the efforts of Fire Chief Samuel Webber and his twenty-five men. High winds sped up the blaze. It damaged both businesses and homes on Main Street and in the residential section beyond.

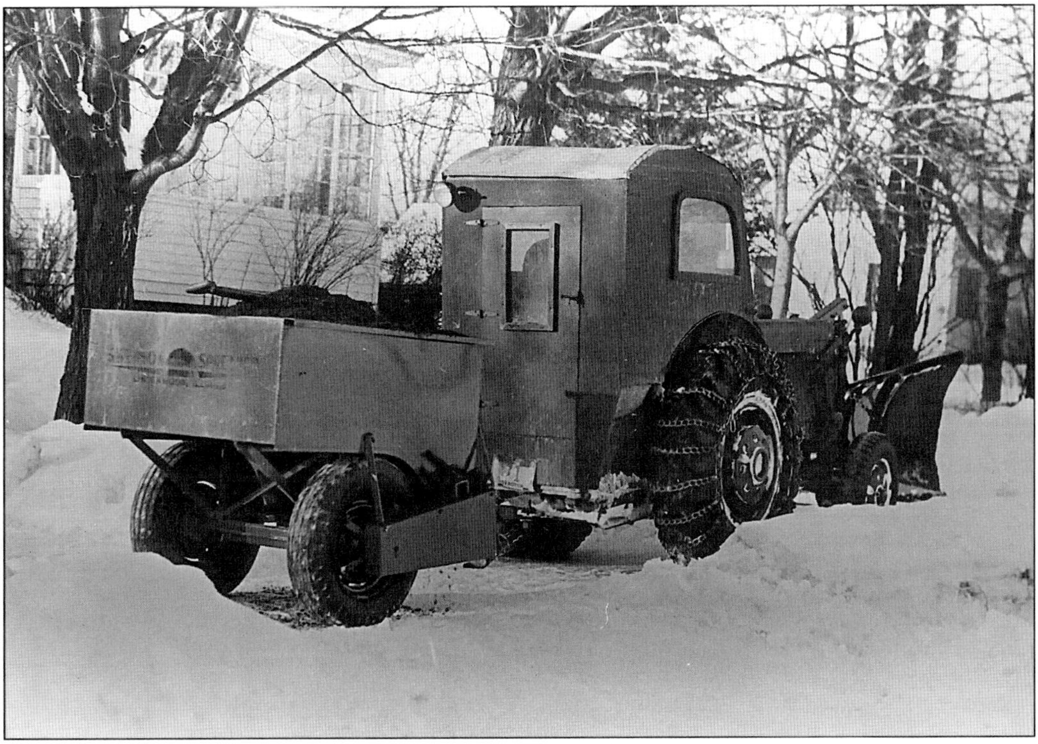

By 1947, Houlton had a very good idea of how to handle snow!

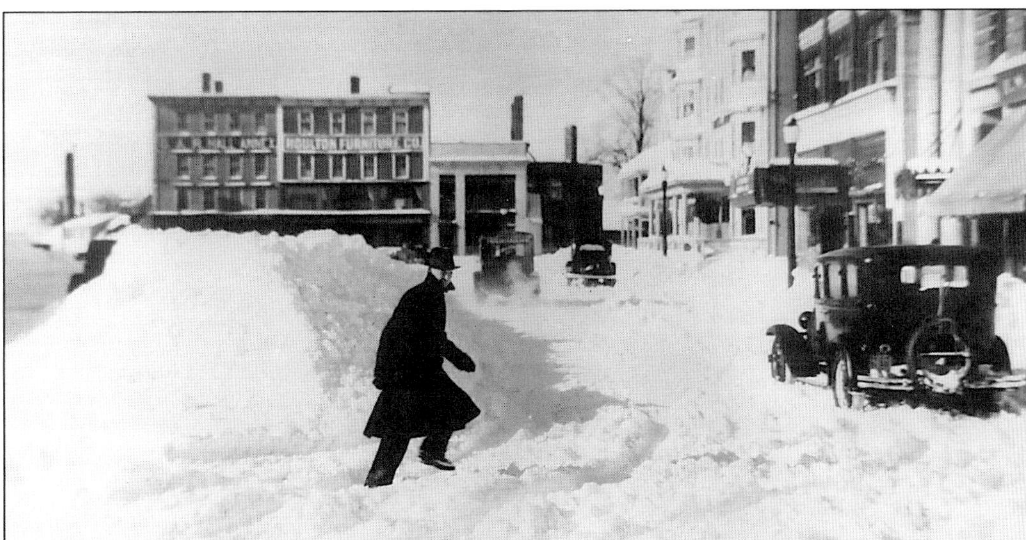

And there still was plenty of snow. This is Market Square during a Thanksgiving Day storm in 1937.

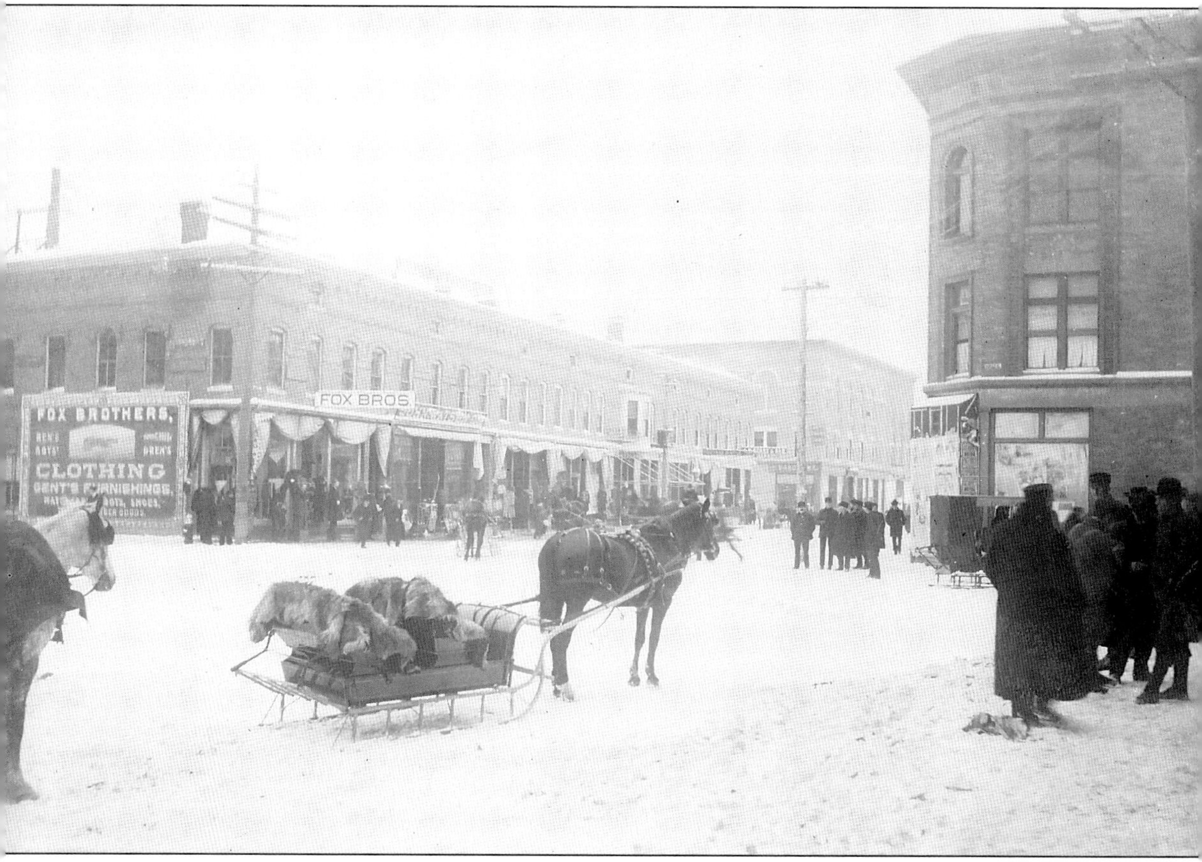

It wasn't much different earlier. This was the Fox Block in 1905. Horses in Houlton certainly became used to working in the snow.

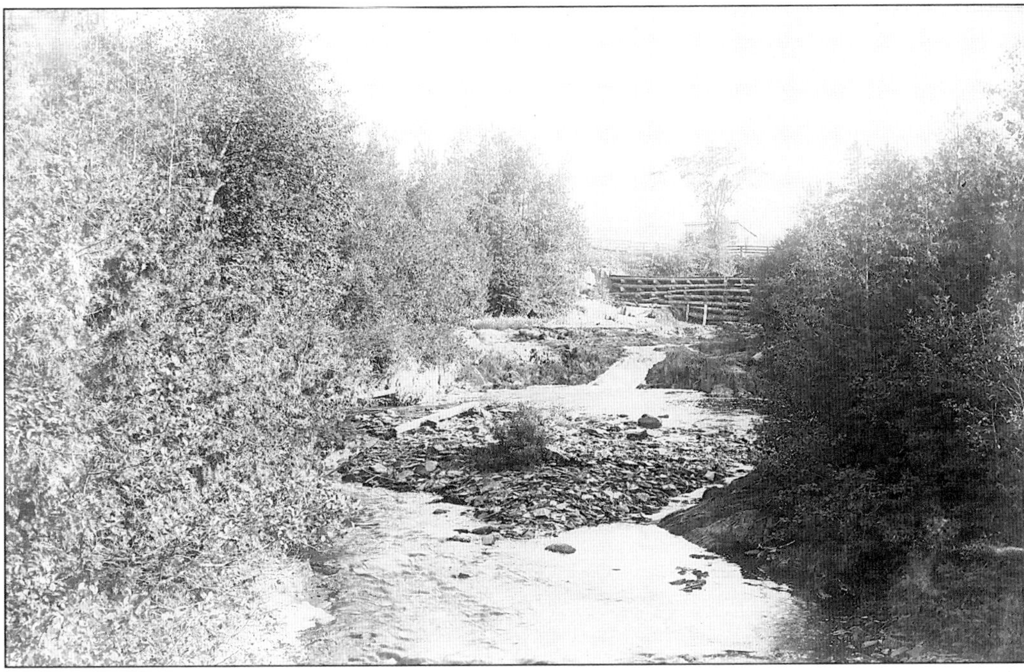

Ah, the beauty of that snow—and ice. This was Cary's Mills in 1905, gleaming in the sunlight, possibly after a storm.

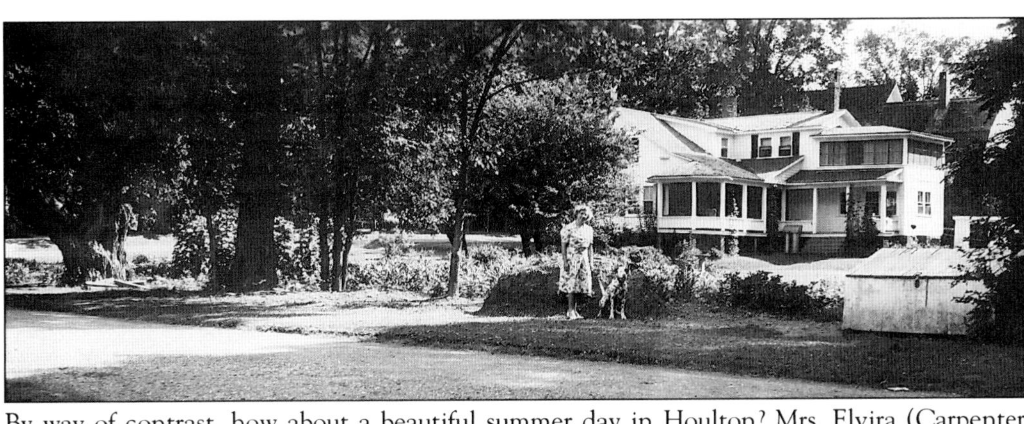

By way of contrast, how about a beautiful summer day in Houlton? Mrs. Elvira (Carpenter) Johnson and her dog Laddie stand in front of "The Moorings", her Pleasant Street home in June, 1952.

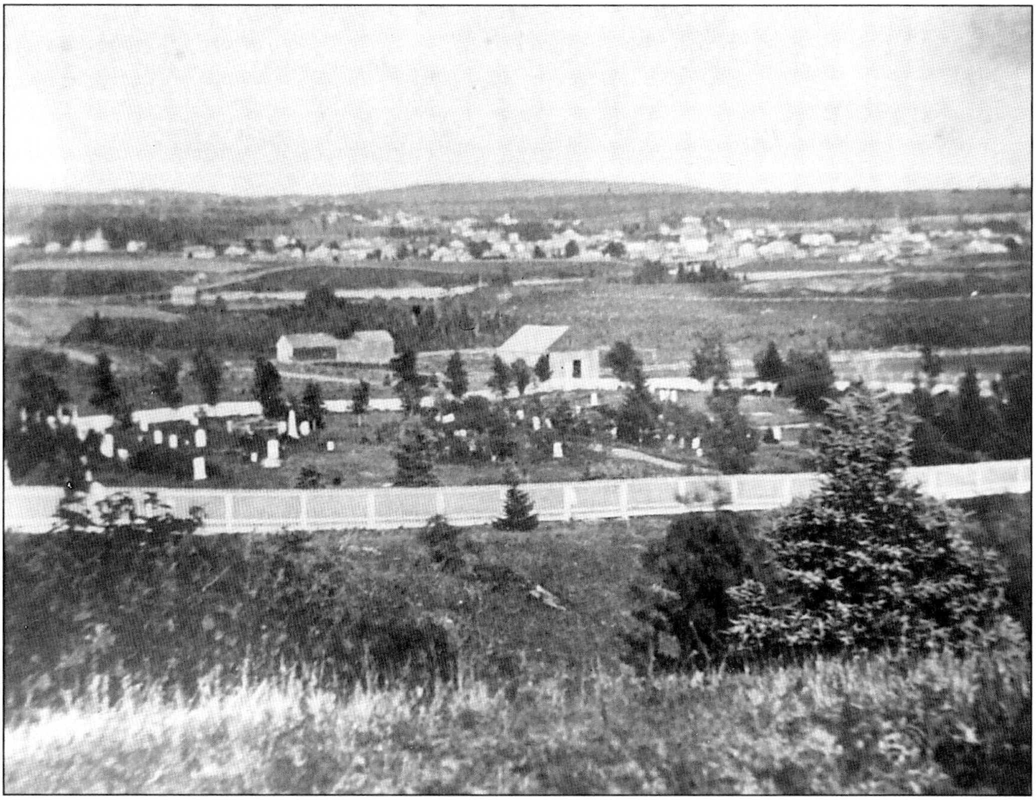

Every community has a cemetery and in Houlton it is Evergreen. This was the early part of that cemetery. The village is in the distance. Evergreen was later extended to the hill beyond.

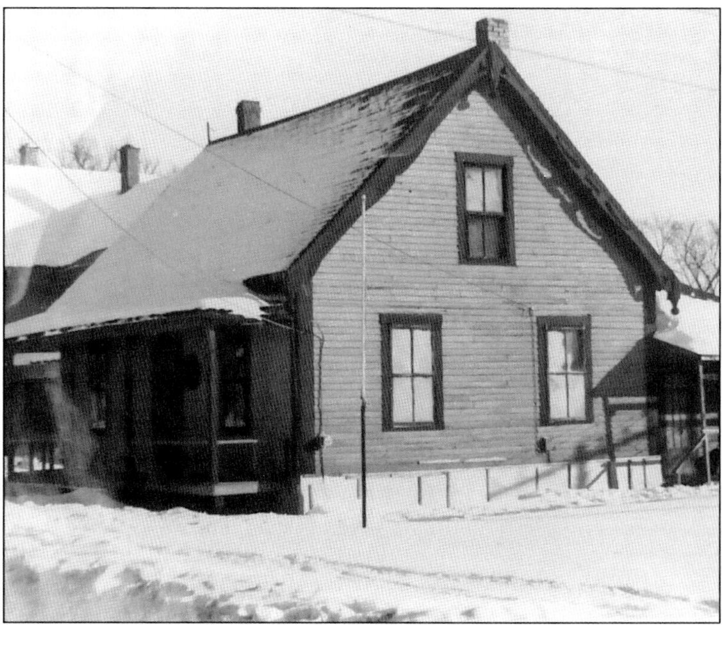

The first frame house ever built in Houlton was erected in 1810, only three years after the first settlers arrived. My grandmother Sleeper lived in the house for many years. It was eventually torn down after she died to make way for the Peabody insurance office.

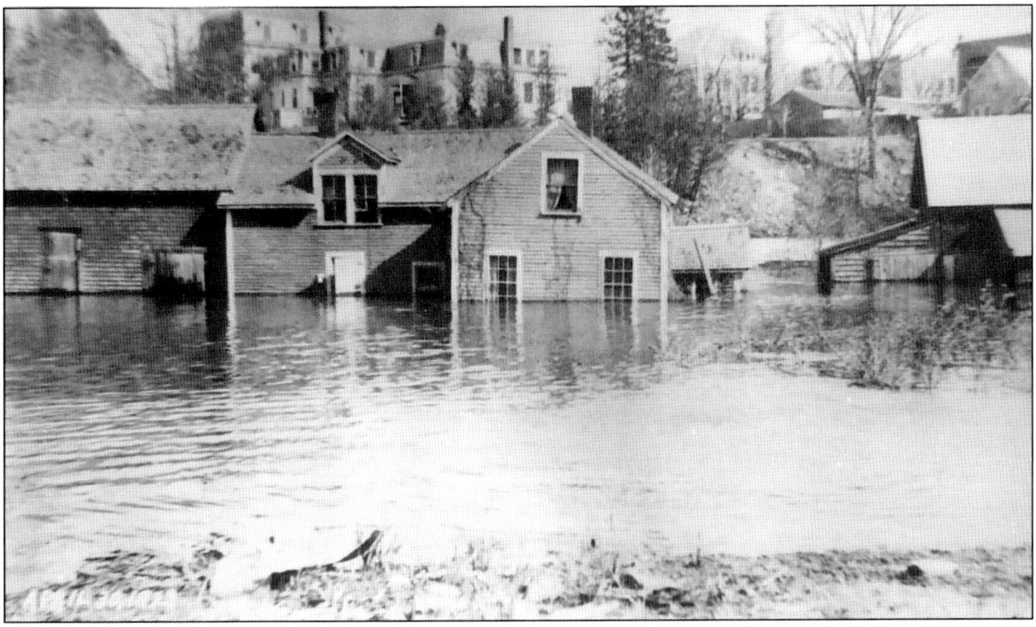

To go along with fires, Houlton also had floods. This is one example, the 1923 Meduxnekeag River flood at Putnam's Flats.

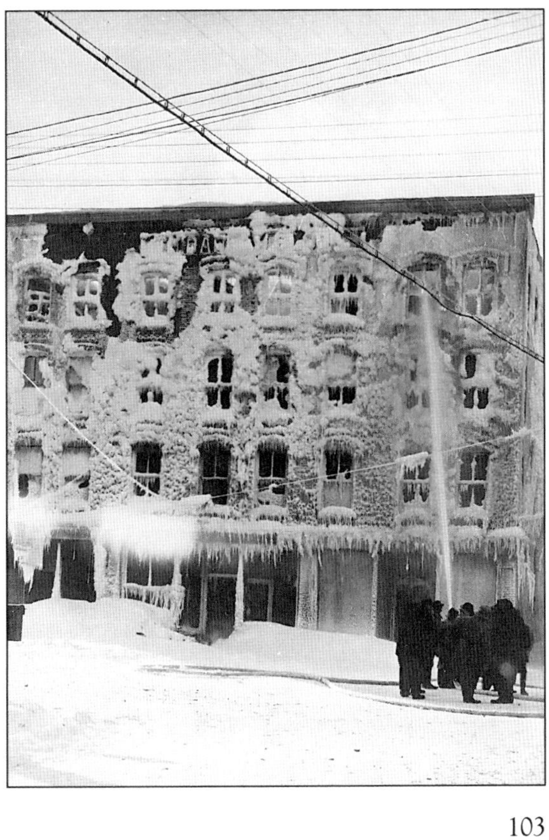

Firefighting and its results in the winter can be quite beautiful. This was the Hotel Lafayette in the Thibodeau Block. It was owned by Henry and William Thibodeau and sold to P.M. Ward, A.E. Astle and Frank Dunn after the fire, then repaired to become the site of Dunn Furniture Co. when that business was on Main Street.

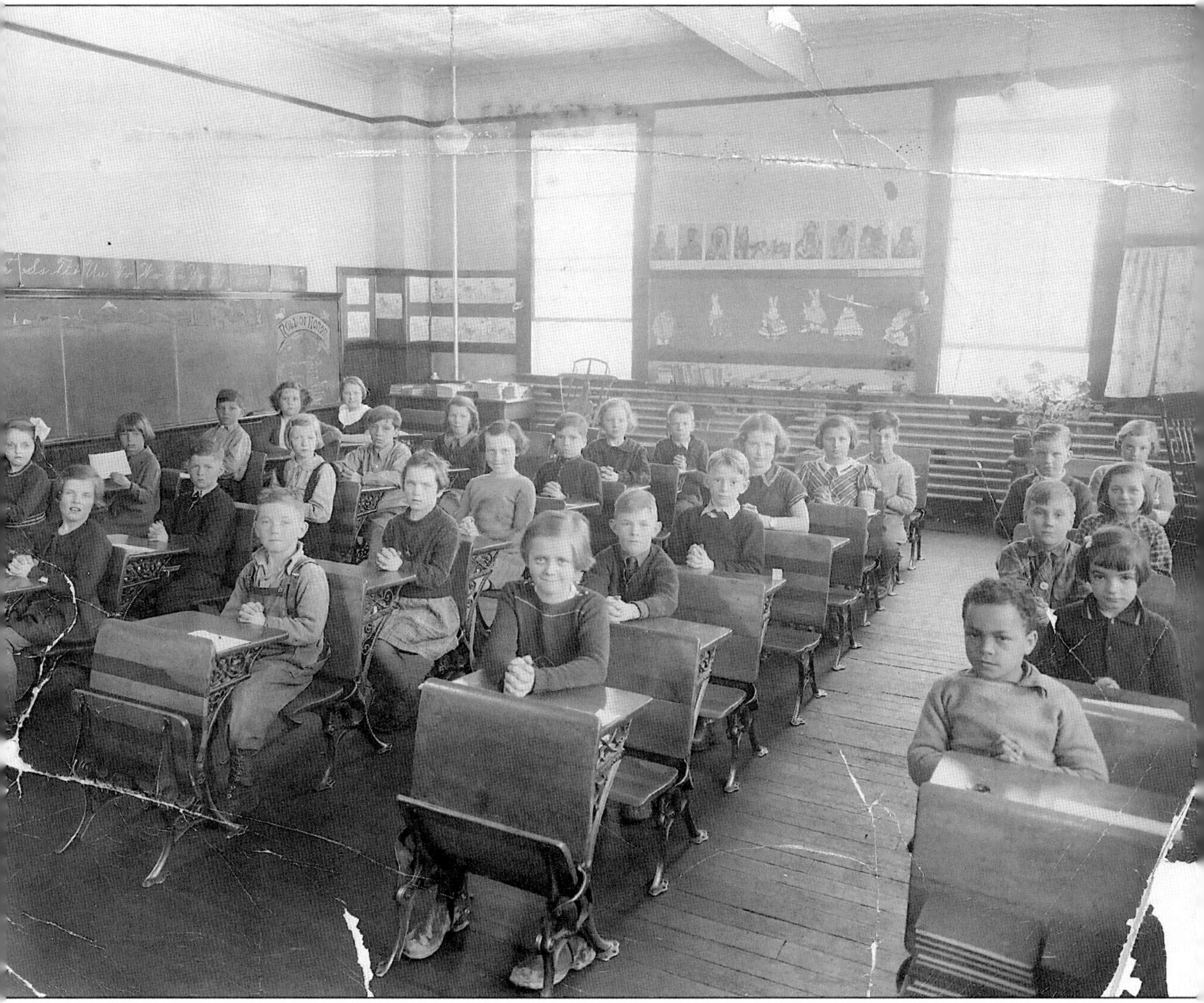

Education has always been of the utmost importance in Houlton. Here we see the third grade at the Fair Street School in 1941 when Miss Barbara Wilson was the teacher. In the first row are: Ralph Erther, Glenice ?, Englise Tompkins, Beatrice Sweet, Keith Antworth and Jaqueline Hall; second row: Elizabeth Conway, Earl Dunphy, Richard Hall, Jeannette Gartley, Belle Ricker and Richard Tompkins; third row: Ray Brewer, Jean Lambert, Mary Shaw, Vaughn Steen, Geraldine Grant and Percy Hall; fourth row: Betty Miller, Lorn Scott, Margaret Cummings, Almond Morris and Sarah McGaffin; and fifth row: Florence Patton, Bette Carpenter, Robert ?, Clara Gartley and Eunice Porter.

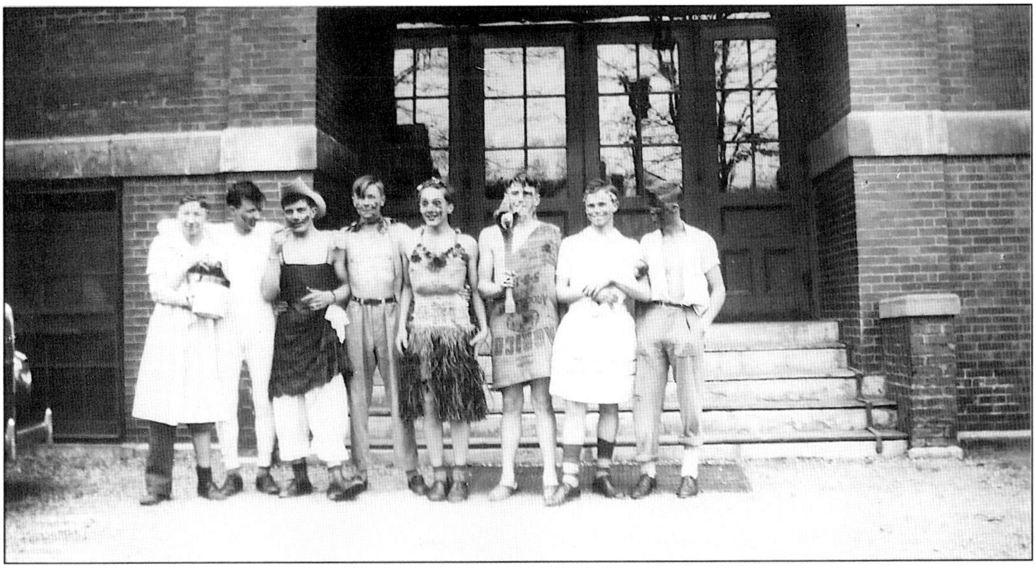

A group gathers after initiation at Houlton High School in the early 1940s. Included are, left to right: George Pray, Stan Greaves, Bob McCormack, unknown, David Dunn, unknown, Ted Hawkins and Jack MacNair.

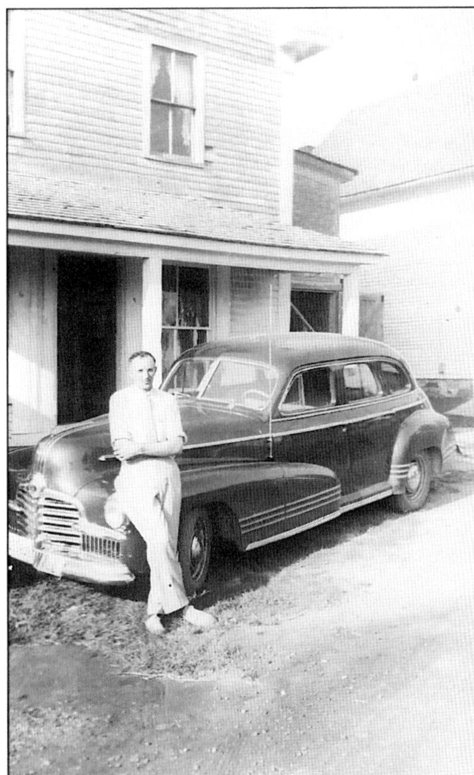

Fred C. Greaves, manager of seven towns around Houlton in the early 1950s, stands by his car in Hodgdon in 1942. Greaves traded in his car for a new one every year.

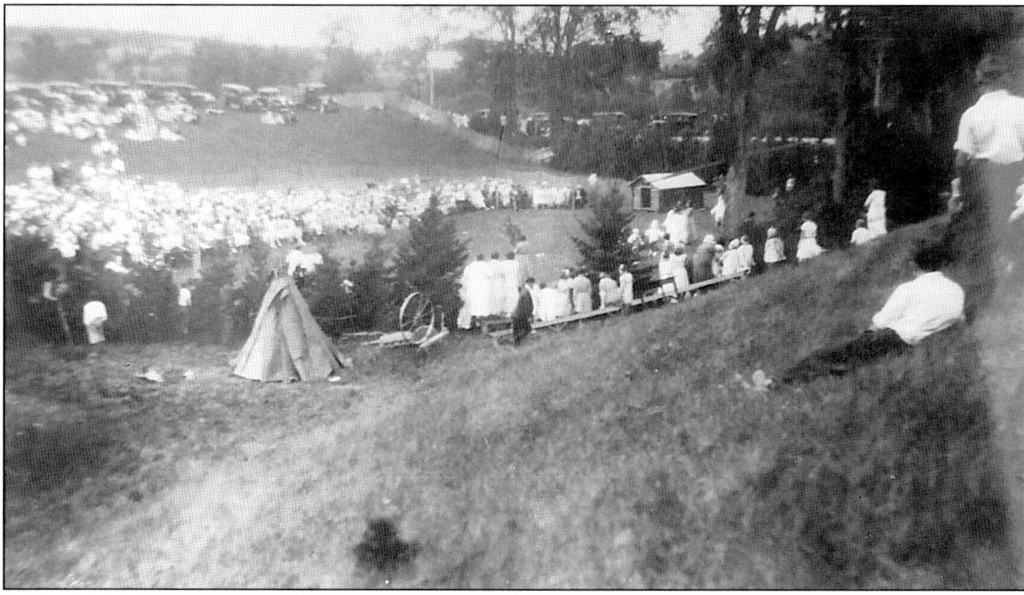

This was a pageant held in Hodgdon in 1932.

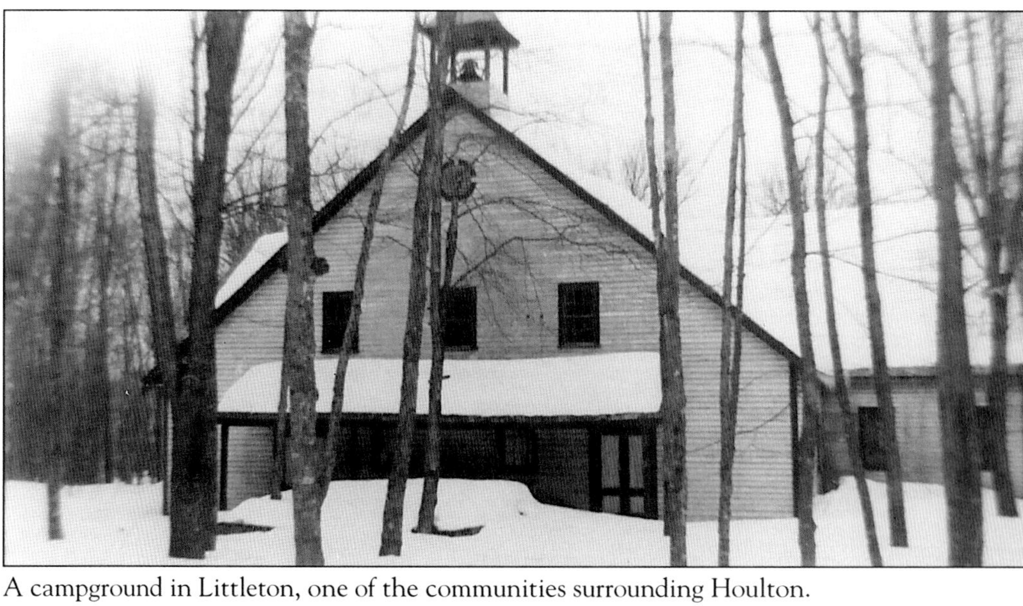

A campground in Littleton, one of the communities surrounding Houlton.

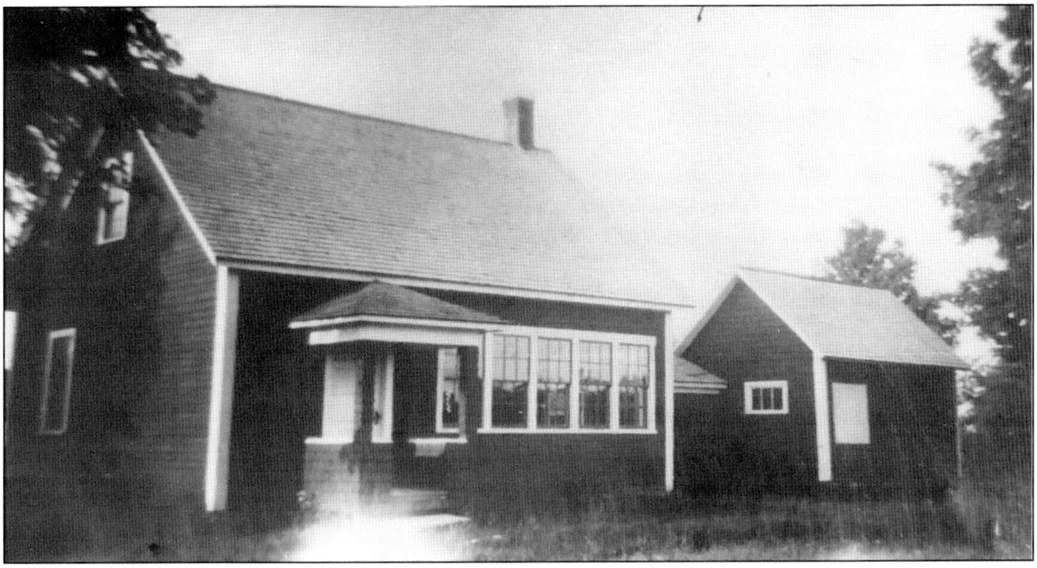

This photograph of North Amity School was taken in 1937.

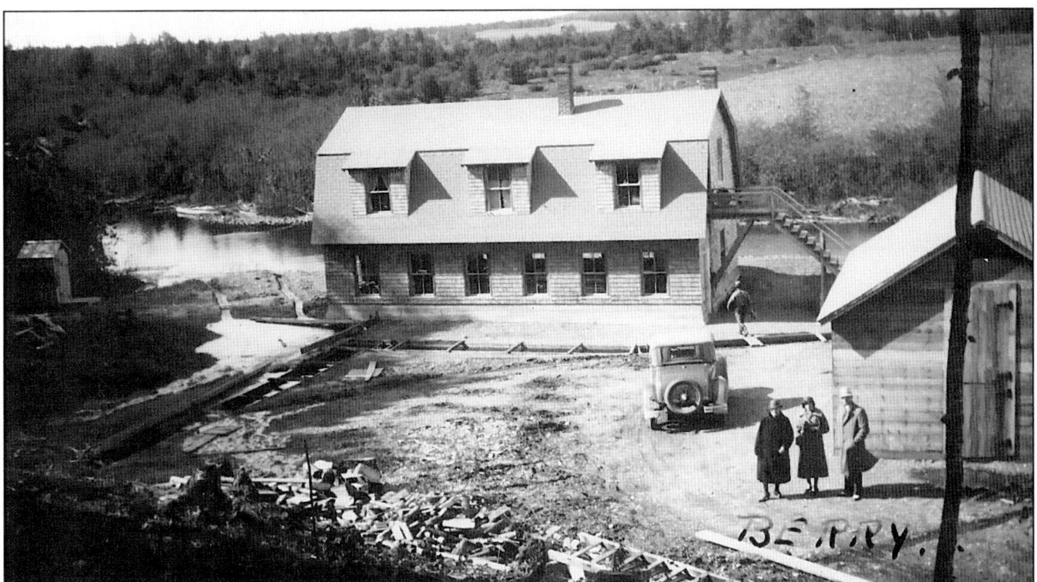

Littleton also possessed a fish hatchery as recorded here in the 1920s.

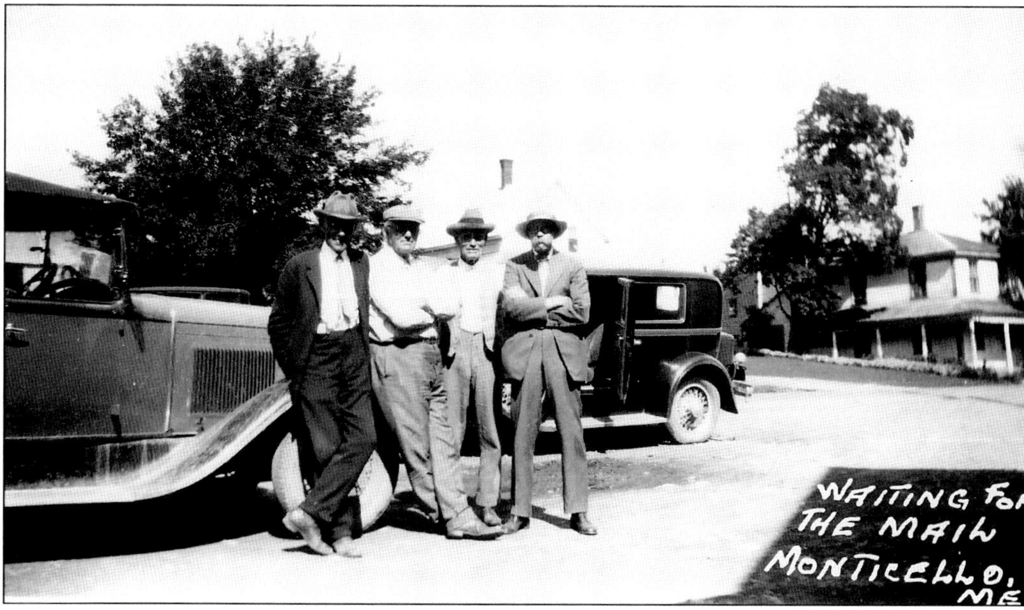

A group is waiting for the mail in Monticello in the 1920s. Left to right are: Perley Bubar, Postmaster Foster, Archibald Arnot and Dr. F.O. Hill with false mustache and glasses.

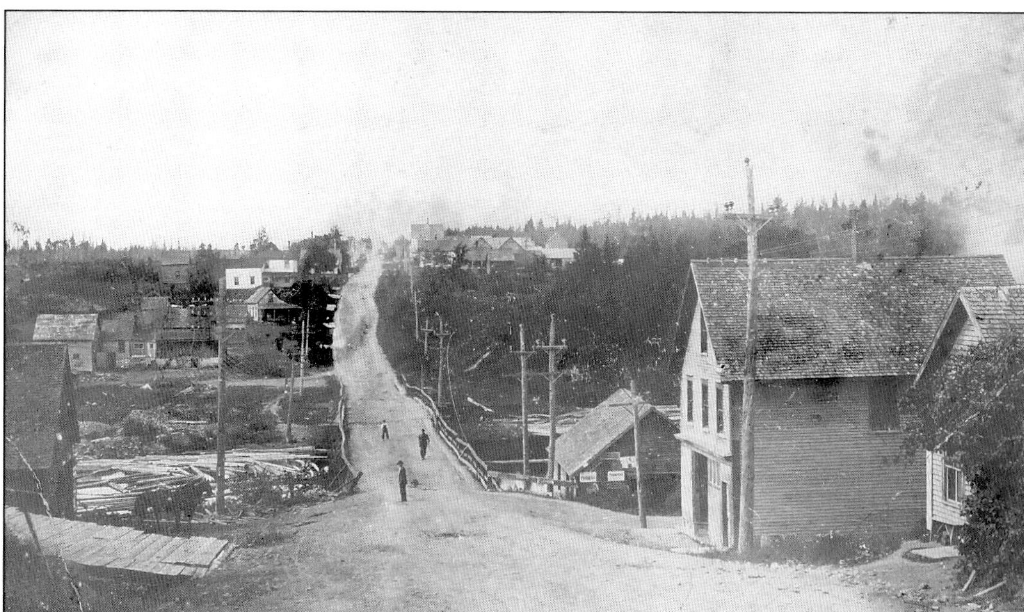

A view of Monticello's Main Street (Route 1) in the 1900s.

Six

Houlton Is Doers and Shakers

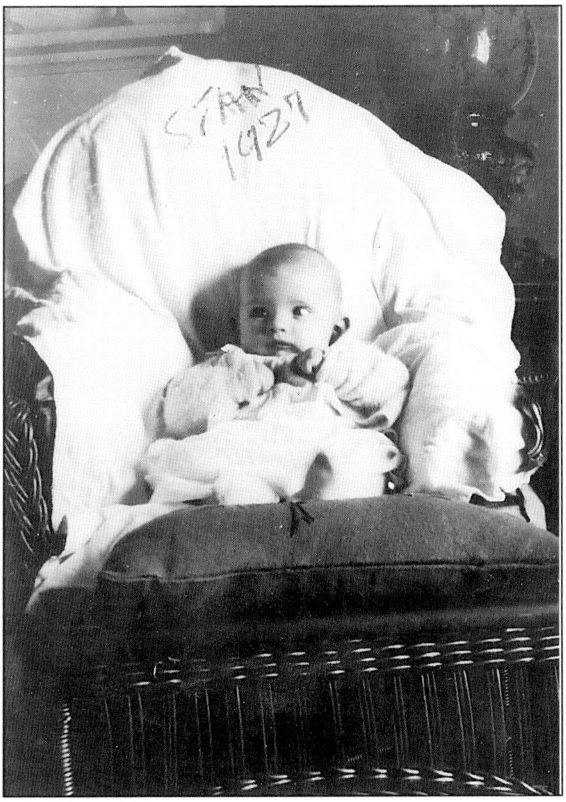

Stanley Greaves, later to become the executive vice-president of the Maine Potato Council, is cooing in 1927 (the year he was born).

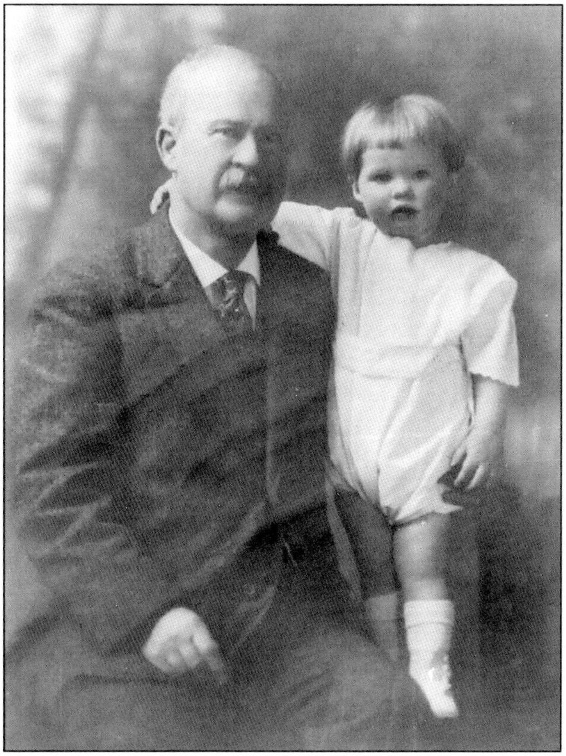

John A. Millar, for whom a building at the Houlton Fairgrounds has been named, sits with John A. Millar, his grandfather, about 1921. Millar was three years old at the time.

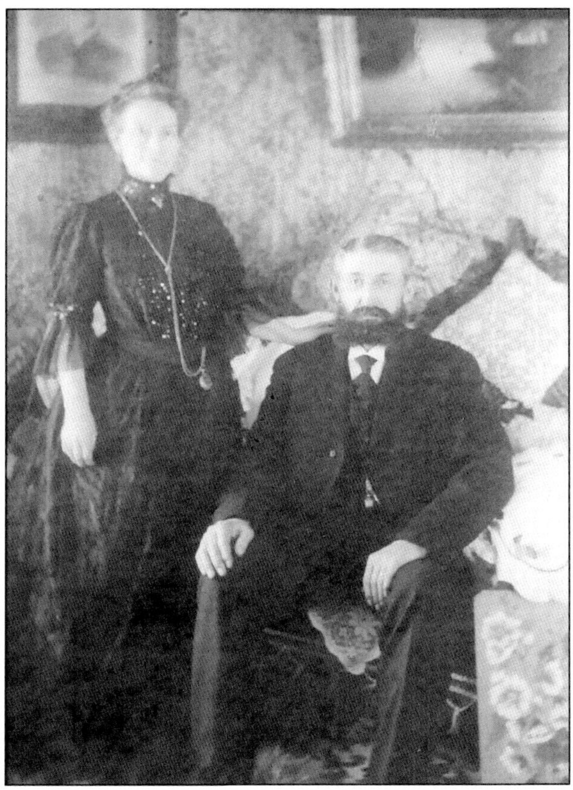

Mr. and Mrs. C.D. Getchell brought the first car into Houlton. Getchell was once owner of the Snell House, Houlton's best known hotel.

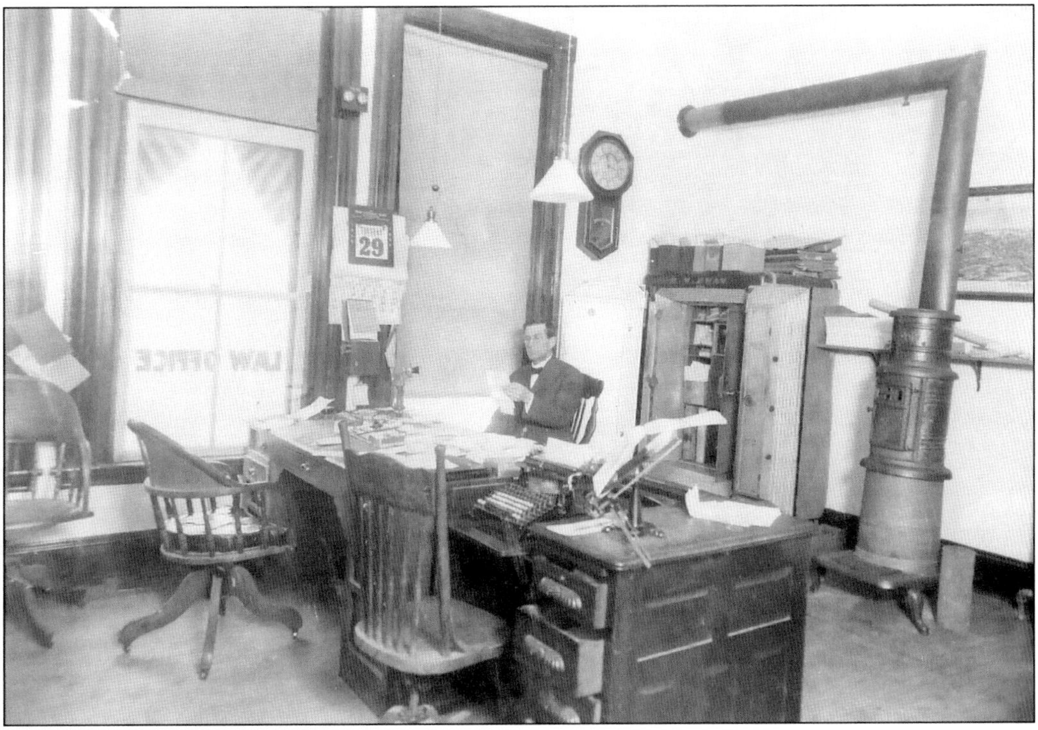

Ransford Shaw sits in his Houlton law office on 29 December, 1908 at 18 minutes past 11 a.m. Shaw was to become a Maine attorney general and was founder of the Maine Historical and Art Museum. His office was in the French Block.

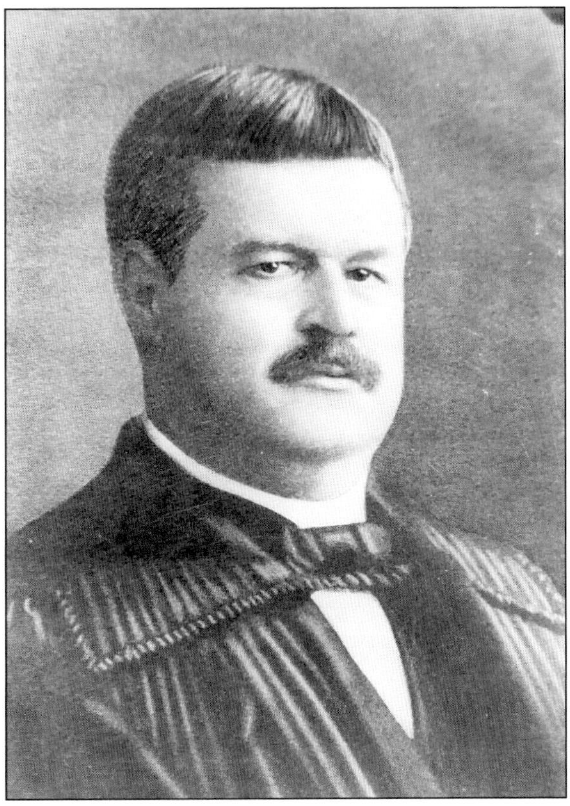

Frederick Powers was a Maine Supreme Court justice from 1900 to 1907 and Maine attorney general from 1893 to 1896. Houlton's third attorney general, Michael Carpenter, has recently announced that he will not seek that position again.

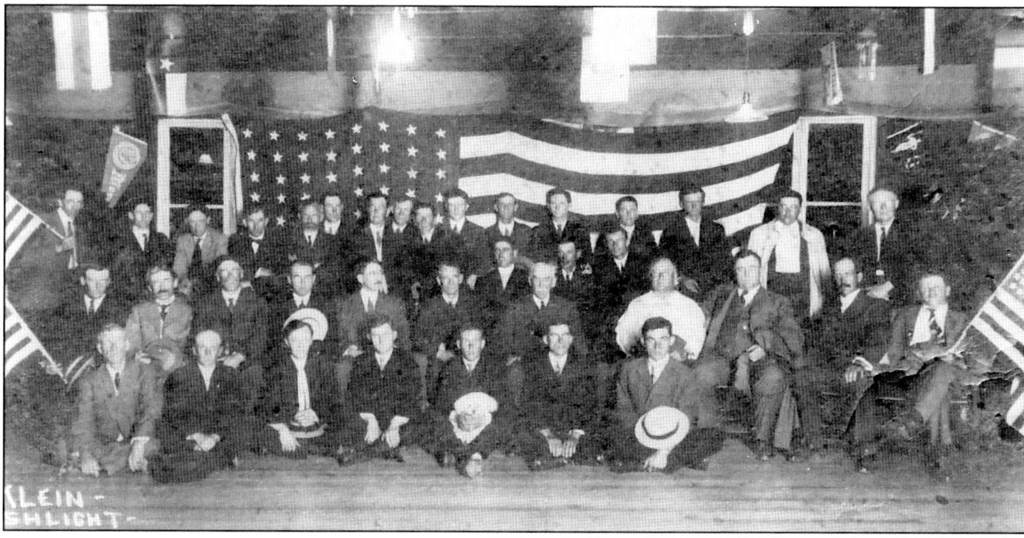

A 14 July, 1914 banquet was held at Crescent Park at Nickerson Lake honoring Frank Hume, who had just retired after having served as postmaster from 1897.

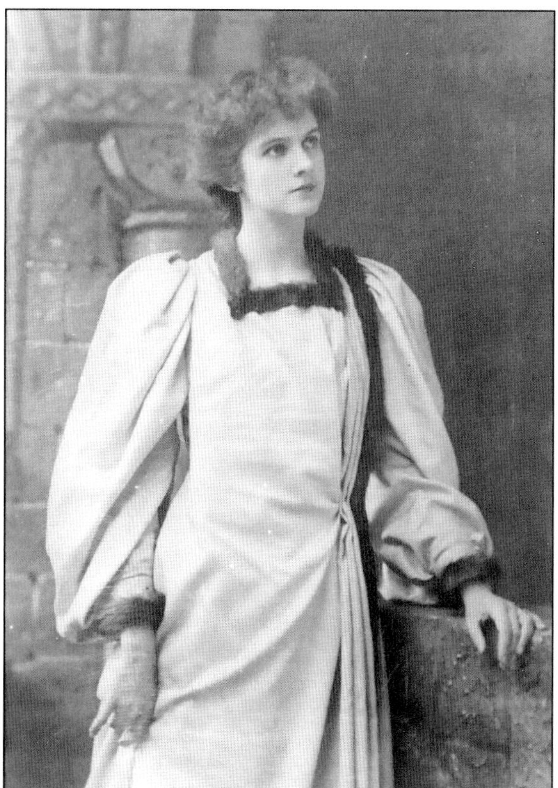

Faye Davis was born in Houlton in 1868, and lived there for about twelve years. She went on to become one of the leading Shakesperian actresses in England, dying there in 1945.

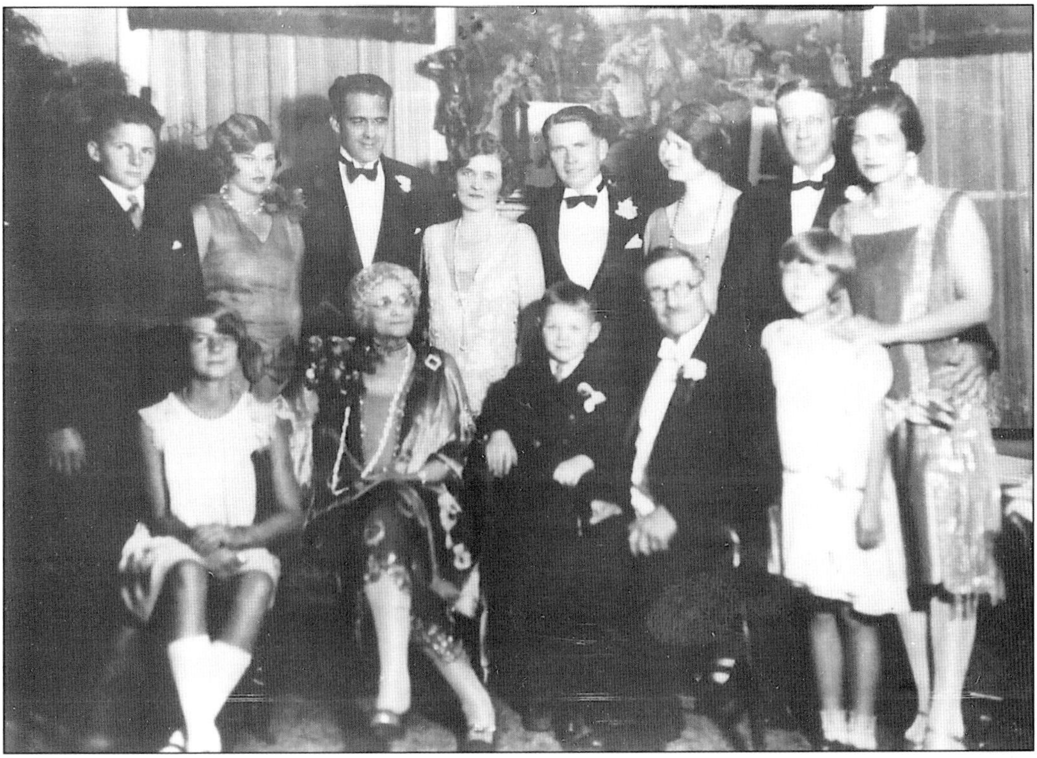

The family of Maine attorney general Ransford Shaw poses in front of their home in Houlton. Included are: Mary Shaw, John Lakin, Ransford, Ardith Lakin, Sliz Lakin, Dick Shaw, George Shaw's wife, George Shaw, Pennette Shaw, Hershel Shaw, Dora Shaw and Jack Lakin.

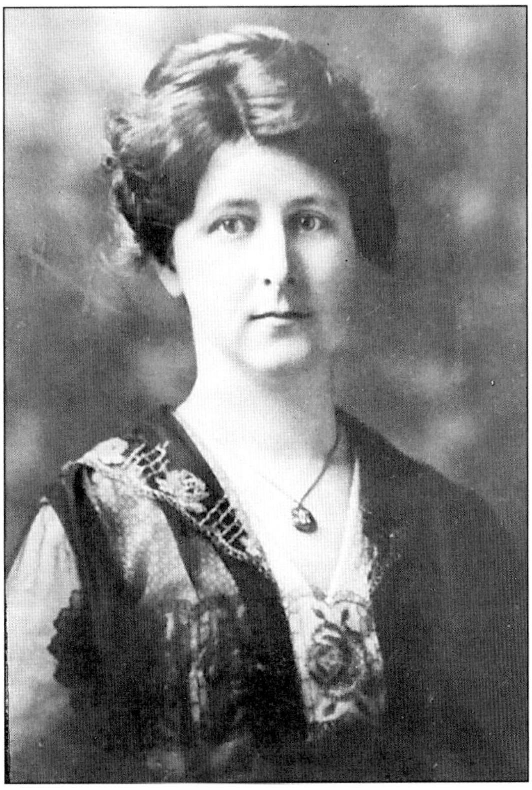

Edna B. Gentle was the donor of the Gentle Memorial Recreation Building to the citizens of Houlton. The building continues in operation and has proven to be a very valuable facility.

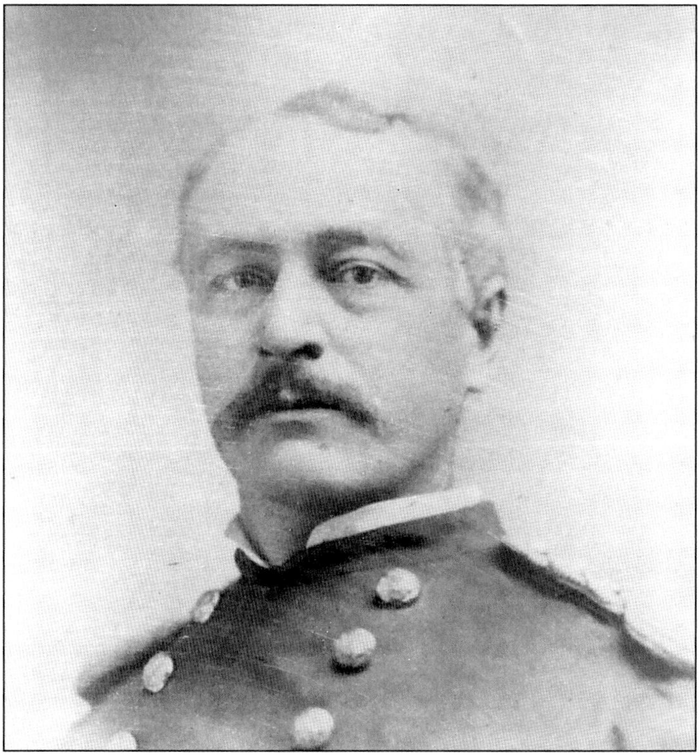

Major General Henry Clay Merriam, born in Houlton in 1837, was the only native of the town ever to win the Congressional Medal of Honor for his services in the Civil War. He stayed in the regular army after the war, rising to the rank of major general. Merriam invented an infantry pack that was used in the First World War.

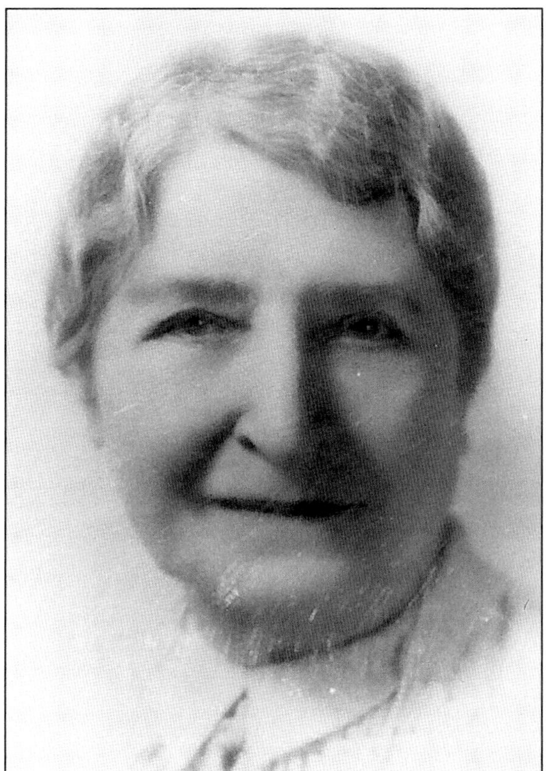

Mrs. Stella King White was the donor of the building which now houses the Aroostook County Historical and Art Museum and the Greater Houlton Chamber of Commerce. Her husband operated White's Drug Store for many years.

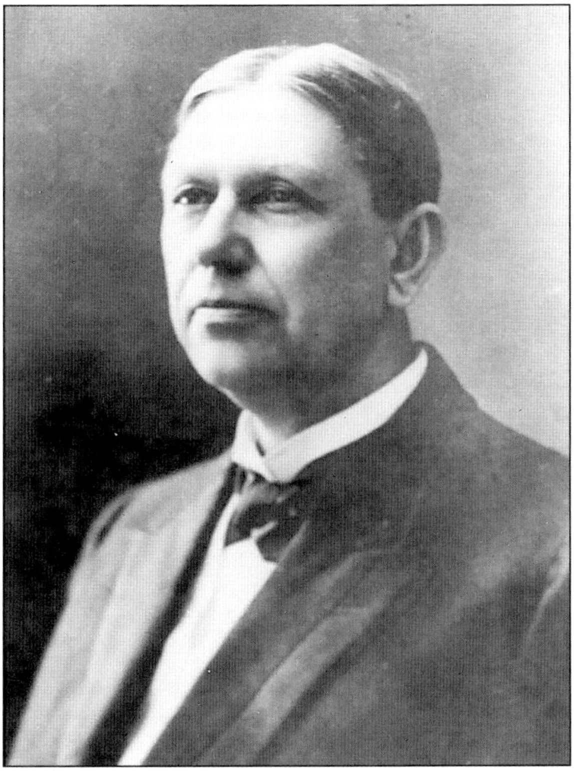

Ira Greenlief Hersey, born in Hodgdon, was a US Representative from 1917 to 1929. A Republican, he had earlier been a state representative and president of the Maine State Senate.

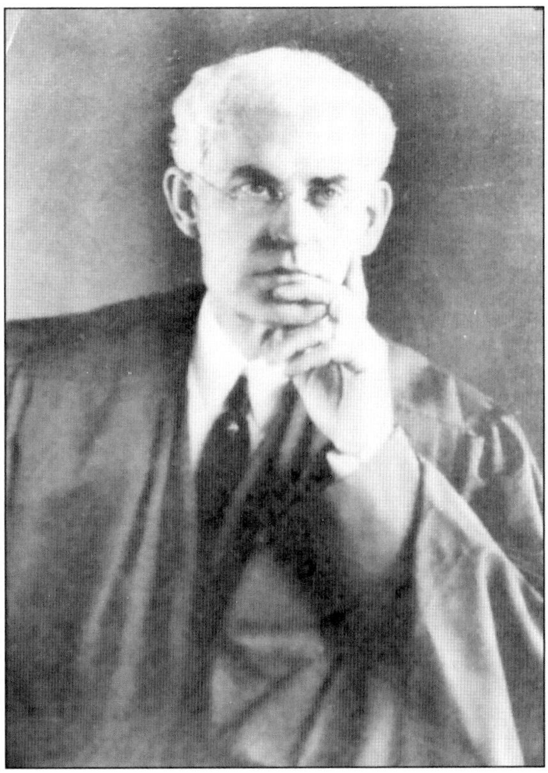

Charles Putnam Barnes was Chief Justice of the Maine Supreme Court from 1939 to 1941, serving on that court from 1924 onwards. He is the only Houlton native ever to be chief justice of the state's highest court.

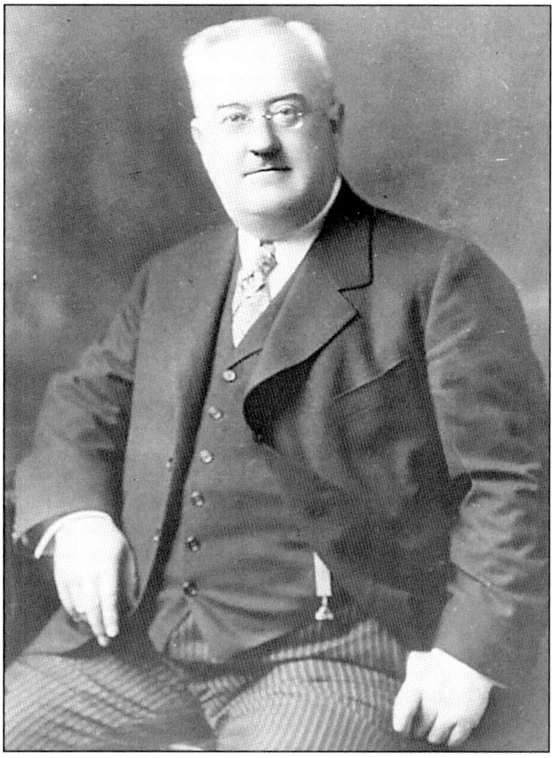

John B. Madigan served as an associate justice of the Maine Supreme Court from 1916 until his death in 1918. He helped Houlton in many ways: equipping Madigan Memorial Hospital, named for his family; starting the Houlton Agricultural Society and serving on the Houlton Board of Education and as a trustee of Ricker Classical Institute.

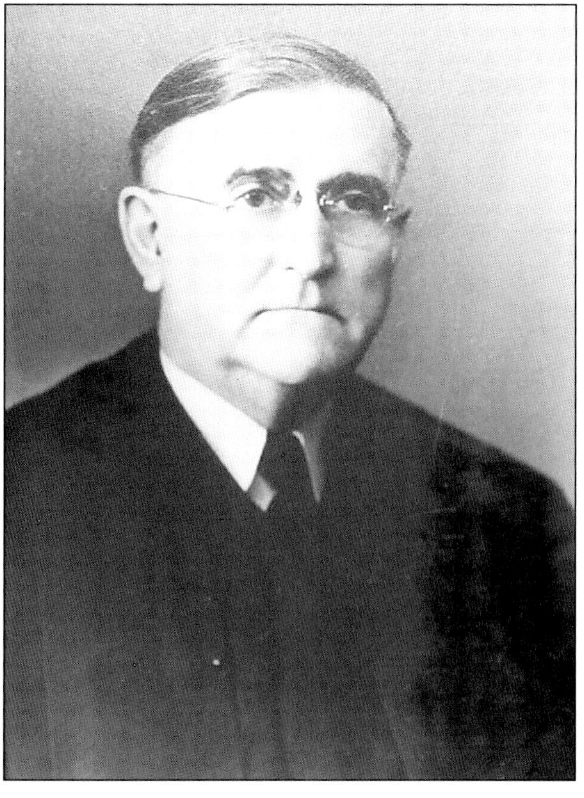

Another Maine Supreme Court justice from Houlton was Nathaniel Tompkins who served from 1945 to 1949. Tompkins, a Republican, had previously served as speaker of the Maine House of Representatives and president of the Maine State Senate.

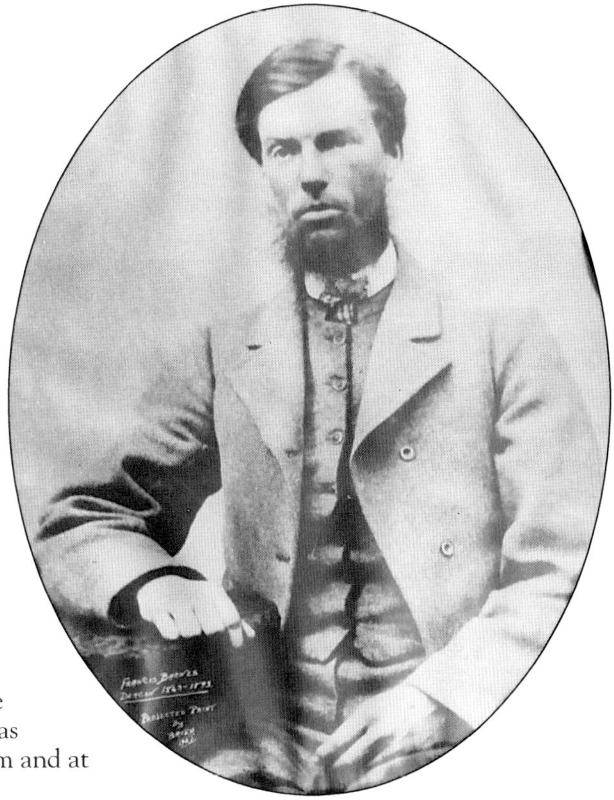

The second historian of Houlton was Francis Barnes, another member of the illustrious Barnes family. His history was written in 1885. Barnes operated a farm and at one time owned a cheese factory.

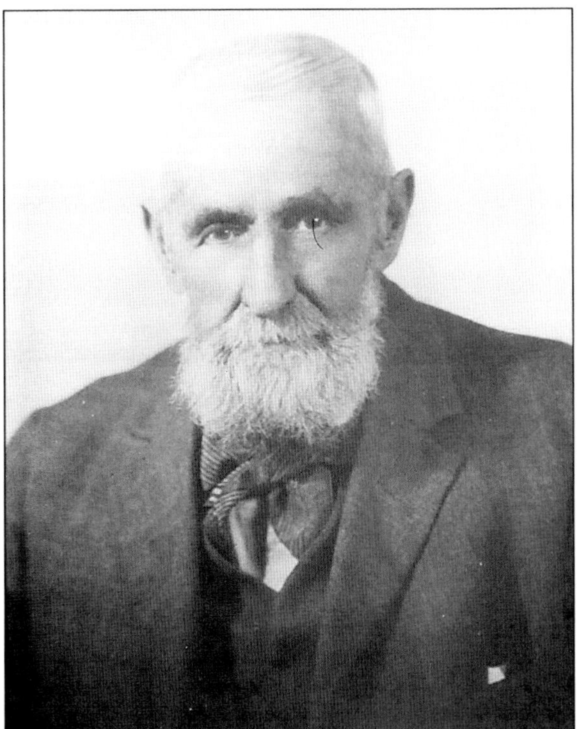

The man who made the Almon H. Fogg Co. grow rapidly was Clarence H. Pierce. Pierce worked for sixty-seven years at the Fogg Company.

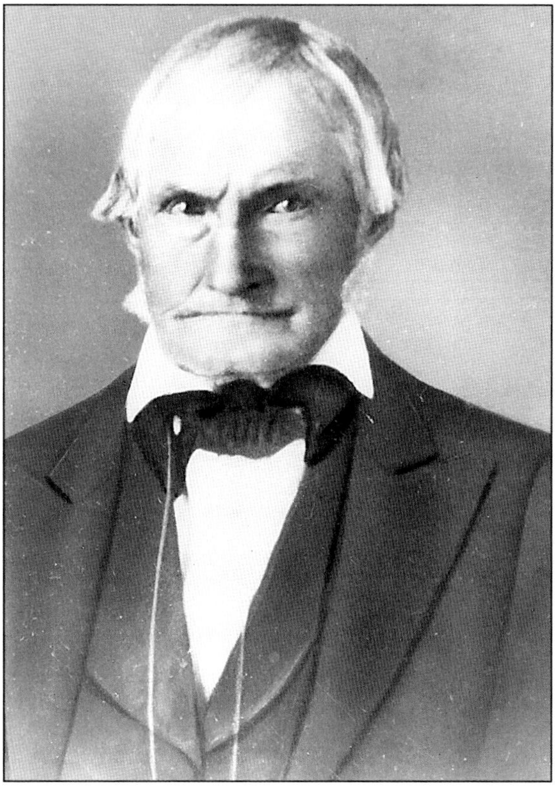

Don't be fooled by looks. Samuel Cook, Esquire, was one of Houlton's first settlers and the man called upon to bring petitions to make the settlement a plantation and a town to Augusta. Cook was Houlton's judge of probate and a spokesman for the entire community.

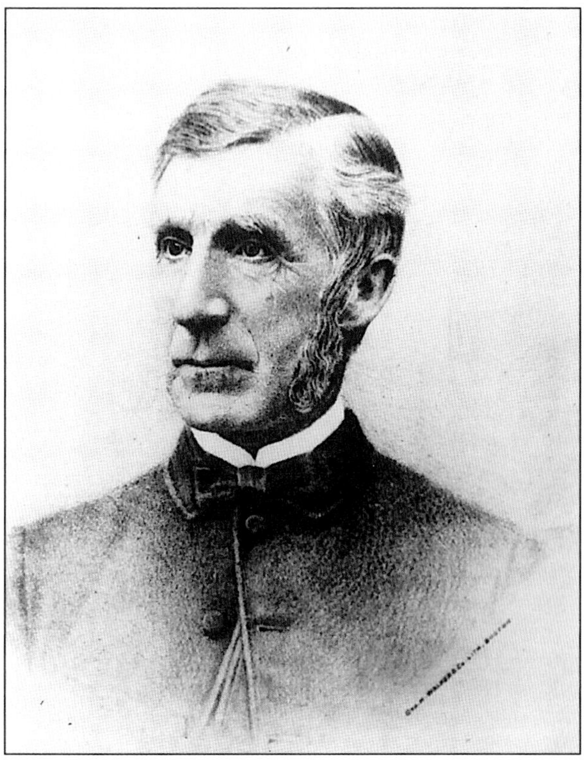

Dr. Joseph Ricker was a Baptist missionary who suggested to the people of Houlton that the financially suffering Houlton Academy might be saved by making an arrangement with Colby College. The plan worked in 1887 and the school's name was immediately changed to Ricker Classical Institute.

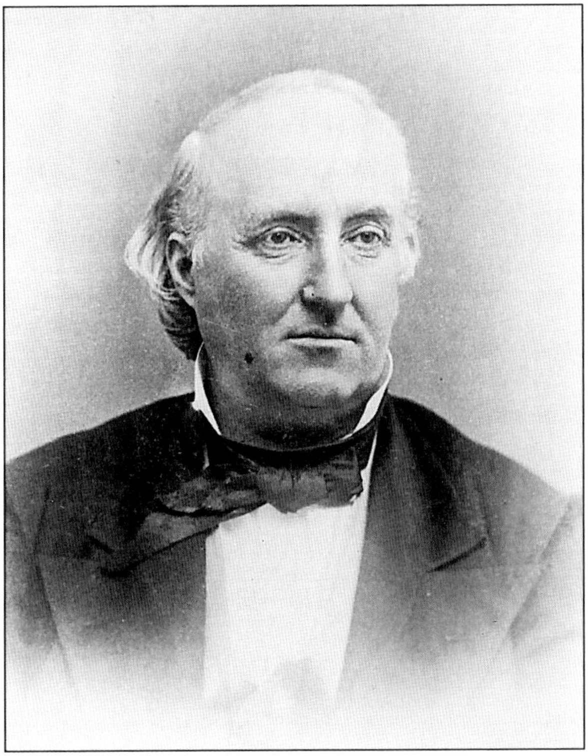

The founder of Houlton's illustrious Madigan family was James Cortrill Madigan, Sr. Coming from Fort Kent in 1850, he built the home which was later to become Madigan Memorial Hospital, was proficient in French, organized schools for the Franco-Americans in the St. John River Valley and was collector of customs at Houlton from 1853 to 1857.

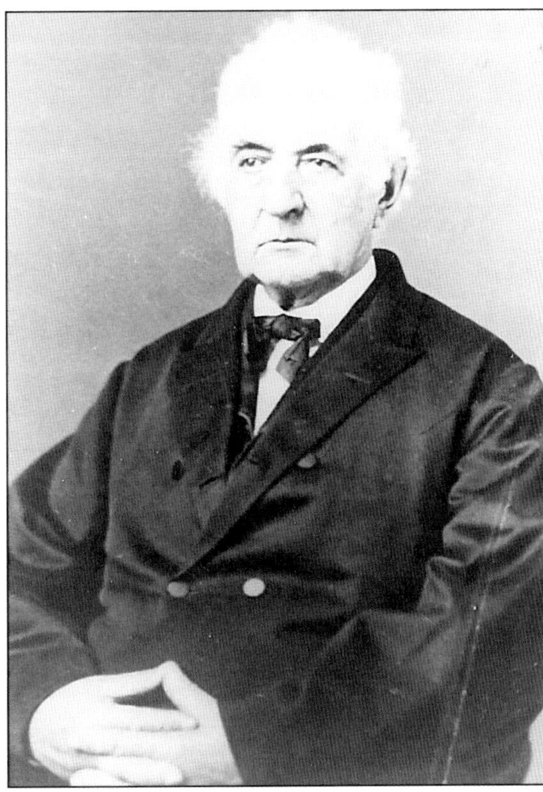

"Squire" Leonard Pierce was born in Dorchester, Massachusetts. Pierce later became a Houlton selectman and postmaster. He was the founder of the Pierce branch of the Madigan-Pierce alliance in Aroostook's shiretown.

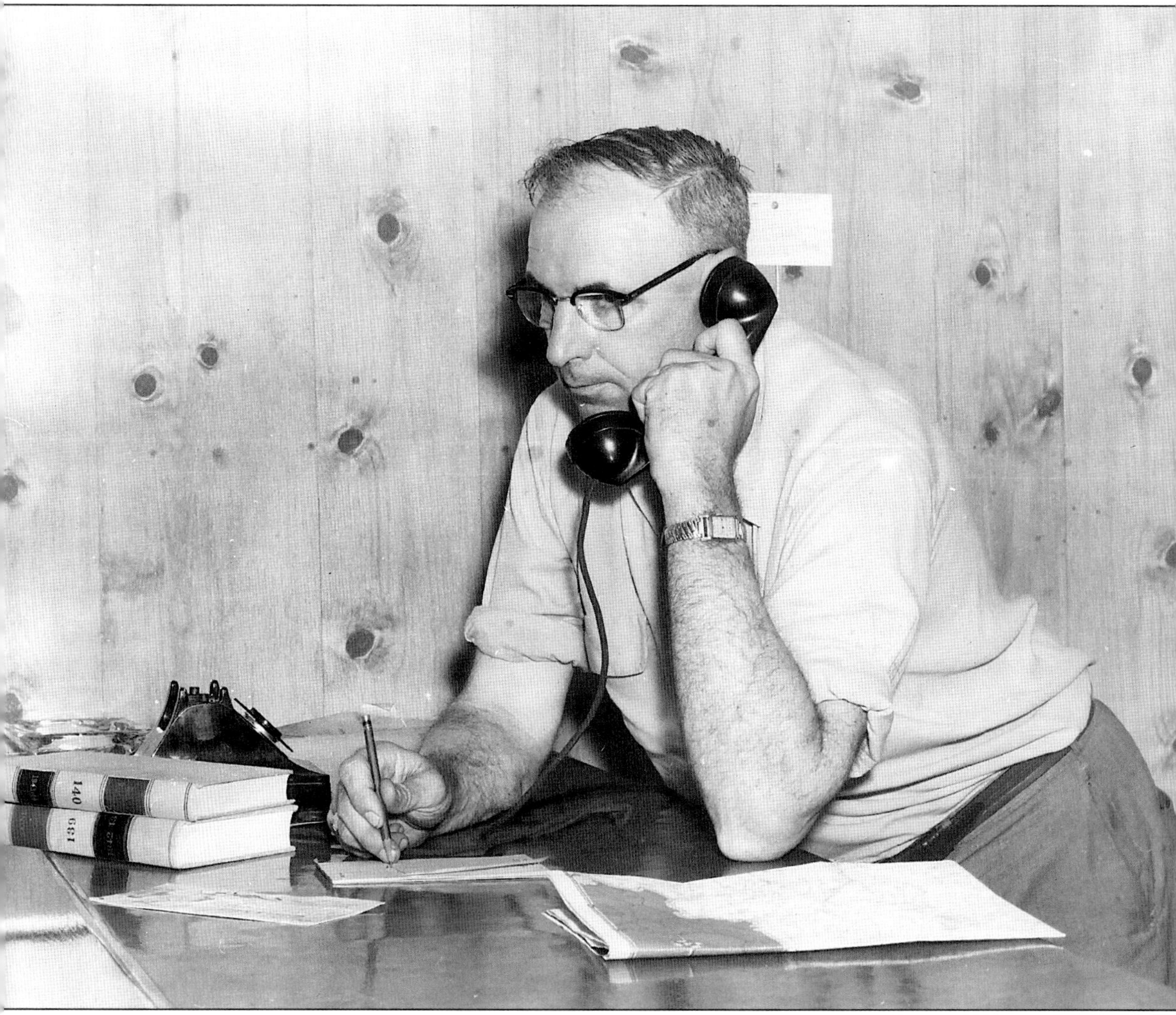

Fred C. Greaves at work in the Hodgdon Town Office. Largely self-taught, Greaves was able to return several Maine communities to financial stability after they hit the doldrums during the Depression. He became, among other things, a specialist in welfare rules and regulations as they applied to Maine's small towns.

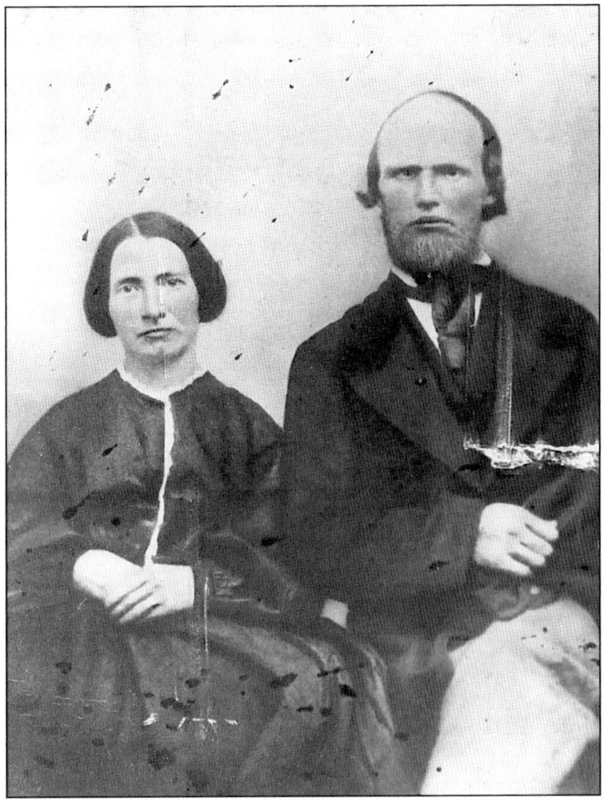

Let's go way back. This is Levi Houlton Putnam (1820–1890) and his wife, Sarah Bradbury Putnam. Levi was the oldest of seventeen children of Amos and Christiana (Wormwood) Putnam. The two were parents of Amos Putnam (1863–1936).

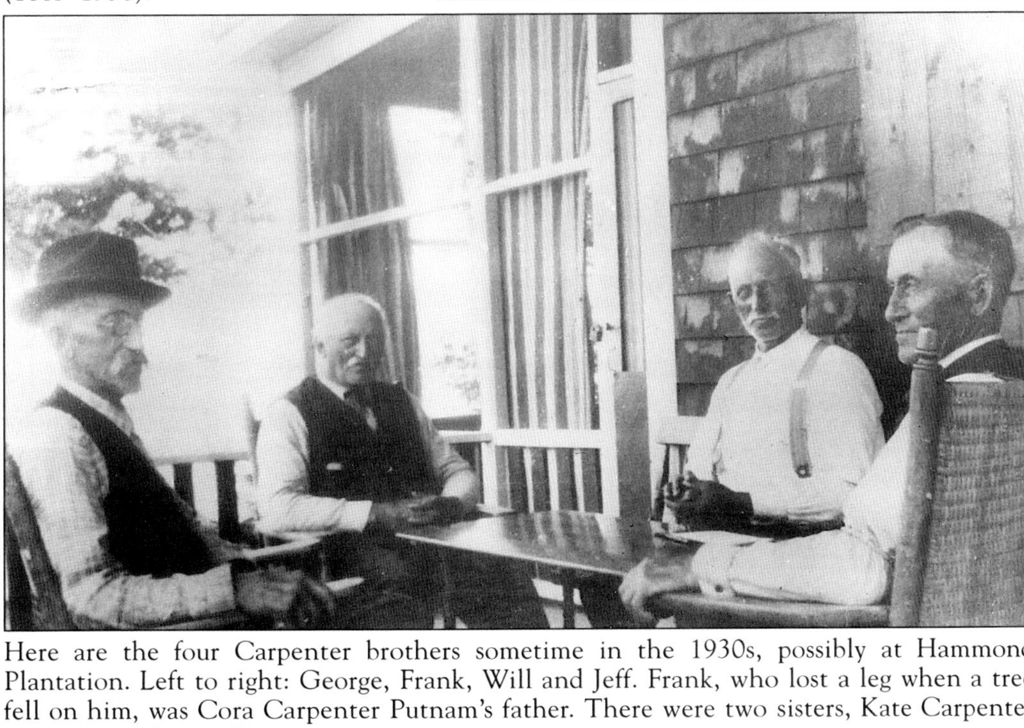

Here are the four Carpenter brothers sometime in the 1930s, possibly at Hammond Plantation. Left to right: George, Frank, Will and Jeff. Frank, who lost a leg when a tree fell on him, was Cora Carpenter Putnam's father. There were two sisters, Kate Carpenter Watson and Annie Carpenter.

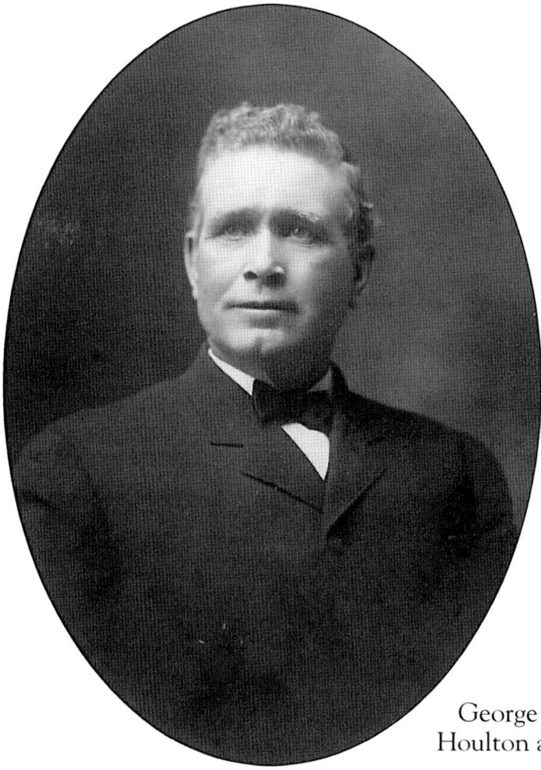

George MacNair built many of the homes in Houlton and was father of Leonard MacNair.

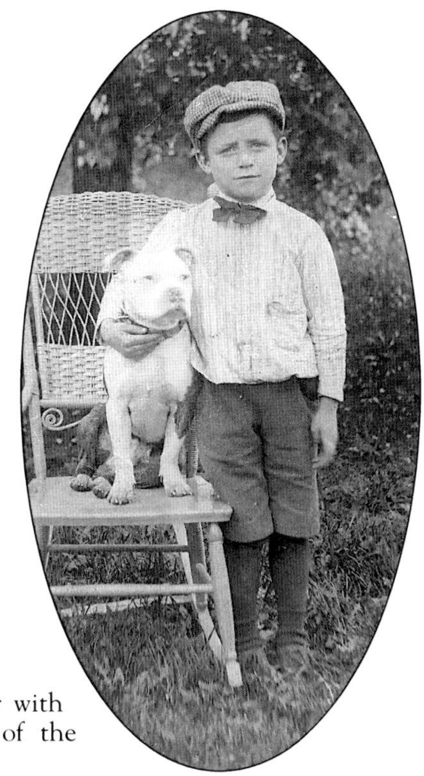

Leonard MacNair, future president of L.E. MacNair with Tootsie. Potato bags and pesticides were staples of the MacNair company.

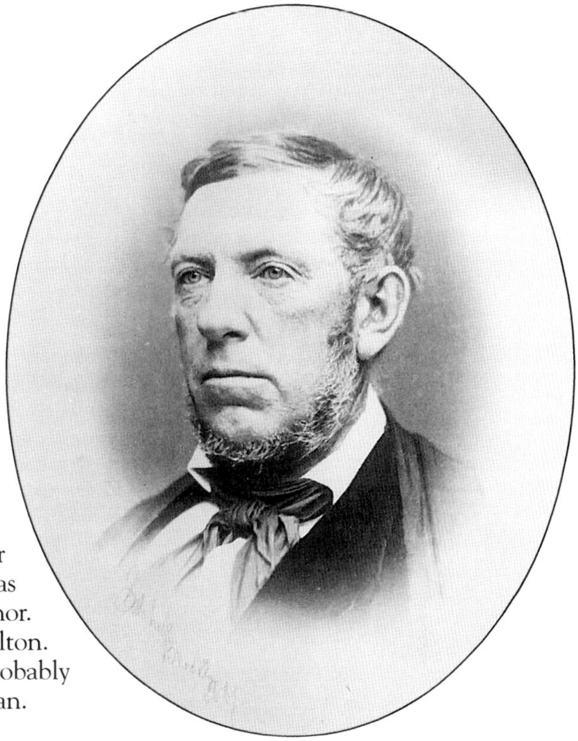

The early business and political leader of Houlton was Shepard Cary. Shep Cary started with a retail store close to the Hancock Barracks on Garrison Hill, expanded into lumbering all over Aroostook, built and operated a grist mill, was a congressman and was defeated for governor. Several places are named after him in Houlton. He came from New Salem and was probably Houlton's first really prominent businessman.

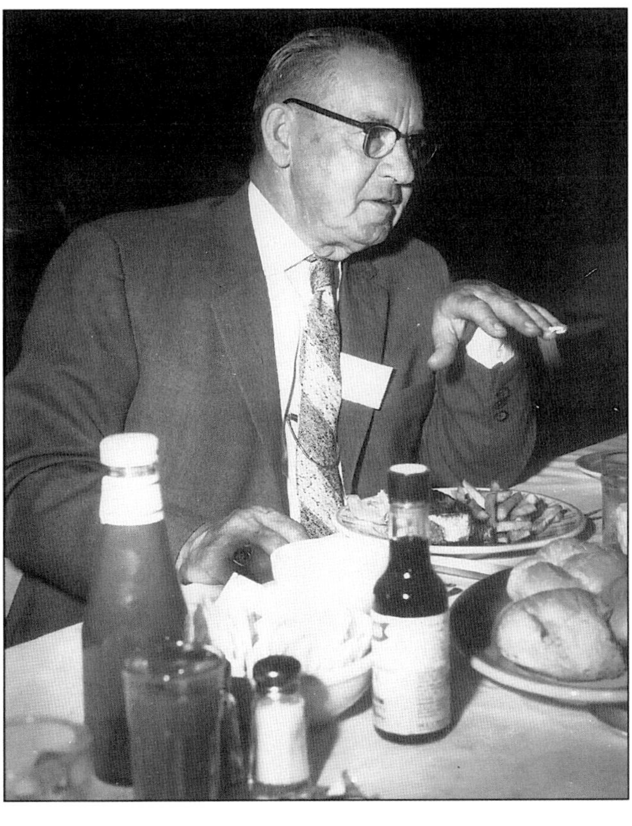

John Hall of Houlton rose from a dispatcher to become head of the Bangor and Aroostook Railroad's northern sales office.

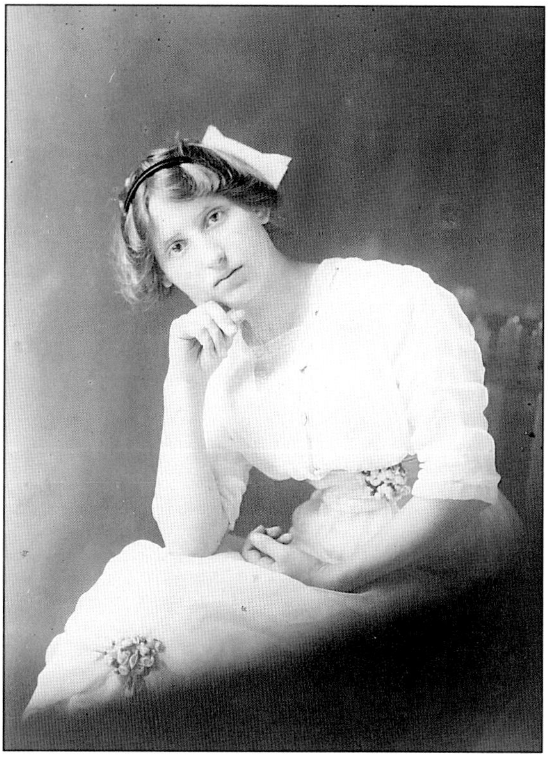

Margaret Putnam Greaves was for years teacher of Latin and French at Houlton High School. She is about twenty years old in this photograph.

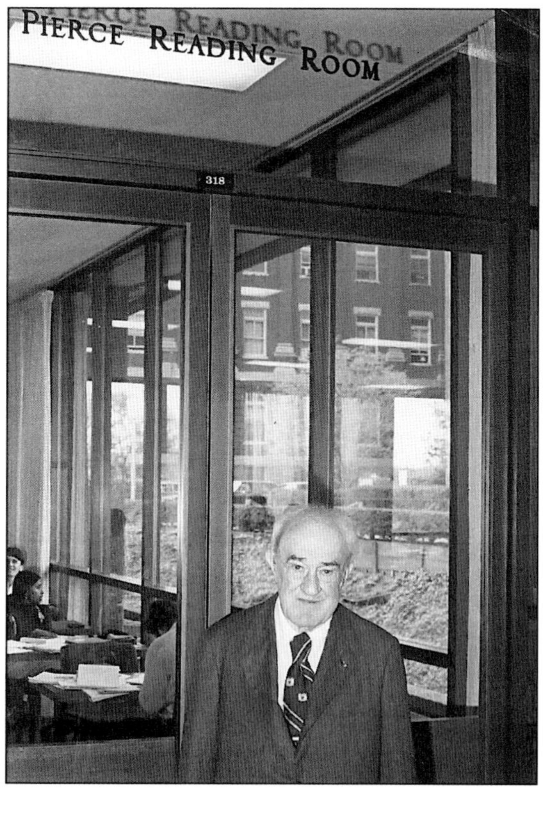

James M. Pierce of Houlton stands in the Pierce Reading Room which he donated to Catholic University in Washington, DC. The president of both A.H. Fogg Co. and the First National Bank of Houlton, Pierce was one of the most outstanding Catholic laymen in Maine history. He was also a great lover of the outdoors, bred by the timberlands interests of the Pierces and Madigans.

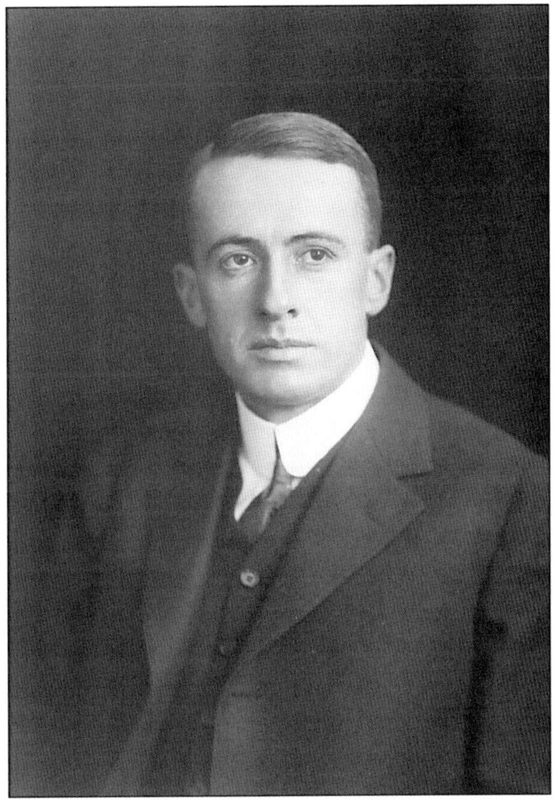

Leonard Augustus Pierce, Houlton native and lawyer, moved to Portland and was the primary lawyer for Central Maine Power Co. for many years.

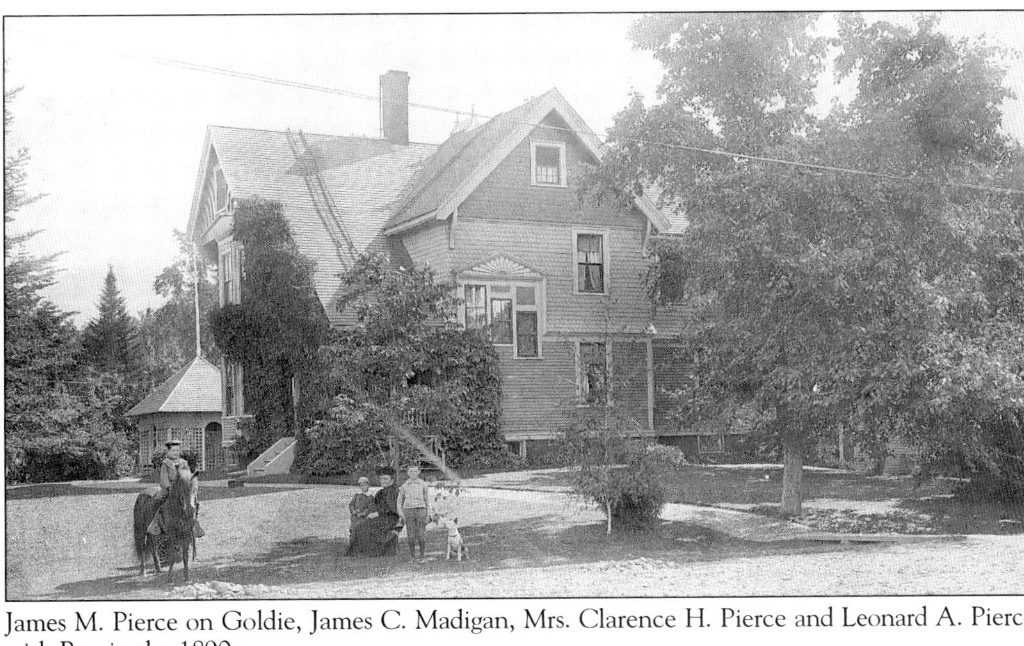

James M. Pierce on Goldie, James C. Madigan, Mrs. Clarence H. Pierce and Leonard A. Pierce with Rex in the 1890s.

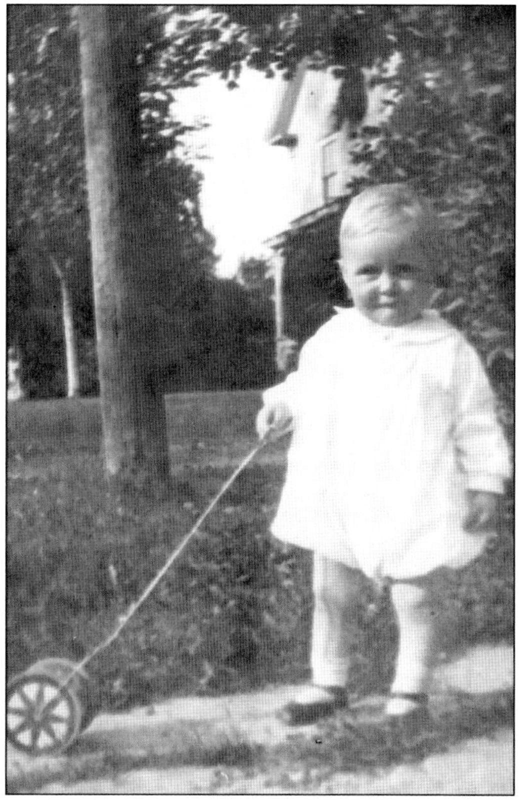

Jotham Pierce, a prominent Portland attorney, in Houlton at the age of two.

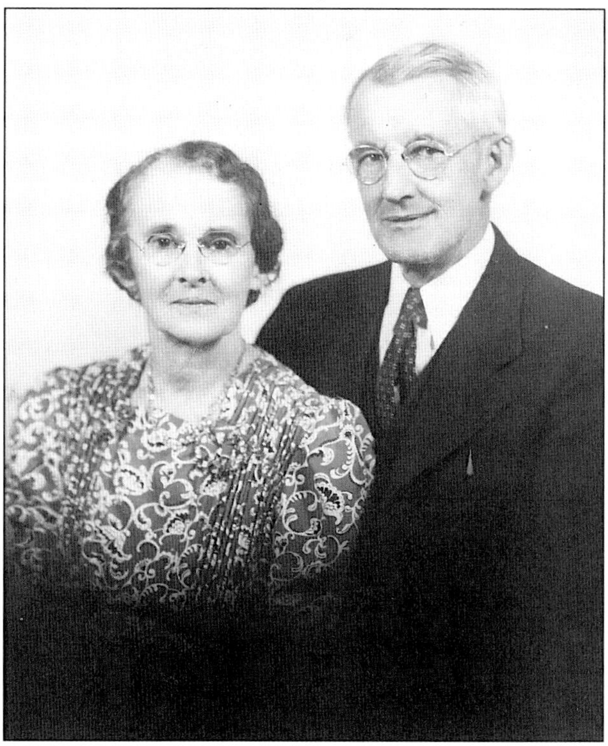

Lewis and Nellie Hall, parents of John Hall, as they appeared on their fiftieth wedding anniversary.

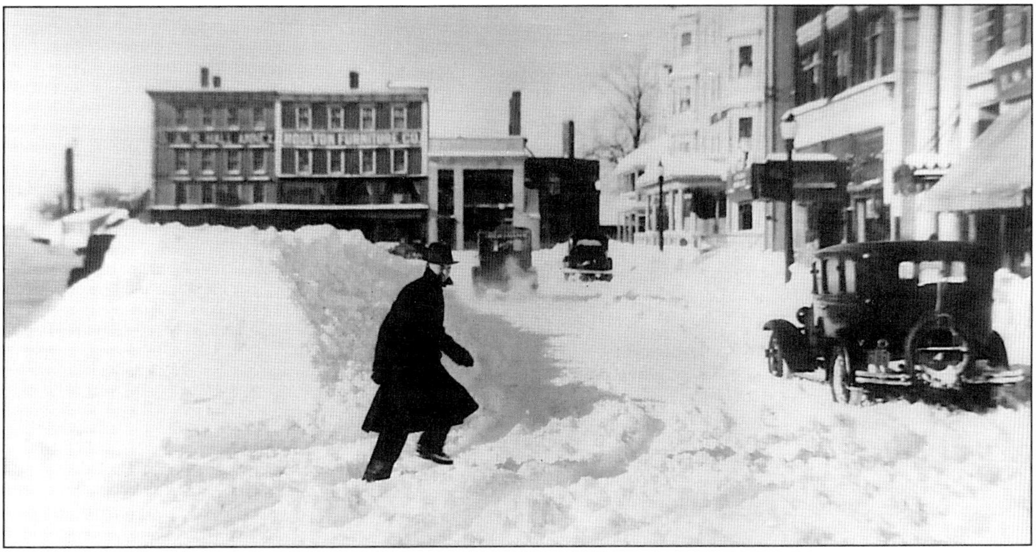

To conclude, we return to potatoes and snow, two of the factors Houlton has had most publicity about. First comes another Thanksgiving Day snowstorm in Market Square.

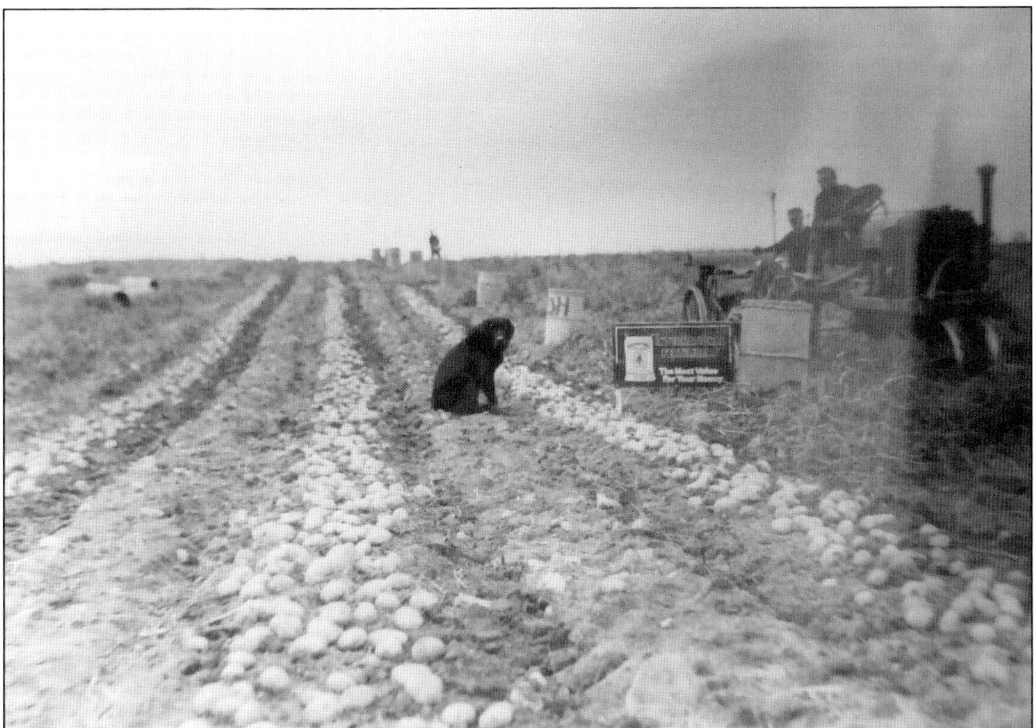

Finally, we take a look at the David Hammond potato farm in Houlton. They grew and grew and grew them.

Acknowledgements

A memorable start for this book was provided by John and Donald Dunn of Dunn's Funeral Parlor in Houlton. Never has nine hours on the floor of a funeral parlor produced so many pictures, largely duplicates of the photographs appearing on the walls at Dunn's; the Dunn Collection.

Hand in hand with the Dunns, credit must go to Betty Fraser (head librarian), and Laurie McQuarrie (assistant librarian), at Cary Memorial Library. They were co-operative beyond all belief.

Mrs. Barbara O'Donnell, president of the Aroostook County Historical and Art Museum, and John Millar, one of the museum's directors, were very helpful, and the Maine Humanities Council was kind enough to give a $1,200 grant to the museum, part of which was an aid in compiling this book.

Others to be thanked, usually for the photographs they supplied and in no particular order include: Alice Mary Pierce of Portland (trustee of the Maine Historical Society), Joyce Daigle McCormack of Houlton and her daughter, Pamela Green of Portland; Stan and Jackie Greaves of Presque Isle; Dorothy Fitzpatrick of Houlton; Barbara Edwards of Houlton; John Folsom (vice-president of the museum); Pamela Dill Dombek of Iowa; Dolly Dombek Daigle of Gray; Terry and Kenneth Larson of Houlton; Frank Gooch and his wife, the former Eleanor Ingraham of Cape Elizabeth, Maine; Graden Swett; Mildred Peabody; Doris McPherson; and Mark Russell of the US Immigration and Naturalization Service.

There were others, I'm sure. It was a pleasure to return to Houlton, even with a 500-mile round trip commute once a week for several weeks. The tingle is still there.